More Death Records from Missouri Newspapers

1810-1857

by
Lois Stanley
George F. Wilson
Maryhelen Wilson

Please direct all correspondence and orders to:

www.southernhistoricalpress.com
or
SOUTHERN HISTORICAL PRESS, Inc.
PO BOX 1267
375 West Broad Street
Greenville, SC   29601
southernhistoricalpress@gmail.com

ISBN #0-89308-442-5

Printed in the United States of America

After the publication of our earlier books covering deaths in this period, we discovered a number of newspapers we had not included. Some had simply not been available on microfilm at the time; we had overlooked a few issues of some others.   ·

At the same time, we still had in our files the death records of hundreds of children, who had not been included in the earlier books because of space limitations.

All of these deaths occurred between 1810 and 1857. Few, if any, tombstones survive from that early period. The great majority of these people died before the census of 1850; in the case of women (who seldom left an estate) and children, their names may well be unknown to their present-day relatives.

There are about 2900 records here, taken from 65 newspapers - - starting with the Missouri Gazette, the first newspaper published in Missouri territory, and including papers from 20 of the state's earliest counties.

A list of newspapers, and codes, is on the following page.
Note: an Addenda from the St. Louis Missouri Democrat 1854-1857
        starts on page 120.

Code	Newspaper	Location
BEA	Beacon	St. Louis, city and county
BGDB	Democrat-Banner (	Bowling Green, Pike Co.
BGRAD	Radical	
BOBS	Observer (	Boonville, Cooper Co.
BORE	Register	
BOLT	Boonslick Times	Fayette, Howard Co.
BRUNS	Brunswicker	Brunswick, Chariton Co.
CANE	Northeast Missourian (	Canton, Lewis Co.
CANP	Plebeian	
CGWE	Western Eagle	Cape Girardeau, city and county
COMB	Commercial Bulletin	Boonville, Cooper Co.
COP	Patriot	Columbia, Boone Co.
FARW	Far West	Liberty, Clay Co.
FAME	Farmer's and Mechanic's Advocate	St. Louis, city and county
FULT	Telegraph	Fulton, Callaway Co.
GLWT	Weekly Times	Glasgow, Howard Co.
HAG	Gazette	
HAJ	Journal (	Hannibal, Marion Co.
HANT	Tri-Weekly Messenger	
HWU	Western Union	
INJN	Journal	Independence, Jackson Co.
INP	Independent Patriot (	Jackson, Cape Girardeau Co.
JASO	Southern Advocate	
JEFRE	Republican	
JEM	Metropolitan (	Jefferson City, Cole Co.
JINQ	Inquirer	
J-MOH	Missouri Herald	
KCEN	Enterprise	Kansas City, Jackson Co.
LADB	Democrat-Banner	Louisiana, Pike Co.
LEXA	Appeal (	Lexington, Lafayette Co.
LEXP	Express	
MIN	Intelligencer	First Franklin, then Fayette, Howard Co. Later in Columbia, Boone Co.
MODE	Missouri Democrat	Fayette, Howard Co.
MOAR	Missouri Argus	
MOG	Missouri Gazette	
MORE	Missouri Republican (	St. Louis, city and county
MORP	Missouri Reporter	
MOSN	Missouri Saturday News	
MPSC	Missouri Patriot	St. Charles, city and county
NERA	New Era	St. Louis, city and county
OSIN	Independent	Osceola, St. Clair Co.
PWH	Whig	Palmyra, Marion Co.
SASE	Sentinel	Savannah, Andrew Co.
SCMO	Missourian (	St. Charles, city and county
SCNT	Chronotype	
SCOMB	Commercial Bulletin	St. Louis, city and county
SCWR	Weekly Reveille	St. Charles, city and county
SGPD	Plain Dealer	Ste. Genevieve, city and county
SJA	Adventure	St. Joseph, Buchanan Co.
SLAM	American	
SLDU	Daily Union	
SLINT	Intelligencer (	St. Louis, city and county
SLMD	Missouri Democrat	
SLNL	News Letter	
SLOB	Observer	
SMAD	Southern Mo. Advocate	Jackson, Cape Girardeau Co.
SOV	Shepherd of the Valley	St. Louis (a Catholic newspaper)
SPAD	Advertiser	
SPRIG	Whig (	Springfield, Greene Co.
SPRIM	Mirror	
SRJ	Salt River Journal	Bowling Green, Pike Co.
STGAZ	Gazette	St. Joseph, Buchanan Co.
SWERE	Weekly Reveille	St. Louis, city and county
WARV	Visitor	Warsaw, Benton Co.
WEJ	Journal	Weston, Platte Co.
WEM	Western Emigrant	Boonville, Cooper Co.

Most of these newspapers are available at the Newspaper
Library, State Historical Society of Mo., Columbia.
Some are at the Missouri Historical Society, Jefferson
Memorial, Forest Park, St. Louis. The St. Louis County
Library HQ, South Lindbergh Blvd., has the old SLMD.

ACHENBACH, Louisa, daughter of Herman and Christine, died   MORE 18 Feb 1853
                        Thursday ae 5.

ADAMS, Cornelia Scott, daughter of John and Emily C.,   MORE 12 May 1849
                        10 May ae 21m 21d.

        Caroline Teese, daughter of Rudolph and Sarah,   MORE 8 Sep 1846
                  ae 1y 9m. Funeral from the home,
                  4th-Green. Frankfort pc

        Children of John H. and Caroline: (St. Louis)
                  Charles V., eldest son, 9 Jan ae 5y.   MORE 10 Jan 1853
                  John Henry Jr. 29 Apr ae 1y 9m 4d.   "   1 May 1847

        Cyrus in Pike Co. 18 May.   NERA 26 May 1845

ADRIANCE, children of William and Mary Elizabeth:
        Martha Harrington 16 Sept ae 18m 19d.   MORE 17 Sep 1847
        Cornelia Hyde, eldest daughter, 14 Dec ae 9y 6m.   " 15 Dec "
        James Edward 6 Jan ae 8y 7m.   "   8 Jan 1849
        Family home was at 248 6th St.

ALDRICH, Nahum 12 Apr in his 50th y. New York pc   MORE 14 Apr 1850

ALEXANDER, Edward, infant son of B. W.   MORE 2 Jul 1846

        R.W., funeral notice.   MORE 24 Jan 1851

ALFORD, Col. J. H., Clerk of Jefferson Co., 1 July   NERA 6 Jul 1849
                        of cholera.

        Margaret, daughter of J. H. and Adaline, at   MORE 17 Feb 1842
                  Herculaneum 3 February ae 7y 6m.

ALLEN, George H.: funeral from his home, 7th St.   MORE 10 Jul 1849
                between Franklin-Wash.

        James H., son of Abraham and Catherine,   MORE 27 Mar 1848
                  20 Mar ae 1y 10d.

        John, "many years a pilot on the lower Mississippi"
                4 Mar ae 30. Lived on Morgan St. between   MORE 5 Mar 1850
                17th-18th. Philadelphia pc

        Luther Pendleton, son of R.L. and P.A., ae 16m.   MORE 15 Sep 1849

        Mary, infant of James and Elizabeth, 9 September.   " 10 Sep 1840

        John, son of T. R. and D. S. "survived his mother
                but a few days." Ae 19m 3d.   MORE 29 Jul 1851

        Frances Mary, daughter of Thomas and Ann Russell,   "   3 Apr 1846
                ae 9m 25d.

        William Pratt, infant of S. H. and A. R., 21 July.   " 25 Jul 1848
                Worcester MA pc

        Elizabeth, infant of William and Clara, 17 Sept.   " 19 Sep 1853

        Sterling B., of Berry & Allen, Springfield MO
                merchants, 19 July.   JEM 3 Aug 1847

        Susan Ann at Warrenton 5 August after a long,
                painful illness.   NERA 10 Aug 1849

ALLEN, cont. Dr. V. S. in Warsaw 8 October.   NERA 17 Oct 1845

ALLISON, Lucinda, daughter of Nathaniel and Ruth, ae 23d.   WEM 29 Aug 1839

      Mrs. Mary, consort of Samuel, at her home in   LADB 26 Nov 1849
            Pike Co. 11 Oct ae 42. Wife, mother.
            Cumberland Presbyterian.

      Robert H. at his home in Buffalo Twp., Pike Co.,   LADB 16 Aug 1847
            29 Jul ae 40.

ALMEIDA, children of William H. and Mary E. : (St. Louis)
      William, only son, 3 Dec ae 2y 17d.   MORE 6 Dec 1847
            Baltimore and Washington pc
      Mary Theresa died 18 May, age not shown.   "   20 May 1848

AMES, children of Benjamin: (St. Louis)
      Alfred Clair, Thursday night (cholera epidemic).   MORE 30 Oct 1832
      Louise Octavia, Tuesday night. "   "   "   "
      (Their father was killed at the racetrack in
        1841 by Daniel Brady.)

      William, son of William and Margaret, Tuesday last   MORE 28 Jun 1845
        in Manchester MO, ae about 11m.

AMISS, Mrs. Thomas, 11 Jan. Funeral from 328 Morgan.   MORE 13 Jan 1850
      Buried in the Baptist Cemetery.

AMOS, Adella D. in her 9th year. Funeral from the home of   MORE 24 Nov 1851
      her aunt, Mrs. Douthitt.

      Emma G., eldest daughter of W. W. and Emma J.,   MORE 20 Oct 1845
        last Friday ae 4y 25d. (possibly in SWERE)

AMSDEN, L. H. Sunday night ae about 30, after a long,   JEM 11 Jan 1848
      severe illness.

ANDERSON, Charles Winton, son of C. R. and Eliza of   MORE 13 Feb 1849
            St. Louis, in Cincinnati
            5 Feb., age not shown.

      Frederick Gustavus, son of Gust. A. and Jemima,   MORE 22 Sep 1849
        in Pinckney 11 Sep ae 1y 10m.

      Robert Woods, son of W. J. Jr. and Anna, ae 4m 11d. " 4 Sep 1849

      Sarah in Paris, Monroe Co., 16 Feb in her 19th y.   BGDB 1 Mar 1845

      Sarah W., daughter of Thomas J. and Fannie M.,   GLWT 7 Apr 1853
        26 Mar ae 2y 4m.
      Thomas L., infant of Thomas of Lindenwood,   PWH 26 Sep 1840
        St. Charles Co., 17 September.

ANDREWS, Josephine, youngest child of Thomas and Ann, ae 3.
            Lived on 3rd St. between Olive-Locust.   MORE 13 Oct 1847
            Buried in Methodist Cemetery.

      Mary Isabel, daughter of John and Harriet W.,   BORE 17 Sep 1844
        12 September ae 3y 7m.

ANGEVINE, children of Jonathan: (St. Louis)
      Joseph Stephen Saturday evening last ae 1y 8d.   MORE 1 Nov 1833
      Ann Margaret yesterday ae 20m.   "   23 Aug 1836
      Julia Elizabeth 14 June ae 21m.   "   16 Jun 1838

2

ANGNEY, Stephen G. in Pulaski Co. ae about 30, after   JEM 26 Nov 1848
          a short illness.

ANNIS, James W., son of Asa and Cecelia, 29 Jul ae 2y 6m.   MORE 31 Jul 1848

APPLEBURY, Mrs. Frances H., consort of the late William S.,
               at her home near Prairieville. LADB 18 Jun 1849
               Native of VA, in MO 6 years.
               Lynchburg pc

APPLEBERRY, William S. at his home in Calumet Twp. 12 Feb   LADB 21 Feb 1848
              in his 57th y. From Albe marle Co.
              VA to MO in the fall of 1843.

APPLETON, William Whitley, oldest son of William, late of MORE 18 Jul 1834
              PA, 13 July ae 5y.

ARCHER, Children of Edward E. and Mary A.: (St. Louis)
           Edward E. ae 22m 25d.   MORE 27 Feb 1847
           Eliza Lynch 28 Feb ae 3y 3m 13d.   "   1 Mar 1847
      Both funerals were from the home of Thomas Shore,
           Walnut between 6th-7th.

      Julia, daughter of Mr/Mrs. Lawrence, 19 July   SJA 26 Jul 1850
                  ae 15m.

ARMAND, Frances 11 August at the home of Mme. Bouju.   NERA 11 Aug 1849

ARMISTEAD, William, son of Robert and Eliza, 26 June   MORE 29 Jun 1851
          ae 18m 20d.

ARMSTRONG, Almira, daughter of Col. Robert, Sunday,   MORE 27 Oct 1829
          25 October ae 6y.

ARNOLD, William Trimble, son of Thomas L. and Eliza,   MORE 21 Sep 1844
              19 September ae 2. Louisville
              and Paris pc

ARTHUR, Abner in Benton Co. 29 October.   JEM 3 Nov 1846

      Mrs. Adeline Amanda 23 April of consumption, age   HAJ 3 May 1849
              illegible, member of the
              Methodist Church in Ralls Co.

      Samuel A. in Hannibal 17 June of cholera.   HAJ 21 Jun 1849

ASBURY, Daniel, only son of David R. and Jane, of Canton, CANE 21 Sep 1854
          19 September age about 2.

ASHBURN, James F. at his home in Warren Co. 9 February of MORE 20 Feb 1850
          consumption in his 37th year. Last of
          11 brothers, a sister survived.

ASHDOWN, Mary Ann Nesham, daughter of the late William, MORE 10 Jul 1849
             ae 21y 11m. Family home was on
             Pine St. between 3rd-4th.

ASTON, Richard M., formerly of Manchester, ENG, 17 Jan.   SLINT 19 Jan 1850
          of pneumonia ae 20.

ATCHISON, an infant son of George Jr., 12 February./SWERE? MORE?15 Mar 1847

      Capt. John T., 2 June after a short illness.   MORE 3 Jun 1850
            Funeral from home of Geo. W.
            Atchison on 5th St.

ATKINS, William, son of William and Jane, ae 3y,
                 Wednesday last.   SLDU 25 Sep 1846

        Family of General Henry:
            Henry, son of Gen. Henry, in Louisville
              7 September ae 18m.   MORE 16 Sep 1828
            Mary Diana Louise at Jefferson Barracks
              ae 11m.   "   3 Apr 1832
            Miss Annie at the home of her mother in
              Louisville ae 19.   " 17 Jan 1845
        (Gen. Henry died in St. Louis in 1842.)

        Hester, consort of John, 26 July of bilious   NERA 27 Jul 1849
            diarrhoea ae 48.

AUGUSTINE, Amanda, eldest daughter of Michael, in her
              5th year; family home, 57 Locust St.   MORE 4 Nov 1840

AUGUSTIN, Emile, parents not shown; died 18 February at
              79 Locust St., ae 5y 3m.   MORE 19 Feb 1849

AUSTIN, Daniel, infant of John and Mary, 2 Jul ae 6m.   COMB 4 Jul 1846

        Family of William J. and Caroline: (St. Louis)
            Clara Virginia, infant daughter, at the
               home of James S. Lane.   MORE 30 Jan 1840
            Edwin Fimister, youngest son, 17 Mar ae 1.   " 18 Mar 1850
            Henry Augustus, youngest son, in Manchester
               3 Sep ae 1y 6m.   SLDU 5 Sep 1846
            William Phelps, only child, 8 Sep ae 14m.   " 12 Sep 1838
        Family of William J. only:
            Mrs. Mary Ann, consort, Thursday.   " 14 May 1833
            Elijah P., son, 30 September ae 5m.   " 15 Oct "
            William Henry Savage, only son, 8 Jan at
              Beardstown IL ae 2y 2m.   " 23 Jan 1834

AVERY, Laura Susannah, daughter of Charles and Salina L.,
              ae 7m. Funeral from the home of   MORE 28 Aug 1848
              Moses Stout, 6th betw Olive-Locust.

AVIS, Ellen Elizabeth, daughter of Thomas and Elizabeth,
              1 Oct ae 1y 8m. Family home on   MORE 2 Oct 1841
              Washington Ave.
    Thomas Cobb, son of Elizabeth, 14 May ae 1y 5m 3d.   " 15 May 1847
              Funeral from home of the late Thomas,
              Washington near 4th St.

AXTELL, Hannah Mary, daughter of Thomas R. and
              Electa Jane, ae 1y 20d.   MORE 10 Jul 1849
    Thomas Hall, son of Thomas H. and Electa, Friday   " 11 Mar 1843
              ae 2y 4m 6d. Funeral from family home,
              3rd St. between Spruce-Almond.

AYRES, Robert W. Sunday ae 32. Funeral from the home of MORE 5 Mar 1850
              John Daggett.

      William J. J., of White and Ayres, Warsaw, formerly NERA 25 Dec 1845
              of Berlin MD, died 23 December.

BABER, Emily, daughter of Hiram H. and Harriet M., in Jefferson City ae 7y 5m.   MORE 27 Oct 1845

BACON, Edwin, in his 60th year; lived on Vine St. Between 7th-8th. New York pc   MORE 1 Oct 1849

   Henry, son of James of St. Louis, 20 April at Farmer's College, OH ae 12.   MORE 26 Apr 1849

   James, ae 71, near Manchester; formerly of Albemarle Co. VA, in MO 20 years.   MORE 23 Sep 1849

BAILEY, Maj. James in Lafayette Co. 29 September; had once represented St. Charles Co. in the State Legislature; an 1812 veteran.   NERA 8 Oct 1845

   Lucinda, daughter of Clifton and Mary, 22 Oct in St. Louis Co., ae 15y 1m 10d.   MORP 28 Oct 1845

   Missouri, only daughter of George and Mary, 20 May ae 1y 8m.   MORE 22 May 1848

   Thomas, son of William and Elizabeth H., 13 August ae 2y 8m.   MORE 14 Aug 1846

BAIRD, Caroline, ae 16, at the home of David Andrews.   BORE 14 May 1844

   Thomas J. in Louisiana, MO yesterday in his 45th year, a resident 10 years; husband, father.   LADB 14 Dec 1846

BAKER, Catherine, relict of Martin, 22 Mar in her 52nd y. She had come from Louisa Co. VA, 1842.   MORE 16 Apr 1844

BALDRIDGE, Mildred, daughter of William and Elizabeth, died 16 August; born 28 Aug 1833.   PWH 23 Aug 1849

BALDWIN, Baker G., infant of Thomas and Elizabeth, 21 May ae 9m 12d.   CGWE 2 Jun 1848

   Pauline Amanda, daughter of Capt. John and Amanda Trallen Baldwin, yesterday ae 12.   MORE 4 Jun 1852

BALL, Martha Virginia, adopted daughter of S. W. and Isabella, 27 March ae 5m.   MORE 28 Mar 1850

BALLENTINE, Ada, only child of William and Judith, ae 2y 7m 4d. Brunswick & Louisville pc   MORE 21 Jun 1851

BALMER, Ernest A. at the home of Mrs. Elizabeth Balmer in his 23rd year.   MORE 24 Jul 1849

BALMSLEY, Catherine, daughter of William Warrance, Sunday ae 21y 12d. Funeral from her home in South St. Louis to the Presbyterian Cemetery.   MORE 26 Oct 1841

BARBEE, John, son of Dr. A. B. and Elvira, 25 March in Manchester age about 4m.   MORE 27 Feb 1850

BARBER, William F., son of William B. and Mary, 25 April ae 2y 9m.   MORE 28 Apr 1846

BARBOUR, Sarah, eldest daughter of Dr. Thomas and Sarah, 1 Jan at the U. S. Hotel ae 3y 7m.   MORE 8 Jan 1844

BARCLAY, Catherine Ellen, of St. Louis, died last night. MORE 11 Aug 1840

BARKER, George, in Newton Co. 9 November ae 48. JEM 23 Nov 1847

Sons of Jo., of St. Louis Co.:
    Jefferson Decatur "last night between 10 and
                        6 this morning" ae 10. MORE 11 Jul 1839
    Benjamin Franklin, ae 3. " "

BARNARD, Julius C., son of George and Astella, 20 November
    ae 3y 11m. MORE 21 Nov 1851

BARNES, Caroline Claire, wife of Dr. John and daughter of
    the late Daniel Clark of New
    Orleans, died 31 May. MORP 3 Jun 1845

George W., son of Rev. James, in Randolph Co. of MODE 19/17
    typhoid in his 10th year. May 1847

Louisa F., wife of Henry M. and daughter of
    Capt. R. M. Strother, in her 22nd y. MORE 31 Aug 1849
    Buried Christ Church Cemetery.

Family of Robert A.: (St. Louis)
    Mary Isabella, daughter of Robert A. and MORE 7 Mar 1848
        Louise, ae 13d.
    Julius D., son of Robert A. and Louisa, " 1 Mar 1848
        29 Feb ae 22m 1d. Family home on
        6th between Pine-Olive. Buried
        in the Episcopal Cemetery.

Emma, daughter of William and Mary E., 7 Jan MORE 8 Jan 1848
    ae 2y 8m. Family home on Franklin between
    14th-15th. Buried Episcopal Cemetery.

BARR, Daniel, infant of Robert, last Wednesday ae 1y 8m. MIN 24 Sep 1831

BARRETT, Richard Patrick, son of J. Richard, at the home
    of Mrs. W. P. Barrett ae 7m 9d. MORE 9 Jan 1853
    Springfield IL, Lexington and
    Louisville pc

BARRET, James Joseph, son of William D. and Eliza, ae 16, MORE 6 Dec 1848
    5 December. Funeral from his
    mother's home, Manchester Rd.

BARRON, Sally Ann, daughter of Richard and Elizabeth (nee MORE 18 Sep 1843
    Sappington) 13 September ae 23.

BARROW, George, 13 June ae 38y 5m. NERA 14 Jun 1849

BARRY, Emily S., consort of R. F. and eldest daughter MORE 23 Sep 1849
    of John B. Weber, formerly of Potosi,
    ae 36y 6m.

BARTEE, Ann Maria, daughter of William and Frances, MODE 22/20
    on 10 September. Sep 1847

BARTLETT, Cyrus, infant of Phineas, Sunday evening last. MOG 23 Oct 1818

BARTLING, Henry T. 6 May ae 43; lived on 3rd betw Pine-Olive. MORE 6 May '50

BARTON, Maj. Stephen in Monroe Co. 1 October. NERA 14 Oct 1845

6

BASCOM, Armina Viola, daughter of J. D. and Frances Ann,   NERA 26 Jul 1849
       25 July, age not shown.

    Hiram, son of Mrs. Catherine, 13 February
         ae 2y 10m 21d.   NERA 24 Feb 1846

BASKETT, Mary Jane, daughter of William H. and Mary A.,
       24 May ae 2y 9m 8d.   MORE 25 May 1852

BASSETT, Susan A., wife of P. T. and daughter of the late   NERA 20 Jul 1849
       Isaiah Bray of Yarmouth, MA, 19 July
       in her 39th y.

BATES, Margaret, daughter of Edward, Thursday night last.   MORE 3 Apr 1832

    Mary Malinda 7 August ae 17.   NERA 11 Aug 1845

BAXTER, Rezin, oldest son of Alexander, 22 Jul ae <u>ca</u> 15.   PWH 29 Jul 1843

    Sarah, daughter of John, in St. Louis 8 Nov. ae 2.   JEM 23 Nov 1847

BAY, Harriet Mansfield, 2nd daughter of the late S. M.   NERA 21 Jul 1849
        and Virginia, 20 July at the home
        of Samuel Conway, ae 4y 5m 12d.

BAYLISS, Susan, infant of William and Susan, ae 1 week.
       Funeral from the Planters' House.   MORE 20 Dec 1844

BEAKEY, Mary E., daughter of John and Margaret, 27 March.   MORE 28 Mar 1849

BEAKY, Mrs. John killed in the collapse of the 2nd-floor   MORE 2 May 1850
       hall at Laclede's Saloon, where girls
       from Purkitt's Female Seminary were
       having a party.

BEAL, Elizabeth, wife of James, in Greene Co. 7 August.   JEM 17 Aug 1847

BEAN, Jonathan B., son of Jonathan and Mary, 4 October   MORE 5 Oct 1841
       ae 22m. Buried Presbyterian Cemetery.

BEATTY, Emilie Alcy, daughter of Thomas and Mary Ann,   MORE 7 Aug 1846
       6 August ae 23m.

BEELER, George Washington Jr., only son of G. W. and   MORE 25 Jun 1845
        Martha Jane, in New Orleans
        16 June ae 2y 14d.

BELL, Edward in Benton Co. 6 October.   JEM 13 Oct 1846

    Virginia, infant of Richard J. and Mary A., in   LEXP 6 Aug 1844
       Lexington ae 1y 6m 6d.

BELT, Hanson, son of Capt. F. T. and Caroline, Wed. ae 2y.   MORE 24 Apr 1846

    Mrs. Mary Catherine, Sunday, 22 July. (cholera?)   "   22 Jul 1849

    Hetty M., of cholera, the 5th member of her family
       to die of the disease, Winchester VA   "   23 Aug 1849
       and Baltimore pc

BENEDICT, Rush Fitch, son of Walter, 15 July ae 1y 8m.   WEM 18 Jul 1839

BENIGHT, Thaddeus 10 October, ae about 55.   SJA 11 Oct 1850

BENJAMIN, Sophia, wife of Wm. C. (now absent from the city).
       Left 2 children in care of the Protestant MOSN 10 Feb 1838
       Orphan Assn. Relatives perhaps in Chicago.

BENOIST, children of Louis A. and Esther (Hackney):
    Louis Augustus, youngest son, 14 July ae 7m 9d.   MORE 15 Jul 1842
        Funeral St. Francis Xavier.
    Charles Page, age not shown, 31 Jan. in New Orleans. " 14 Feb 1848

      Eliza, daughter of Louis A. and Eliza (Rector),   MORE 2 Dec 1828
        Monday last, an infant.

BENSON, Lavina Beatrice, daughter of James H. and Ruth P., WEM 10 Jan 1839
        at New Franklin 18 Dec. ae 3y 9m.

    Neva, daughter of James L. and Lucinda Ann, 17 June MORE 18 Jun 1850
      ae 4y 6m. Palmyra pc

BENT, Edward, infant of Silas, Monday last.   MORE 23 Aug 1833

    Robert S., son of the late Judge, 17 October at the MORE 21 Oct 1841
      home of J. L. Bean, near the Arsenal.
      Buried Presbyterian Cemetery.

BENTEEN, Caroline, daughter of T. C. and B., 18 May   MORE 19 May 1853
      ae 1y 11m.

BENTON, James McDowell, youngest son of Thomas H., this SCOMB 3 Aug 1835
      morning, ae about 4. Buried
      Presbyterian Cemetery.

    Prudence, daughter of D. and Susanna, 8 July   MORE 14 Jul 1853
      ae 15y 8m 25d.

BERRY, Lesley E., son of William and Mary, ae 13m.   MORE 29 Jul 1853

    Mary, daughter of William, suddenly at Manchester   " 28 Oct 1847
      on 18 October.
    Cynthia Smith, daughter of Major Berry, in Franklin MIN 23 Oct 1824
      4 October, ae about 3y 6m.

BERTHOUD, Nicholas, ae 63; funeral, Congregational Church. MORE 20 Nov 1849

BETTS, George H., son of George and Mary Jane, 14 May MORE 15 Apr 1850
      ae 3y 5m.

    Laura, infant of John and Grace, 6 Feb ae 3m.   " 7 Feb 1845
      Funeral, 6th St. between Morgan-Green.

    Robert, youngest son of Frederick W., yesterday   " 21 Aug 1840
      ae 18m.

BIBB, Elvira, only child of Richard, last Saturday ae 16m. MIN 20 Nov 1830

BIDFORD, Elizabeth, daughter of William H. and Mary E., SJA 28 Jun 1850
      27 June ae 15m.

BIGGS, children of Joseph and Josephine, of Canton:
    James Elbert 14 August ae 1y.   CANE 26 Aug 1854
    William 20 August ae 2y 6m 27d.
BILLINS, Lucy Ann, wife of Samuel, ae 31.   MORE 3 Jul 1849

BILLON, children of Frederic L.: (St. Louis)
    Frederick Louis 12 Sep ae 15m 19d. Funeral from MORE 11 Sep 1845
      family home, #69 Pine.
    Josephine Alice, ae 19m 16d; #44 N. 6th St.   " 29 Apr 1848
      (continued)

8

BILLON, children of Frederic L., continued:
        Sophia Emily, Friday last ae 16m.   MORE 10 Jul 1832
        Augustus on 22 October ae 6y 22d.   SWERE 25 Oct 1847

        Theresa Sophia, youngest daughter of Charles P.
                    and Frances, 8 May. Buried   MORE 9 May 1842
                    Episcopal Cemetery.

BINGHAM, sons of John of St. Louis Co.:
        Paul L. on 10 September ae 9.   MORE 30 Sep 1839
        Carberry, ae 3, date not shown.   "   11 Oct 1844

        Taylor, son of William and Ann, ae 2y 9m.   "   8 Oct 1851

BIRCH, Crittenden, son of Thomas and Elizabeth, in
                Plattsburg 17 September ae 18m.   MORE 31 Oct 1851

        Richard Nicholls, son of Hon. James H., at Prairie
                Park, Clinton Co., 18 Feb ca 3m. LADB 10 Mar 1851

        Thomas Erskine, son of Col. James H. and Sarah C.,
                25 September.   BOLT 2 Oct 1841

BIRD, Joseph Sprigg, son of G.A., 9 February ae 17m. MORE 19 Feb 1828

BIRMINGHAM, William in Independence 2 September ae 24. JEM 21 Sep 1847

BLACKSTONE, Charles C., native of St. Mary's Co. MD,
              23 March ae 47. Funeral from the MORE 23 Mar 1850
              home of his brother, N., on
              Collins St,

BLAINE, daughters of John L. and Margaret (or John I.),
        address shown as Locust between 6-7:
        Annie, died 29 September ae 19m.   MORE 30 Sep 1848
        Kate R., no date, ae 11m 16d. Buried in " 12 Aug 1853
              Wesleyan Cemetery.

BLAIR, daughters of Montgomery:
        Lucy, only child, 11 August ae ca 15m. MORE 12 Aug 1840
        Caroline, age not shown, 29 May (her mother " 10 Jun 1844
              had died in January)

BLAKEY, Eugene, infant of Granville, Saturday night last. PWH 2 Apr 1845

BLANCHARD, Adeline C., only child of Sidney and Cornelia,
              yesterday of scarlet fever ae 3y 7m. MORE 27 Dec 1845
              Boston pc

        Emilie Corinne, daughter of Elzear and Amilina,
                23 September ae 8m.   MORE 25 Sep 1846
        George Homer son of Elzear and Amerlia   " 13 Aug 1849
              ae 2y 1m 19d.

        F. T., child of Benjamin and Virginia,   " 26 Jul 1853
              25 July ae 23m 7d.

BLAND, Serena Ann, oldest daughter of Mary and ? , in
              Warren Co. (paper folded)   MORE 13 Aug 1835

BLANKENSHIP, James in Warren Co. 21 September. NERA 27 Sep 1845

9

BLANTON, daughters of Wash L., in Fayette:
           Harriet H. on 18 April in her 8th year.   BOLT 26 Apr 1845
           Margaret L. on 3 December, no age shown.   "   10 Dec 1842

BLATCHFORD, children of Rev. John:
           Alexander, in Quincy IL 9 Oct. in 8th year. MORE 15 Oct 1847
           Frances A. on 6 June in her 14th year.   PWH 25 Jun 1846

BLEDSOE, Robert, estate in Chariton Co.; letters of
           administration, with will annexed, to   BRUNS 10 Jun 1854
           Felix Laforce on 6 June.

BLISH, Susan, infant of Oaks S. and Maria, 9 August.
                    Philadelphia pc   MORE 13 Aug 1844

BLOCK, Isaac Newton, only son of Jacob and Catherine,
           6 September ae 1y 11m.   LADB 7 Sep 1846

BLOW, Eugenia Susan, daughter of Peter E. and Eugenia,
           at Richwood Mines, Washington Co.,   MORE 21 Jul 1846
           ae 5y 9m.

BOARDMAN, Charles, youngest son of Wm. J. and Mary Agnes,
           in Baltimore 29 April ae 4y 8m 7d.   MORE 10 May 1844

BODLEY, Sarah Howard, daughter of Henry J., 18 June ae
               <u>ca</u> 6. Franklin & Lexington KY pc MORE 20 Jun 1849

BOEHM, Martin 15 May of cholera ae 20.   NERA 16 May 1849

BOGY, children of Lewis V.:
        Lewis Jr., 3 April ae 14m 10d. Family lived
           8th-Olive. Buried Catholic Cemetery.   MORE 4 Apr 1842
        Bernard Sire 21 February ae 7m 21d.   "   22 Feb 1844
        Mary Felicite 2 June ae 3y 8m.   "   3 Jun 1845
        Mary Aime 25 January ae 2m 13d.   "   28 Jan 1847

BOHANNAN, Maria, infant of William A. S. and Angeline,
           16 June, age not shown.   MORE 21 Jun 1845

BOILVIN, John W., son of Nicholas and Elizabeth,
           Tuesday last in his 7th year.   MORE 27 Feb 1840

BOLGIANO, Mary Elizabeth, only daughter of Francis and
           Mary Jane, 17 Jan. ae 4y 6m 17d. MORE 20 Jan 1837

BOLTON, Celestia A., daughter of Dr. William, 10 Sept. ae 3. JEFRE 14 Sep'39

BONFILS, Francis D., son of Dr. S.F. and Maria D. of
           St. Louis, in Lexington KY ae 21m.   MORE 17 Aug 1846

BOON, Children of Hampton L. and Eliza, of Fayette: BOLT 26 Sep 1840
        Jesse Green, infant, 20 September.
        Hampton L. at Jefferson City 15 December. "   3 Jan 1846

      Ratliff, son of Baily H. and Elizabeth S., 12 Feb. LADB 25 Feb 1850
        ae 4y 10m 3d. Evansville & Newburg IN pc

BOOTH, Samuel C., youngest child of James W. and Sophronia, MORE 10 Oct 1848
           at Clarksville ae 21m.

BOURGOIN, Joseph 28 January ae 42; lived on Lombard St. MORE 29 Jan 1850
           between 2nd-3rd.

BOUTON, Annie, eldest daughter of Mr. and Mrs. H. B.,   KCEN 24 Jan 1857
            11 January ae 3y 5m 2d.

BOSSERON, Julia, yesterday ae 18.   SOV 27 Apr 1833

BOURKE, Ann, daughter of Patrick, 18 July. Buried in   MORE 19 Jul 1851
            the Catholic Cemetery.

BOURNE, Elizabeth, daughter of Joshua, in Palmyra   MORE 28 Jun 1833
            of cholera.

BOUTELLE, Charles at Monroe House 4 March ae 23. Friends   MORE 5 Mar 1850
            of Mr. Farwell invited to the funeral,
            at the Unitarian Church.

BOUVIER, Maurice Anthenor, son of Joseph and Laura, of   MORE 17 Mar 1853
            typhoid 16 March ae 4y 2m.
            Catholic Cemetery.

BOVERIE, Jule A. in Ste. Genevieve 9 July of cholera,   MORE 19 Jul 1849
            ae 11y.

BOWEN, Mary B., daughter of John and Harriet, 151 N. 4th,   MORE 26 Mar 1849
            on 25 March ae 15m.

BOWLEN, children of Hon. James B. and Margaret V.:
    BOWLIN   William Sublette on 17 July ae 8m   MORE 18 Jul 1844
                  Funeral 3rd St. between Pine-Chestnut.   or 1845?
                  Edward, infant, on 12 July.   "   13 Jul 1846

BOWMAN, Capt. John H., formerly of Boston, 16 January.   MOSN 19 Jan 1839

        "All of spotted fever or cold plague:"   LADB 1 Jan 1849
        McDonald, son of John, 27 Dec ae 10m
        Nancy, daughter of John, 28 Dec ae 3y
        Harrison, son of John, 31 Dec ae 15y
            (all apparently in Louisiana MO)

BOXLEY, John Samuel 1 June at the home of James Bibb in   MORE 14 Jun 1849
            Franklin Co., ae 7y 10m. Son of
            William S., of St. Louis Co.
            Richmond pc

BOYD, Ann, consort of Joseph, in Callaway Co. 27 July.   JEM 17 Aug 1847
      Cyntha Ann, daughter of Maj. Joseph, 23 March.   FULT 6 Apr 1849

      Henry Clay, son of John M. and Catherine, 19 Nov.   SLDU 20 Nov 1846
            ae 23m 29d.

BOYDEN, Henry, agent for a new edition of the Bible to be   JEM 13 Oct 1846
            published in NY, 25 Sept. in Platte Co.

BOYERS, Robert Morris, infant of Cincinnatus and Margaret Ann,
            at Independence 24 Sept. ae 13m 13d. WEM 17 Oct 1839

BOYLE, children of Hugh and Sarah, 6th (or 7th) nr Spruce:
            Ellen on 12 March ae 2y 8m.   MORE 13 Mar 1844
            George 8 July ae 5y 9m. Philadelphia pc   "   9 Jul "
            George, infant.   "   1 Jan 1852

BRADFORD, Alice, daughter of John and Frances, in her   MORE 10 Jul 1849
            6th year.

11

BRADLEY, Theresa, consort of Stephen G. and daughter of
      Rev. Norman Parks, in Monroe Co. 29 Aug.   JEM 14 Sep 1847

BRAMBLE, Emma Cora, only daughter of H. L. and Alice,
  (see Addenda)   29 April ae 6 m. Buried Wesleyan.   MORE 30 Apr 1853

BRANAGAN, Charles A., son of William and Margaret, on
      1 September, age not shown.   SWERE 9 Sep 1844

BRANDON, Mrs. Mary Ann in this city 1 February.   LADB 5 Feb 1849

BRANT, Sarah Benton, youngest daughter of Col. J.B.;
      family lived at Washington-4th St.   MORE 7 Jul 1849

BRASSELL, Elizabeth, widow of Dr., formerly of
      Keosauqua IA, 15 July of cholera.   NERA 25 Jul 1849

BREEZE, sons of Robert: (St. Louis)
          Henry Cook ae 3y 5m.   MORE 23 Nov 1836
          Archibald H. R. 17 April, ae not shown.   " 18 Apr 1840

BREITENBAUGH, Martin at the home of N. H. Whitmore, of
      cholera, in his (69th?) year.   NERA 6 Jul 1849

BREVARD, children of Albert H. and Juliet W.: (Jackson)   JASO 6 Oct 1838
         Robert ae 3y 14d.   /MO
         Frank, ae about 12m.   " 20 "
         Mary Gayle, ae 4, of scarlet fever.   " 27 "

BREWER, Eastll? (not clear) of Canton, Lewis Co., at
      Elk Lick Springs, Pike Co. MO, of   HAJ 30 Aug 1849
      consumption, 26 August.

BRICKEY, Susan Hoard, daughter of John S., at Potosi
      26 November ae 10y 2m.   MORE 5 Dec 1834

BRIDGE, Julia, 2nd daughter of Hudson E. and Isabella,
      ae 20m 16d.   MORE 20 Mar 1845

BRIDGEFORD, Richard, 23 May in his 60th year. Funeral
      from the Christian Church.   HAJ 24 May 1849

BRIGGS, children of Joseph and Susan (or Susannah):
      Joseph on 9 March ae 17m.   MORE 13 Apr 1846
      Mary on 21 July ae 1y 3d.   " 24 Jul 1848
      (possibly may have been in SWERE?)

BRISON, Fanny B., youngest daughter of Benjamin,
      23 April ae 3y 7m 28d.   MORE 26 Apr 1853

BRIZENDINE, Louis in Ralls Co.   NERA 22 Jul 1845

BROKING, Harman D. 17 August, ae about 40.   NERA 20 Aug 1849

BROLASKI, George, son of Henry and Eliza of St. Louis,
      in Hannibal 6 August ae 10m 2d.   NERA 8 Aug 1849

BRONSON, Ella Tuttle daughter of D., ae 10m. Funeral
      from #18 7th St.   MORE 29 Jan 1850

      Leon Kinkead, only son of Delos and Anna C.,
         ae 1y 6m. Funeral from home of   MORE 14 Jun 1848
         Capt. Boyce, 6th-Morgan.

BROOKS, children of Edward and Virginia C.: (St. Louis)
        Edward S. died 6 January ae 22m.   MORE 7 Jan 1843
        John Bell, eldest son, in his 9th year. Family " 25 Jun 1844
          home on Walnut near 7th St.

BROSSER, William M. in Carroll Co. 24 February.   NERA 25 Feb 1846

BROTHERTON, Aurelia, daughter of Marshall and Elizabeth, MORE 28 Mar 1853
        27 March ae 6y 10m 5d. Family lived
        at Broadway & Chambers.

      William drowned Sunday, body found Tuesday.   MORP 29 Jul 1845

BROWN, children of J. M. and Louisa: (St. Louis)
        Henry died ae 21m, no date.   MORE 27 Jul 1849
        Warren ae 4y 4d; family home, 85 N. 4th. " 7 Nov 1849
     Henry St. Louis, only son of Dr. R. B., 17 February MORE 19 Feb 1840
        of scarlet fever ae 2y 9m.
    Isaac M., son of Isaac and Lydia, 7 Jan. ae 8y 5m 5d. " 10 Jan 1850

     John Jefferson, son of T. W. and Lucy, 21 March SRJ 13 Mar 1841
            ae 7m.
     R. P. at the home of his brother, T. W., in LADB 11 Dec 1848
        Cuivre Twp., Pike Co., 30 November.

     Sabra, relict of William, 3 May near Brunswick, MORE 18 May 1850
        ae 74; before her death she had freed
        16 of her 17 slaves.

     Susan Elizabeth, daughter of Robert, 26 December MORE 19 Jan 1853
        in Jackson MO ae 11y 1d.

     Thomas Griffith, son of James and Mary, 9 December MORE 10 Dec 1847
        ae 8m. Funeral from home of
        Mrs. Wilson, 6th-Morgan.

BRUFFEY, Mrs. Mary D. 2 August in her 45th year. Friends NERA 2 Aug 1849
        of S. V. and E. H. Farnsworth
        invited to funeral.

BRUIN, Timothy in St. Charles Co. 16 August in 73rd year. JEM 24 Aug 1847

BRUNTY, Elizabeth, consort of Barnabas B., near Elk LADB 17 Mar 1851
        Springs 28 February; short, painful illness.

BRYAN, David E. in Monroe Co. 13 June.   NERA 27 Jun 1845

     John Saunders, son of John and Elizabeth, MORE 9 Aug 1847
        8 August ae 19m.

     Jonathon in St. Charles Co. 11 August ae 87; born SLNL 29 Aug 1846
        in NC, married a sister of Daniel Boone,
        to MO 47 years ago.

     Thomas Theodore, youngest son of Dr. John G. and MORE 1 May 1845
        Eveline, Friday at Potosi in
        his 6th year.

BRYANT, James, in Paris, Monroe Co., 22 January HAJ 3 Feb 1848
        ae 61y 6m 8d.

BUCHANAN, Elizabeth, eldest daughter of Robert, formerly MORE 2 Apr 1840
        of Cincinnati, 27 March.

BUCHANAN, family of George: (St. Louis)
      Ann Scott, daughter of George and Mary,
                  Thursday ae 6y.   MORE 3 Jan 1848
      Mary, wife of George and daughter of Edward
          Berry, 19 July in her 39th year.   NERA 20 Jul 1849
      Catherine Craig, daughter of George,
          24 July ae 10d.   "   25 Jul "

      Joseph Angevine, son of S., Friday night.   MORE 25 Jan 1831

BUCKLEY, Henry, son of James M., suddenly in St. Joseph
      27 September in his 11th year.   STGAZ 6 Oct 1852

BUEHRMANN, Miss Augusta suddenly 25 January at the home
      of her brother.   CGWE 2 Feb 1849

BUFORD, Jeremiah B. in Jackson Co. 7 March.   NERA 2 Apr 1845

BULL, Letitia, youngest daughter of John and Eliza,
      15 September ae 9m 10d.   MORE 16 Sep 1853

BULLARD, children of Rev. A.: (St. Louis)
      Edward Payson, youngest son, ae 2y 11m 23d.   MORE 13 Jan 1848
      Ann Eliza, only daughter, ae 5y 3m 15d.   "   15 Jan "

BULLOCK, Ervin 22 February of typhoid in his 35th year;
      lived at 192 Fourth St.   MORE 23 Feb 1850

BUMGARDNER, Daniel Halsted, son of Lewis, formerly of
      Fayette, died at Mt. Solon VA on   MODE 18/
      23 July in his 9th year.   16 Aug 1847
      William, infant of Lewis and Hetty Ann.   BOLT 8 Oct 1841

BUMPASS, Oliver, of Gasconade Co., 12 Oct. in his 22d y.   JEM 20 Oct 1846

BURCH, Susan Mary, daughter of William R. and Elizabeth,
      at the home of Judge Viley, ae 5m.   MODE 6 Sep 1848

BURCHARD, children of Mortimer and Louisa: (St. Louis)
      Henry Clay, ae 7m, 29 Sept. of gastro-anochnitis. SLDU 30 Sep'46
      Henrietta M. of cholera 13 May, ae 19m.   NERA 15 May 1849

BURCKHARTT, Nancy, consort of J. E., in Texas Co.   MORE 9 Nov 1849

BURDEAU, Emily Aglia, daughter of Capt. J. T. and Aglia,
      8 July ae 7m 4d, at 61 6th St.   MORE 9 Jul 1847

BURDEN, Thomas T., ae 10, drowned in the Missouri River
      opposite Liberty Landing, Clay Co.   BRUNS 12 Aug 1848

BURKE, Isabella, consort of John and daughter of William
      and Mary Ann Humphreys 21 September   NERA 23 Sep 1845
      of consumption, ae 19.

BURKITT, Caroline, infant of Charles, Sunday last.   JEM 27 Jul 1847

BURKS, Samuel 11 September in his 52d year. Native of VA,
      to MO about 20-30 years ago, mostly in   SLDU 12 Sep 1846
      St. Louis. Had been ill for some time.

BURNETT, B. F., of the Louisiana MO vicinity, died at
      Snye Island, Pike Co. IL, ae 41; a   LADB 25 Aug 1846
      resident of the Louisiana area 25 years.

BURNETT, James H., son of the late John, Thursday last in his 10th year. — LADB 30 Apr 1849

BURNS, James, son of Lewis and Nancy, 6 May in Weston ae 7y 1m 6d. — MORE 5 Jun 1853

BURNS, children of William C. (possibly BARNES?):
Edward S., ae 8, in Washington IN 15 November. MORE 12 &
Frances W. in St. Louis 6 December. 14 Dec 1839
Late of Jefferson Co. VA.

BURRESS, John stabbed and killed at Weston "last Monday week." (Weston Journal) — SPRIG 23 Oct 1848

BURROUGH, Mary Jane, daughter of James Jr., 2 June ae 1y. — MORE 4 Jun 1845

BURROUGHS, Hannah F., wife of James "devoted wife, kind mother, exemplary Christian." — MORE 7 Jul 1849

BURRUS, Benjamin Henry, son of Davenport and Anne E., 10 September at the home of George Cason, ae 5m 15d. — MODE 19 Sep 1848

BURTON, Jane, wife of Thomas C., 22 November of consumption ae 26. — MORE 23 Nov 1849

BURTS, William, son of Stephen and Elizabeth, died on Lick Creek 8 November ae 3y 7m. — BGRAD 12 Nov 1842

BUSH, Mrs. John, of Marion Co., Friday last of cholera morbus. HAG 9 Sep '47

Owen R. on 19 July, ae 35. — NERA 21 Jul 1849

BUTLER, Virginia, daughter of Richard and Mary, 28 October ae 8m 8d. — MORE 30 Oct 1841

BYRNE, Gregory, of consumption in his 42nd year; lived corner Biddle-Collins. NY & New Orleans pc — MORE 3 Jul 1849

James, only son of Dr. Edward of Byrnham Wood, Clark Co., 2 April ae 6y 8m. Baltimore pc — SLDU 3 May 1847

BYNUM, Gray, son of Joseph and Elizabeth of Chariton Co., MODE 19/
8 August ae 11m 28d. 17 Aug 1846

CABANNE, Alexander McNair, son of Julius and Stella, ae 15m 3d. — MORE 7 Apr 1853

Ann Maria, daughter of Charles and Virginia, 8 February ae 10. — MORE 10 Feb 1841

CABELL, John L. B. in Keytesville, Chariton Co., 29 Jan. — NERA 16 Feb 1846

CABLE, Isaac Chauncey, son of Isaac and Mary, ae 2y 6m 10d. MORE 20 Nov 1851
John Louis, son of Isaac Chauncey and Mary, of " 21 Jan 1848
21st-Morgan, ae 2y 3m. Buried in the
Methodist Cemetery.

CALDWELL, Ann Isabella, consort of Timothy, 8 December in her 75th year near Sharpsburg; a Presbyterian 60 years. Philadelphia pc — HAG 12 Dec 1847

Edward Eppelsheimer, son of James G. and Mary Ann, HAG 22 Jul 1847
of Hannibal, 19 July in
his 24th year.

CALDWELL, Ephraim at his home in Salt River Twp., Pike Co., 12 June ae about 60; an acting J.P., useful citizen, "loss deeply felt."　LADB 18 Jun 1849

    James G., formerly of Philadelphia, 8 November.　HAJ 15 Nov 1849

    Timothy, a soldier in the Revolution, 6 March ae 89.　Philadelphia pc　" 9 Mar 1848

CALL, Richard Daniel, son of Dr. George W., 7 May.　MORE 8 May 1832

CALLAWAY, Stephen, infant son of John B. of St. Charles, died 27 April.　MOG 9 May 1812

CALTON, Hugh in Barry Co. 20 August.　NERA 8 Sep 1845

CALVERT, George W., infant of John, 26 September.　MORE 27 Sep 1837

    Henry, son of L. N. and Mary, 10 March ae 2y 9m.　" 13 Mar 1846

CAMDEN, family of John B.:
    Eliza, wife of John B. of St. Louis, 13 September in Danville KY. Member 1st Presb. Church.　MORE 15 Sep 1849
    Thomas Hunter, infant of John B. and Eliza, Saturday 29 April.　" 1 May 1837
    Abram Miller, only child of J.B. and Eliza, at the home of P. G. Camden 11 May ae 2y 11m.　" 14 May 1838

CAMRON, Noel, oldest son of Capt. Niel and Frances, at
CAMERON   Saverton 1 July.　MORE 15 Jul 1851

    Willie, son of Prof. William and grandson of Joseph Shewalter, 2 August ae 19m.　LEXP 9 Aug 1854

CAMPBELL, Alexander B. in Dardenne Twp. 2 October.　NERA 8 Oct 1845

    Diana, only child of Mrs. Mary Ann, 10 Feb.; funeral from home of J. A. Wherry.　MORE 11 Feb 1842

    George W., of the City Hotel, 20 June; recently from Clinton Co.　SJA 21 Jun 1850
    John Quincy, son of Capt. James, 24 February ae 11y. Recently of Bedford Co. VA.　MORE 24 Mar 1836
    Mrs. Parmelia M. in Howard Co. 23 May.　NERA 6 Jun 1845
    Margaret Elizabeth, only daughter of D. C., of St. Louis Co., 18 Dec.　MORE 22 Dec 1838

    Children of Robert and Virginia:　(St. Louis)
        Hugh, 15 February ae 6d. Funeral from Planters' House, Episcopal Cemetery.　MORE 17 Feb 1844
        James Alexander ae 7y 1m 4d; family lived at Elm-5th.　" 19 Jun 1849
        Robert, of scarlet fever, 12 February ae 1y 4m.　" 14 Feb 1852

    Mrs. Sarah E., at the home of Alex Askins, 17 December in her 86th year.　HAJ 20 Dec 1849

    William N., in St. Louis, yesterday after a long illness. Funeral 2nd Presbyterian.　SLINT 1 Jan 1850

CANFIELD, John Edwards, eldest child of John E. of   MORE 29 Oct 1839
         Springfield, IL, at the home of
         A. Hayward, ae 3.

         Lucretia, wife of H. D. and daughter of Dr. Wm.   "   4 Jan 1850
         Beaumont, 2 January.

CANTER, Sarah M., widow of Emanuel, in her 36th year.   MORE 12 Sep 1849

CAPLES, Robert, infant of Rev. W. B., in Keytesville Wed.   BRUNS 14 Oct 1848
         (His mother had died in April.)

CAREY, Thomas Jr., son of Thomas and Elizabeth, 18 Jan.   SWERE 22 Jan 1849
         ae 3y 6m.

CARR, children of Archibald and Alletta: (St. Louis)
         Mary Augusta died Sunday, ae 4m.   SWERE 10 Feb 1845
         Thomas Randolph, 19 October ae 10m 11d.   MORE 21 Oct 1847

    Children of William C.:   (St. Louis)
         Charles Elliott, only son, Friday ae 12.   MORE 28 Sep 1826
         George Washington, infant, Saturday night;   "   19 Aug 1839
           buried Presbyterian Cemetery.
         William, ae <u>ca</u> 5, at their home on   "   14 Jul 1840
           St. Charles Rock Road.
    (Note: Wm. C.'s wife had died in August 1826.)

    Charles Berry, son of Capt. W. C. and Caroline,   MORE 23 Aug 1853
         21 August ae 3y 14d.

    Martha Elizabeth, daughter of Wm. C. and Dorcas,   "   13 Sep 1849
         10 September ae 5.

CARROLL, Eleanora, relict of John, 2 August ae 50.   NERA 5 Aug 1845

    John W., of cholera, 13 Jul ae 28.   "   14 Jul 1849

    Joseph, son of John, ae about 2.   MORE 28 Jun 1831

CARSON, children of Henry G. and Mary M.: (St. Louis)
         William Henry on 9 January ae 3y 9m.   MORE 10 Jan 1846
           Family home, Morgan-13th.
         Eugene, no date, ae 3y 9m. Buried in   "   18 Aug 1847
           the Methodist Cemetery.
         Melissa Sophia, daughter of William and Alethea,   PWH 16 Jul 1845
           9 July in her 8th year.

CARTER, Laura Ann, only daughter of John T., ae 5m 6d.   MORE 25 Aug 1853
         Rushville MD pc

    ___, child of William C., in St. Joseph 10 Aug.   "   19 Aug 1851

    William Henry, son of Henry A., 2 Sept. ae 11m.   "   6 Sep 1839

CARVER, William Allen, eldest son of William, 6 June   BGRAD 10 Jun 1843
         in his 9th year.

CASEY, Francis Charles, son of John and Juliette, at   MORE 19 Aug 1853
         Old Mines 11 Aug. ae 15y 9m 7d.

CASH, George R., son of Thomas and Permelia, 29 April   LADB 30 Apr 1849
         ae about 5.

CASHMAN, Mrs. Nancy at LaGrange, Lewis Co., 8 January in   HAJ 21 Jan 1847
        her 53rd year; a Methodist.

CASTLE, E. S. of Andrew Co., mother of Mrs. Alice Beardsley   SJA 9 Aug 1850   .
        of Gallipolis OH; had been visiting there,
        left on the <u>Pocahontas</u> 8 July, died on the
        <u>General Grant</u> after an 18-hour illness.

CASTLEMAN, Almeda, wife of William S. and daughter of
    see Addenda   Rev. Thomas J. Wright, 2 February in   NERA 15 Feb 1846
        Washington Co. ae 22.

CATHCART, John, son of Robert and Hannah, Morgan-9th St.,   MORE 18 Aug 1840
        died yesterday ae 5.

CATHERWOOD, Margaret Ann, wife of Robert, 26 June ae 28.   MORE 27 May 1850
        Funeral from Christ Church.
        Urbana & Wooster OH pc

CAYCE, Adaline F., only daughter of Milton P., in   NERA 28 Sep 1849
        Farmington 22 September.

        Newton F. of congestive fever in St. Francois Co.
        22 September in his 48th year; and   JEM 13 Oct 1846
    Louis (sic) his wife, 20 Sept. in her 45th year.

CERRE, Leon Silvester, son of Michael S. and Ellen,   SWERE 8 Nov 1847
        5 November ae 7y 5m.

CHAFFEY, Samuel, son of John H. and Theresa, 15 February   MORE 21 Feb 1853
        in Jefferson City.

CHAMBERLAIN, H. B., member of the 2nd Ward Board of   MORE 6 May 1850
        Delegates, 6 May of cholera.

CHAMBERLIN, Irene Augusta, 2nd daughter of Capt. B. B.,   MORE 8 Oct 1842
        6 October ae 5y 1m 20d.

CHAMBERS, children of David and Catherine: (St. Louis)
        Mary Lawrence, ae 3.   MORE 10 Feb 1840
        William Tyler, 28 February ae 2y 11m. Funeral   "   1 Mar 1843
           143 Market to Episcopal Cem.
      Children of James and Jane: (St. Louis)
          Thomas Jefferson, 27 January ae 4m 2w.   SWERE 31 Jan 1848
        Richard Graham, youngest child, at
          Taille de Noyer ae 15m.   MORE 10 Feb 1840

      James Dudley, infant of A. B.; funeral from
          6th-Walnut. Ae 6m. Buried   "   5 Mar 1839
          Presbyterian Cemetery.

      Charles, infant of Capt. John H. and Alcy,   SWERE 10 Nov 1845
          died 29 October.

      Children of H. S. and E.A., Moniteau Co.:
        Dorothy Ellen K., 2nd dau., 26 Aug. ae 11. JEM 14 Sep 1847
        Lelia Elvira, ygst dau; 27 Aug. ae 3.

CHAPMAN, Delia Maria, infant of Daniel H., 21 October.   MORE 22 Oct 1835

George, son of J. A. J. and H. E., 30 September   STGAZ 5 Oct 1853
    ae 15m. Brunswick & Boonville pc

James A., an attorney in Greene Co., 30 July   JEM 10 Aug 1847
    ae 24.

CHAPOUIL, William Anthony, son of Anthony and Mary, 17 Jan.   MORE 18 Jan 1840
    ae 21m. Lived at 89 Walnut St.
    Buried Methodist Cemetery.

CHARLES, Julia Dimmick, daughter of Edward and Elizabeth,   SLDU 23 Oct 1846
    21 October ae 3y 9m.

CHARLEVILLE, Joseph Alexander, son of Frederic and   SLINT 8 Jan 1850
    Gabrielle, 4 Jan ae 6m.

CHARLTON, Levi, in Montgomery Co.   NERA 11 Sep 1845

CHAUNING, see CHEWNING

CHAUVIN, Jacques J., son of Marie and the late Joseph,   MORE 14 Feb 1852
    last evening ae 13y 3m.

CHAYTER, William, son of Joseph and Theresa, ae 1y 3m 3d.   MORE 19 Sep 1853
    Funeral from home of late Isaac Snodgrass.

CHEATHAM, Alfred C., son of A. C. of DeWitt, 24 Apr. ae 9. BRUNS 28 Apr 1849

CHENOWETH, Sarah Elizabeth, youngest daughter of Alfred W.   SWERE 5 Mar 1849
    and Sarah Jane, 18 Feb ae 1y 14d.

CHEW, Sally, daughter of Mme. Manuel Lisa, "after a   MOG 22 Feb 1809
    distressing illness of about 12 days."

CHEWNING, family of John, of Vicksburg MS:
    James J., infant, 1 August at the home of   MORE 13 Aug 1838
        John Chewning ae 1y 24d.
    Sarah M. "in this city" Sunday last, ae 5.   " 16 Oct 1839

CHILDERS, Sarah, daughter of T. D., in Greene Co. 9 August. JEM 17 Aug 1847

CHILD, children of Alonzo and Mary: (St. Louis)
    Payton G., only son, yesterday ae 11m 12d. Family   MORE 1 Jul 1841
        lived at 144 N. 4th.
    George Franklin, infant, 18 July; lived 9th-Olive. "   19 Jul 1847

CHILDS, children of Joshua and Elizabeth: (St. Louis)
    Nathaniel, 18 June, ae 22m 5d. Cincinnati and   MORE 19 Jun 1849
        Baltimore pc
    Edward B., ae 7 or 8m.   " 23 Jun "

CHILES, children of Nathaniel: (St. Louis)
    Nathaniel Jr. 7 May ae 1y 4m; lived Franklin Ave. MORE 8 May 1839
    William Anderson 23 September ae 1y 26d.   " 24 Sep 1847
        Buried Wesleyan Cemetery.

CHOUTEAU, children of Henry: (St. Louis)
    George Lewis, Wednesday last.   MORE 7 Jun 1833
    Louise Euphemie, Sunday last.   " 9 Feb 1836
    Victoria, infant, night before last.   " 21 Feb 1840

CHRISTY, Ellen, youngest daughter of William T. and
        Ellen P., 28 January ae 2y 3m.   SWERE 31 Jan 1848

    Joseph A., son of the late S. C. and Melanie,
        23 July ae 15y 9m.   MORE 31 Jul 1843

    Louise Duquette, daughter of William, 6 August in   "
        St. Charles "of the prevailing   20 Aug 1833
        epidemic" ae 11y 9m 11d.

    Louisiana, daughter of Maj. William, Monday night. "   8 Mar 1810

CHURCHILL, sons of Samuel B. and Amelia C.: (St. Louis)
        Leo Walker 8 January ae 2y 28d. Lived on   MORE 10 Jan 1848
          5th St., buried Episcopal Cem.
          Louisville pc
        Walter, only surviving, 31 March ae 5m 2d.   SWERE 3 Apr 1848

CLAGGETT, children of William H.:   (Palmyra)
        Martha C., infant, "two weeks since."   PWH 28 Jan 1843
        William Henry, infant, Saturday night.   "   26 Mar 1845

CLAMORGAN, children of Louis and Julia: (St. Louis)
        Louis St. Eutrope 28 September ae 3y 5m.   MORE 1 Oct 1846
        Appolline, 21 March, ae not shown.   SWERE 27 Mar 1848

CLARK, children of John B. and Elenor: (in Fayette)
        * Philip, on Monday last.   MODE 28 Mar 1848
        Cornelia Hickman on 10 April.   "   18 Apr "
        * Philip Turner, Monday week ae 6y 7m.   BRUNS 6 Apr "

    Fanny, only daughter of John W. and Agnes, in   "
        St. Louis 31 December 1847, ae 2y 7m.   13 Jan 1848

    Dr. Isaac at Westport ae 26, late of Callaway Co.   JEM 26 Oct 1848

    James, infant of Huston and Eliza, yesterday.   MORE 13 Apr 1844

    James S., son of Samuel B., in Frankfort KY at
        the home of his uncle James Shannon; a   LADB 8 Mar 1847
        young man, was there to study painting.

    John Sanford, only son of Capt. John B., at the
        home of Alexander Sanford near   MORE 15 Jun 1842
        Florissant, ae 18m.

    Sarah Elizabeth, only daughter of Edwin D. and
        Henrietta, 5th-Green, ae 3m 13d.   MORE 24 Jan 1846

CLARKE, __, eldest son of A. B., of the St. Louis Theatre,
        drowned while bathing, ae 7.   SLDU 20 Aug 1847

    __ little daughter of Charles A., ca 18m, fell
        into scalding water. (Osage Yeoman)   BOLT 3 Feb 1844

    Maria T., daughter of W. G. and Julia, ae 11m.   MORE 7 Jan 1849

    Amanda, an orphan living with the family of
        Augustus Farnham, killed in a spirit gas "   18 May 1846
        explosion (two Farnham children died also).

CLARKSON, Catherine Dunlop, eldest daughter of Col. Charles
        and Charlotte, at the home   NERA 6 Jul 1849
        of Dr. Rannels, St. L. Co., 4 July.

CLATWORTHY, William in St. Joseph 26 April en route to CA;   JEM 21 May 1850
         of apoplexy; formerly of Jefferson City.

CLAYTON, Robert in Jackson Co. 5 April.   NERA 22 Apr 1845

CLAY, Amira wife of George, at Little Rock, 8 September
         ae 48, and their son George 4 September ae 15. MORE 24 Sep 1846
         Lexington KY pc

CLELAND, Martin, infant of Beriah, 15 February.   MORE 21 Feb 1832

CLIFFORD, William M. in Clarksville 25 June in his 39th
         year. A Mason, left wife, children.   LADB 2 Jul 1851

CLINE, Frederick, living on 7th St. Between Franklin-
         Morgan. Ae illegible. Fredericksbg VA pc   MORE 1 Nov 1849

COBB, Mrs. Elizabeth in Farmington 14 October. Born in
         Co. Tyrone IRE 1768, to Newcastle DE   SLOB 30 Oct 1834
         with mother and 5 siblings after father's
         death. Married Richard Cobb ca 1797.
         He survived, with one son. (Family
         emigrated about 1796.)

COBURN, Frances, daughter of Thomas and Eliza, 11 November SWERE 15 Nov 1847
         ae 6m 11d.

COCHRAN, Philip Gaw, son of Rev. and Mrs. W.P., 9 October   PWH 4 Oct 1849
         ae 2m 6d.

         James, formerly of NY, suddenly ae 23.   NERA 3 Dec 1845

CODY, Miss Bridget 4 July ae 19. (Cholera?)   NERA 6 Jul 1849

COFFEY, Jane, daughter of the late Thomas, ae 3y 9m.   MORE 11 Jun 1849
         Lived at 5th-Carr.

COGLEY, D. H., formerly of MI, drowned en route to CA.   "   14 Oct 1849

COHEN, Sallie, daughter of Albert and Sarah, ae 3m 24d.   MORE 25 Apr 1849
         Funeral from home of J. W. Owings.

         George, son of William and Emily, 18 October ae 4y. MORE 25 Oct 1847
         (family apparently of Hannibal; see below)
         William Jr., son of William of Hannibal, 6 Sept.
         in St. Louis.   HANT 9 Sep 1852
         (Emily Cohen died in St. Louis in 1851)

COLBURN, Walter, son of John, of Carondelet, 4 July   MORE 5 Jul 1833
         of cholera.

         Nancy, daughter of Norris, 27 September ae 1y.   "   28 Sep 1841

         Samuel, only child of Frederick M. and Martha, SWERE 3 Dec 1848
         27 November ae 2m.

COLEMAN, Caroline, consort of Samuel, 20 November.   HAJ 30 Nov 1848

         Fanny, daughter of Nathan and Frances, infant, MORE 17 Jul 1844
         yesterday; lived Morgan between 12-13.
         Frances, wife of Nathan and daughter of the late NERA 2 Aug 1849
         Josias Dallam, 1 August ae 37.

COLLIER, Catherine Emily, daughter of George, 6 August in   MORE 11 Aug 1829
         St. Charles ae 6m 17d.

COLLIER, Frances Euphrasie, daughter of George and Sarah, 27 February ae 4y 7m.   NERA 2 Mar 1846

    Mary Jane, consort of William of St. Louis, at the home of R. K. McLaughlin, Vandalia.   MORE 21 Aug 1849

COLLINS, George Sr. in Warren Co. 30 August.   NERA 23 Sep 1845

COLVIN, Anna Maria, daughter of John W. and Mary Elizabeth, 11 August ae 1y 8m.   MORE 13 Aug 1847

COMFORT, Fanny, only child of James H. and Mariette, ae 10m; buried Bellefontaine.   MORE 22 Jun 1851

COMPTON, William, infant of W.T.S. and S.R., Saturday.   MORE 9 Nov 1843

CONDON, William A., son of Albion and Eliza, 13 September ae 2y 3m 10d.   MORE 14 Sep 1853

CONN, children of Joseph H. and Elizabeth: (St. Louis)
    Sally Ann, infant, 19 March; funeral from home of Maj. W.C. Anderson.   MORE 20 Mar 1844
    Sally Ann, ae 17m, 19 February; funeral from home, Pine near 14th St.   SWERE 19 Feb 1849
    Joseph, ae 4y 4m 9d, on 7 June.   MORE 9 Jun 1849
    Charles Anderson, ae 9y 24d, on 17 June.   NERA 24 Jun 1849

CONNELLY, Fannie Alice, infant of William and the late Elizabeth; funeral from home of Mrs. Kiger.   MORE 26 Jun 1851

CONWAY, Lovett, son of Eugene and Johanna, ae 8m 3d. Memphis & NY pc   MORE 12 Aug 1853

    Mary Elizabeth, youngest daughter of Frederick R. and Martha L., 5 Jan. ae 2y 3m. (MORE 6 Jan. says 2y 2m 26d, buried Methodist Cemetery.)   SWERE 10Jan 1848

COOK, Adelaide, wife of Robert of St. Louis, 18 July near Wilmington Delaware.   NERA 19 Jul 1849
    Martin, infant of Robert, 18 July near Wilmington DE.   "   26 "

    Annie, daughter of Dr. M. C. and Emily, ae 14m.   MORE 4 Jul 1849

    Mary Elizabeth, wife of George Freeman, ae 28.   "   10 "

    Mary Ellen, daughter of Henry and Ellen, 20 September ae 8m 19d.   PWH 23 Sep 1843

    Margaret Josephine, daughter of Langford and Lydia, Wed. last ae 7m 15d.   MODE 12 Aug 1846

    Theresa, at the home of Mrs. E. Herford, 11 May.   SWERE 14 May 1849

COOLEY, Dr. Lawson at his home near Herculaneum 22 July of cholera, in his 47th year. Formerly of Hartford Co. MD.   NERA 2 Aug 1849
    Lawson, only son of Dr. L. and Amanda, 18 Jan. at Clinton, Jefferson Co., ae 3y 3m.   SWERE 7 Feb 1848

COOLIDGE, children of Curtis and Catherine P.: (St. Louis)
        Frances Adelaide 22 November ae 3y 10m.   MORE 23 Nov 1843
                Funeral 3rd-Cedar.
      Helen Rebecca, only daughter, Saturday ae 11m. " 16 Jan 1844 .

COONS, Benjamin F., son of George W. and Semphronia, at the MORE 27 Sep 1851
        home of Gen. Lanham in Bonhomme Twp.
        ae 5y 7m 10d.

      Joseph, ae about 6, on 22 January.   PWH 3 Feb 1848

      William Dellord, son of Dr. A. J. and Fanny, of MORE 26 May 1850
           St. Louis, at Fredericksburg VA
           ae 15m.

COOPER, Sarah, mother of the late Jacob of St. Louis, in NERA 20 Jul 1849
        St. Louis Co. in her 93rd year; widow of
        William of VA, a Revolutionary soldier.
      Hardage Lane, son of Jacob, 26 August ae 14m. MORE 27 Aug 1841
        Lived at 74 S. 7th St.

      Children of Thomas R. and Eurania Bouis:
(see Addenda) Frances Twichell, 20 Dec ae 4y 8m 20d. SWERE 24 Dec 1848
        Taylor W., infant, 29 November.   " 3 "

COORMAN, Marcella, daughter of James and Ellen, 3 May MORE 4 May 1853
        ae 4y 5m 3d.

COPELIN, Mary, daughter of John R. and J.M.D., ae 3y 8m. PWH 17 Dec 1846

COPES, Mrs. Mary Louise, consort of Thomas P., 31 Dec. SLNL 3 Jan 1846
        in St. Charles in her 47th year,

CORBIN, Frances Doan, only child of Rev. A. D. and Mary MORE 22 Jul 1842
        Edgerton, at Kemper College Tuesday.

CORDELL, Annette, 2nd daughter of E.B., 25 July ae 17. JEM 30 Jul 1850

      Fanny, daughter of the late John, in Jackson MO MORE 19 Jan 1853
        (Cape Girardeau Co.) 4 January.

      Presley, native of VA, ae 70.   MORE 15 Jul 1849
      Amelia, consort of Presley, ae 65.   " 16 "

CORDER, James Henry in Lafayette Co. 27 October. NERA 11 Nov 1845

CORNELIUS, Mary Frances, infant of William, last MIN 23 Feb 1833
        Tuesday in Columbia.

CORSE, William, son of William and Cornelia, 6 July ae MORE 7 Jul 1841
        11m 13d. Lived 5th near Convent;
        buried Methodist Cemetery.

CORTAMBERT, Emilia St. Xavier, daughter of Louis and MORE 6 Jul 1848
        Susan, 5 July ae 9m 17d.

CORWIN, Rebecca H. wife of Joseph in Louisiana MO 7 June LADB 10 Jun 1850
        ae 28y 3m 19d; and their infant,
        Martha Jane, in Cape Girardeau 8 June.

COULTER, Perrine McMichael, youngest son of George W. and SWERE 15 Aug 1847
        Margaret, 10 August ae 19d.
        Greenburg PA pc

COURTNEY, James Clendenin, son of Thomas J. and M.A., 19 June ae 16m.   MORE 22 Jun 1853

COUTE, George J. C., son of Clement W. and Sarah, of scarlet fever, 19 November.   MORE 20 Nov 1848

COUZINS, infant of James W. and P.J., 15 August; buried Episcopal Cemetery, mother died same day.   "   16 Sep 1841

COWIE, Jane, consort of John, 2 August in her 16th year.   NERA 4 Aug 1849

COWLES, Dr. Franklin, recently of St. Louis, formerly of Farmington CT, en route to CA.   MORE 2 Aug 1849

* COX, Annie, daughter of John and Bridget, ae 1y 8m 4d.   MORE 23 Jan 1852

COXE, Henry, formerly cashier of the Branch Bank of US, many years a resident of St. Louis, ae ca 47, at Planter's House. Funeral from Christ Church, buried O'Fallon cemetery.   SLINT 16 Jan 1850
Henry S., son, 21 April in his 11th month.   MORE 26 Apr 1833
Walter, only child, 28 October ae 23m.   "   29 Oct 1841

CRAIN, Rev. Caleb, in Cape Girardeau Co.   NERA 7 Jul 1845

CRANDALL, Rev. A.J., pastor of Ebenezer Chapel.   MORE 13 Sep 1849

CRANE, children of Dr. Josiah M. and Adaline: (St. Joseph)   STGAZ 9 or 16
Mary Lunette 12 May ae 3y 6m   Jun 1852
Oscar J. 8 June ae 18m

George W., eldest son of J. W. and Emily; lived 4th betw Pine-Locust. Louisville pc   MORE 26 Nov 1849

CRAPSTER, Frances B., wife of John and daughter of John Short of Emmetsburg MD, 10 May. Buried St. Vincent's.   MORE 11 May 1850

CRAWFORD, Harriet, daughter of George, 3 Oct ae 18y 7m. Member Baptist Church.   WEM 24 Oct 1839

Rachel of Chariton Co., Letters of Administration to Edwin T. Hickman.   (no date shown)   MIN 5 Sep 1828

Rev. William M. 31 May at the home of George W. Caplinger, in Hannibal, in his 37th y. Methodist, IOOF, born in Georgetown KY.   HAG 10 Jun 1847

CRENSHAW, William E. T., son of Robert A. W. and Anne, 27 August ae 1y 21d. Buried Wesleyan.   MORE 29 Aug 1853

CROMWELL, Phebe Ellen, daughter of Richard, 7 March in Columbia ae 7y.   MIN 15 Mar 1834

CROPP, Albert L., son of Lewis T. and Mary Jane, 3 June ae 13y 5m 3d.   MODE 27 Jun 1848

CROSS, Barbara M., wife of John, in Cape Girardeau Co. 8 January.   CGWE 12 Jan 1849

CROW, Medora, infant of Wayman, 8 January ae 10m 27d.   MORE 9 Jan 1838

* See Addenda

24

CROW, Alice Maria daughter of Wayman and Isabella,   MORE   8 Nov 1849
                        ae 4y 8m 17d.

CROWLY, John, son of John and Margaret, 21 March ae 17m16d. SWERE 26 Mar 1849

CROWTHER, Margaret Lavinia, daughter of James and Mary,   SWERE 30 Sep 1844
                        24 September ae 1y 8m.

CULVER, Matilda, widow of Dr. Henry, in Potosi of   NERA 25 Jul 1849
                cholera in her 52d year.

CUMMINS, Jane, consort of John, formerly of Maysville KY,   SLNL   6 Mar 1847
                yesterday ae 54.

CURTISS, Daniel, eldest son of Josiah and Nancy, formerly   MORE   2 Feb 1846
                of St. Louis, in Green Co. IL ae 7y3m6d.

CUTHBERT, George, son of Samuel and Eugenia, 24 January   MORE 25 Jan 1853
                        ae 15m.

CUTTER, Hannah, wife of Moses, formerly of VT, 9 June   SLMD 12 Jun 1854
                in her 80th year.

        Norman, son of Ames and Catherine, ae 3y 3m.   MORE   4 Jul 1849

CUTTING, Harriet Louise, daughter of Amos and Theodora,   MORE 11 Jul 1853
                7 July. Boston pc

DAILY, Thomas, shown on a hospital list: ae 11, born in   MORE 20 Jun 1840
                St. Peters, son of a soldier; blind.

DALLAS, George Abel, son of Alexander J. and Catherine,   PWH 1 Apr 1843
                27 April at West Ely ae 16m 5d.

DALY, Michael 9 May in his 56th year at the home of James   MORE   9 May 1850
                Timon. Funeral Cathedral; Catholic cemetery.

DANIEL, William on 23 July ae 65; Susan, his wife, 27 July
                ae 55; Melinda, their daughter, 27 July   NERA 30 Jul 1849
                ae 15; Jacket G. Emily (sic), their
                daughter, 28 July in her 17th year. All
                of cholera.

DANIELS, children of William and Lois: (St. Louis)
                Jane Ann 11 October ae 6y 4m 22d.   NERA 14 Oct 1845
                Amanda 24 September ae 16m 25d.

        George W., son of W., Sunday last ae 19.   JEM 3 Aug 1847

DANNER, John, recently from NC, in Greene Co. 18 July.   "   "   "

DARBY, Emilie, daughter of John F. and Mary M., 27 April   MORE 28 Apr 1847
                ae 2y 9m. Buried Catholic Cemetery.

DARLINGTON, Charles, infant of J.H., in Livingston Co.   JEM 16 Nov 1848

DARST, Robert Lucien, son of Robert A. and Julie, 5th &   MORE 22 Mar 1843
                Myrtle, yesterday ae 2y 4m.

DAUGHERTY, Joseph, son of Ralph, at the home of his grand-   JASO 17 Nov 1838
                father, Col. George Bollinger, on White
                Water, 10 November ae 7.

DAVENPORT, Martha Jane, daughter of H.C., 9 July ae 6y11m4d. LADB 18 Jul '46

25

DAVIES, William Henry, son of Thomas Warren and Mary A.,   MODE 27 Jun 1848
                injured in machinery at the G. N.
                Douglass carding house, died
                21 June ae 4y 9m.

DAVIS, Carrington ae ca 21d, on 12 October.   BGRAD 14 Oct 1843

    Children of D. D. and Theresa: (St. Louis)
           Emelinda Theresa 11 May ae 14m.   MORE 13 May 1844
           Elizabeth 7 March ae 2m 21d.   "   7 Mar 1846

    David Robert, eldest son of Greer, 26 June in 3rd y. INP 3 Jul 1824

    Alonzo, infant of George, yesterday in this city. MORE 26 Jul 1836

    Jannet Martha, only daughter of Horatio and   MORE 1 Sep 1840
              Elizabeth, 30 August.
    John, infant of Rev. John, 8 July.   "   19 Jul 1831

    Mrs. Mary E., consort of Dr. D. L., at Bowling   LADB 7 Aug 1848
              Green 27 July in 23rd year. Left
              "infant children;" ill a few hours.

    Caroline Augusta, daughter of Samuel C. and
              Caroline, 29 June ae 4m.   MORE 30 Jun 1847

DAVISON, Edward J. at his home near Jefferson City 3 Sep.   JEM 26 Sep 1848
              in his 49th year; brother of Drs. W.A.
              and A.M., native of Frederick Co. VA.
              Wife, 2 children. Heart disease.
        Mary Baldwin, 2nd daughter of Edward J., 19 Nov. " 1 Dec 1846

DAWSON, Emma Philadelphia, daughter of Wm. R. and Ann Eliza, MORE 23 Jul 1851
        in Cape Girardeau 17 July ae 2y 6m 25d.

    Children of Wm. R., mother not shown:
        John Summerfield, ae 22m, at Bellevue,   MORE 28 Feb 1837
           Washington Co., 23 January.
        Frelinghausen, ae 14m 13d, on 15 October.   "   18 Oct 1845
        (Lynchburgh and Richmond VA pc)
        George Washington 30 August at Cape Girardeau, MODE 22/20
           Wm. R. was editor of the Western Eagle.   Sep 1847

DAY, Alice, daughter of Charles A. and Diana E., near   FULT 17 Aug 1849
            Portland 20 July ae 6m 6d.

DAYTON, children of B. B. and Mary F. of St. Louis: MORE 28 Sep 1848
        Amelia in Philadelphia 27 Sept. ae 23m 21d.
        Mary Amelia, only child, 21 November of   SLMD 22 Nov 1854
           convulsions ae 6y. Buried Belf.

DEAN, Isabel, only child of George P. and Ellen M, at   MORE 8 Sep 1851
        Boonville 21 August.

    James Edward, son of J. Parker, 13 April.   MORE 15 Apr 1839

DEANE, Eloise Stella, daughter of Charles and Eloise,   MORE 1 Jan 1850
        249 N. 5th, 1 January ae 18m.
        Middleton CT pc
DEAVENPORT, children of H.C.:   (Louisiana MO)
        Martha Jane 9 July ae 6y 11m 4d.   LADB 18 Jul 1846
        Mary L. 4 November ae 16m 7d.   "   22 Nov 1847

DEAVER, Margaret Augusta 6 January ae 9y 8m.   SLMD 9 Jan 1854

     Sophia Augusta 21 June ae 17.   MORE 22 Jun 1839

DeBANN, Anna Elvira, youngest child of George Jr. and the   MORE 19 Mar 1849 .
        late Sarah Ann, 18 March ae 4m 2d.

DeCAMP, children of James C. and Ellen, of St. Louis:
        John ae 9 and Anna ae 3, in   MORE 26 Nov 1851
                San Francisco.

DECKERS, Mary wife of Albert, of extreme debility,   NERA 8 Aug 1849
        7 August ae 48.

DELAFIELD, Charles, of Milwaukee, at the home of Edw. Mead. MORE 8 Jun 1842

DELISLE, Caroline, wife of J., 27 April in her 37th year.   "   29 Apr 1850

DeMOSS, Elizabeth, consort of Charles, 18 December.   HAG 24 Dec 1846

DENNING, Mary J. of St. Louis, wife of William G., at the   SLDU 25 Dec 1847
        home of her father near Vincennes 20 Dec.

DENNY, William, son of William S. and Anna, 2 Sept. ae 1y 10m. MORE 4 Sep'41

DENT, Mary Ann, daughter of Frederick, 9 October at   MORE 16 Oct 1832
        Gravois ae 1y 11m.

DEPEW, Robert, of St. Louis, on the plains east of the
        Little Blue 25 June, of cholera, ae 62.   NERA 29 Dec 1849
        Formerly of Easton PA.

DePREFONTAINE, Frances W., infant of Dr. J.R., of croup,   MORE 24 Nov 1835
        21 November.

DERRICKSON, Henry Brent, son of Charles and the late Emily, BRUNS 27 Sep 1849
        yesterday ae 3-1/2m.

DETCHEMENDY, Mary Therese, widow of Pascal, near Old
        Mines 15 November ae 67.   MORP 26 Nov 1845
        Native of Kaskaskia, nee St. Gemme.

DETRO, Edward E., son of E. S. and Ann Maria, ae 5m.   MORE 23 Oct 1849
        Louisville & Baltimore pc

DEVER, Amanda in St. Louis Co., ae about 18.   SLOB 1 May 1834

DEVRAUX, Mrs. Nicholas on Thursday, ae 36.   SLDU 17 Oct 1846

DEVOTION, Louis "last Monday."   MORE 30 Oct 1822

DeVOY, William Nicholas, son of Nicholas and Mary Ann,   SLMD 28 Jan 1854
        of lung congestion, ae 4y 6m.

DEVRICKS, George Millard, son of T. W. and Martha G.,   SLMD 12 Jun 1854
        10 June ae 1y 8m 24d.

DEWARD, Charles Dunning, infant of Charles and Margaret,   MORE 26 Sep 1837
        yesterday. Funeral Florida-Laurel.

DEXTER, Elizabeth Vila, youngest child of James W. and   PWH 30 Sep 1843
        Sarah E., 25 Sept. ae 17m.

DICK, Mildred A., consort of Nathaniel, 9 Aug. ae 32.   HAG 24 Aug 1848

DICKINSON, Wm. Mad., son of N., 8 December ae 4 weeks.   BORE 12 Dec 1843

DICKSON, Harriet Agnes, infant of Rev. W. T., at
    West Ely 4 September.   PWH 17 Sep 1842

DIX, Mary Elizabeth at the home of her son in the country,
    ae 60. Wheeling pc   MORE 17 Aug 1849

DIXON, Eliza Giddings, only daughter of D. W. and
    Mary A., 19 Oct. ae 18m 15d.   SWERE 20 Oct 1847

DOBBIN, Sarah Elizabeth, daughter of Leonard W. of
    LaGrange, drowned in the Mississippi Sunday. PWH 29 Apr 1847

DOBYNS, Sarah, consort of James, 28 July of cholera in
    her 28th year.   NERA 30 Jul 1849

DODGE, Elizabeth Whipple, wife of Ezra and daughter of
    Seth Allen of Providence RI, 21 May.   NERA 26 May 1845

    L. Channing, infant of Luther and Ann, of
      Glasgow, ae 11m.   MODE 29 Aug 1848

DODSON, Rev. Thomas of the Christian Church in
    Greene Co. 4 September.   JEM 14 Sep 1847

DOLMAN, Andrew Craig, son of John H. and the late
    Sarah C.· Zanesville OH pc   MORE 16 Jun 1849

DONALDSON, Chester Butler, son of Dr. A. C. and Phebe,
    3 October ae 2y 11m.   MORE 6 Oct 1846

    Phebe, wife of Dr. A. C., 12 July of cholera
    ae about 38.   NERA 15 Jul 1849

    Sons of James F. and Julia Ann: (St. Louis)
    Henry Clay 27 July ae 16m. Troy OH pc   MORE 30 Jul 1844
    James Lee, only son, drowned off the   " 24 Jul 1846
      Crittenden to St. Louis. Troy OH pc

DONELL, James, son of James and Margaret, 9 Sept. ae 3y10m.
    Lived 3rd betw Chestnut-Market.   MORE 10 Sep 1847

DONELLAN, John 24 September in his 80th year. MORE 25 Sep 1849

DONNELL, Charles Rankin, son of Thomas and Mary, in
    Jefferson Co. ae 2y 6m.   MORE 12 Oct 1844

    Jane, wife of Rev. James, 2 Dec. in Jefferson Co. " 13 Jan 1840

DONOVAN, Francis, brother of Dan H. of St. Louis, 26 Jan.
    in Hangtown CA of an enlarged spleen. MORE 25 Apr 1850

DORMAN, James M., late of McMurray and Dorman, 2 March
    of smallpox in his 33rd year.   MORE 3 Mar 1850

DORSEY, Elizabeth Louisa, only daughter of George and
    Ann Permelia, in Boonville 5 Jan. ae 5m. BOBS 15 Jan 1851

DOUGLASS, George Thompson, youngest son of John T. and
    Cornelia, in Boonville 24 Jul ae 2y 6m. SLMD 2 Aug 1854

    Howard, youngest son of John T., a (11?15?)m. MORE 17 May 1851

    Mary B., wife of Alexander T., 8 June in her   MORE 9-10
    54th year. Funeral from late home of   Jun 1850
    Capt. P. Salisbury. Buried Bellefontaine.

DOUGLASS, William H., son of George N. and Charlotte,   BOLT 30 Aug 1845
          25 August ae 4.

DOWDALL, George Samuel, son of John and America, ae 12m 17d. MORE 14 Aug 1846
          Louisville KY & Hannibal MO pc

DOWLING, Margaret, eldest daughter of Richard and Elenor.   MORE 10 Jul 1849
          Mary Sophia, daughter of Richard and Ellen (sic)   "   14 Apr 1853
          13 April ae 3y 10m.

DOWNS, __, a child about 2 years old, "near camp," strayed   MOG 28 Jun 1815
          from home, found dead the next morning.

DOYLE, Elouise, daughter of James L. and Henrietta, 6m 16d. MORE 18 Jun 1853

          John, at the home of his son William, 3rd-Myrtle, NERA 2 Apr 1845
          1 April ae about 70.

          Lawrence, ae 29.   MORE 27 Aug 1849

DRAKE, Adele, infant of John, 14 August.   MORE 17 Aug 1838

          Harriet Elizabeth, infant of Charles D. and Martha, MORE 28 Jul 1841
          ae 9m 11d. Funeral from J. Charless home.
          Buried Presbyterian cemetery.

          Elizabeth, infant of Silas, 98 Market St.   MORE 1 Apr 1839

DRAPER, children of Edwin and Urania:
          Martha Lucy, 4 January ae 2y 6m.   BGRAD 20 Jan 1844
          Urania L. 12 October ae 3y 8m 18d.   LADB 23 Oct 1848

DRYDEN, Sarah W., infant of John D. S., in Shelby Co.   PWH 6 Aug 1845
          31 July.
          Josephine, daughter of John D. S. and Sarah F.,   " 26 Jul 1849
          Wednesday last ae about 18m.

DUBBS, Susan M., daughter of Martin and Catherine,   SLDU 24 Nov 1846
          23 Nov. ae 6y 11m. (or 4y? 11m)

DUBREUIL, Paul C., son of Charles B., grandson of Rene   MORE 7 Oct 1839
          Paul, 5 October ae 10m.

DUCHOQUETTE, Mme. Baptiste "Wednesday night last."   MOG 10 Jul 1818

          Celeste, widow of Henry, 25 March.   MORP 26 Mar 1845

          Malvina, daughter of Mrs. Henry Lynch, ae 13,   MORE 16 Feb 1850
          Friday at Visitation Academy.

DUFFAY, Walter, son of Capt. Daniel, 1 October of throat
          inflammation ae 8. Lived on Barry   SLMD 2 Oct 1854
          between Carondelet & 7th St.

DUFRENE, Joseph, at the home of his brother Sylvester.   MORE 29 Aug 1849
DUFRESNE
          Celeste, consort of Auguste, ae 44, and their   MORE 8 Jul 1849
          daughter Ellen Antoinette. (cholera?)

DUHRING, Lena (or Sina), youngest daughter of Andrew and   SWERE 19/22
          Mary A., 18 Nov. ae 18m 23d.   Nov 1847

DUMAINE, Amede, infant daughter of Lucien, 8 July.   MORE 9 Jul 1833

DUNCAN, Mary Virginia, infant of T.O. and J.E., Saturday.   MORE 9 Oct 1839

DUNCAN, William Fullerton, infant of Thomas O. of St. Louis, MORE 12 Aug 1834
at the Sulphur Springs 8 August ae 6m.

DUNN, Margaret, wife of John, Barry-Fulton Sts., 12 July. NERA 14 Jul 1849

Mary Jane, daughter of James, in Benton Co. JEM 24 Aug 1847
10 August ae 27.

Mary Jane, eldest daughter of H. B., 5 December. PWH 30 Dec 1847

Meta J. K., youngest daughter of E.W. and Mary B., CANE 2 Nov 1854
25 Oct. at LaGrange ae 17m 7d.

William C., 12th-Olive. Buried Presbyterian Cem. MORE 10 Jul 1849

DUNNICA, Theodore, oldest son of William F. and Martha J., GLWT 4 Sep 1851
2 September.

DURACK, J. H., infant of John and Ophelia, Friday ae 11m. SWERE 28 Sep 1846
(SLDU 26 Sept. gives initials as J.W.,
residence Morgan-13th.)

DURBIN, children of Richard: (Palmyra)
Richard, ae 3, on 5 August; Christina on
9 August, ae 5; Sarah E. 10 Aug., ae 9. PWH 19 Aug 1843
All of scarlet fever.
Elisha son of Benedict, date not shown, also of   "   "
scarlet fever.

DWYER, Catharine, grand-daughter of William, at his home MORE 7 May 1842
on S. 4th in her 10th year.

DYE, children of John: (Palmyra)
Smith P., Friday last, ae 6; Emily, on PWH 12 Aug 1847
Sunday, both of measles.

DYER, Hannah G., wife of Dr. William, formerly of Boston, NERA 27 Jul 1849
22 July. (cholera?)

Samuel, youngest son of L.B. and C.C., ae 3? y 2m. MORE 7 Jun 1850

DYSON, Mary, wife of Abraham, 5 July of congestion of NERA 6 Jul 1849
the brain, in her 37th year.

Parents not shown: Laura Antonio Pauline 6 July
ae 13m; William Taylor 2 July SLMD 8 Jul 1854
ae 2y 4m, both of measles.

EADS, Eliza at her father's home Friday last in 19th year. MOSN 31 Mar 1838

James B., son of James B. and Martha, 15 June ae 10m. MORE 16 Jun 1849

EARICKSON, Gustavus, son of Judge James, 18 August MIN 26 Aug 1825
in Howard Co.

EASTBURN, Thomas, only son of a widow, ae 11. MORE 29 May 1832

EASTERLY, Burnett, only child of Dr. E. and Mary Jane.   "   10 Jan 1853

EASTIN, Kitty Ann, daughter of James W., 15 September. PWH 25 Sep 1841

EASTON, sons of Joseph G.: (Palmyra)
Russell, infant on 22 Feb. (mother Jane) PWH 25 Sep 1841
Langdon, infant, mother not shown, 17 July.   "   23 Jul 1842

30

EASTWOOD, Arthur, of Madison Co. MO, Tuesday in New Orleans. MORE 18 Feb '50

EATON, Harriet Elizabeth 8 May ae 3y 10m, only daughter
               of Nathaniel J. and Harriet H..   MORE 10 May 1841

    William, eldest son of Capt. Eaton, ae 21.   "   31 Aug 1849

ECK, daughters of Joseph and Ellen, St. Louis:
          Fanny, ae 15½m.   MORE 26 Aug 1851
          Ellen, ae 18m.   "   30 Oct 1843

EDDINS, infant of Mr/Mrs. A. D. Monday, ae 4m.   BRUNS 14 Oct 1847

EDDY, Frances E., daughter of George and Catherine, 7 May.   MORE 8 May 1853

    Munson Beach, son of James H. and Mary Jane, 8 July
             in St. Louis ae 18m.   MORE 13 Jul 1836

EDGAR, Edward Sproule, son of Edward, 15 March.   MORE 16 Mar 1838

    Sons of Joseph C. and Lucy W., 5th betw Wash-Carr:
          Cyrus D., ae 1.   MORE 21 Aug 1837
          Joseph Dorey, 2m 25d. Buried Methodist Cem. "   9 Jun 1851
          Joseph Philip 23 March ae 3y 4m.   " 24 Mar 1846

EDGELL, Louisa, daughter of Stephen and Louisa, 17 May <u>ca</u> 3. SLMD 20 May '53

EDMONDSON, Richard H. drowned in the pond in Lindell's
             pasture, ae 17.   MORE 14 Jun 1854

     Rebecca, consort of Dr. B. B., 24 October in her
          34th y. Left 5 small children.   MORP 5 Mar 1845

EDWARDS, Cabanne, son of A.G. and Louisiana, 19 July ae 3. MORE 20 Jul 1841
    Children of A.G. and Mary E., St. Louis:
          Clara Ewing, 23 May ae 1y 10m 17d.   MORE 24 May 1853
          James P., 2 June ae 9m 15d.   "   3 Jun "

    Children of Hiram G. and Martha of Bowling Green:
          Charles Carr 6 August ae 11m
          Mary 12 August ae 3y 6m   LADB 28 Aug 1848
            both of scarlet fever.

    Marcellus, resident physician at City Hospital.   MORE 23 Jul 1849

EFFINGER, Agnes, consort of Rev., at their home 5m west of
          Caledonia 3 February (sic) ae 16y 11m.   SLMD 10 Mar 1854

EGAN, David, a small boy living at 4th-Franklin, drowned
           in a well.   MORP 16 Jun 1845

EHRENHEICH, Wilhelm A. A., only son of Carl A. A. and
          Emilie E., 10 May ae 11m.   CGWE 16 Jun 1848

EIDSON, Morman H. on 31 May of cholera morbus ae 42.   LADB 11 Jun 1851
          Resident a number of years, joined Noix
          Creek United Baptist Church last November.
          Large family, mostly daughters, and wife.

ELIOT, Elizabeth Cranch, daughter of Wm. Greenleaf and
          Abby Adams, 18 December.   MORE 22 Dec 1845

ELLIS, Mary Elizabeth, daughter of M., 31 May ae 14m 5d.   MORE 3 Jun 1852
          Brunswicker & Grand River Chronicle pc

ELLIS, Mildred, widow of William, 13 August ae 71.
        Formerly of Spottsylvania Co. VA.   SLMD 29 Aug 1853

    Rosa, wife of Dr. Robert and daughter of
        Rev. Hiram P. Goodrich, 26 February.   MORE 25 Feb 1850

    Sarah Frances, twin daughter of Charles D. and
        Hannah B., 7 August ae 22m.   NERA 11 Aug 1849
    Thomas Pierce, youngest child of Charles D.,
        14 September ae 1y 9m.   MORE 16 Sep 1847

ELY, Benjamin in Ralls Co., ae 75.   JEM 21 Sep 1847

ELZEA, Kennerly A., son of Samuel, thrown from a horse. HAJ 26 Apr 1849

ERSKINE, Frank, son of Green, ae 19m.   MORE 27 Aug 1833

ESSEX, daughters of James and Rebecca, St. Louis:
        Mary Lee, 24 January ae 2y 8m. Funeral
          from home, 105 Franklin.   SWERE 27 Jan 1845
        Elizabeth, youngest daughter, 18 March
          ae 1y 5m.   NERA 19 Mar 1846

ESTES, Elizabeth, consort of William, 2 August in this city. JEM 13 Aug 1850

    Martha Ann, daughter of W. S. and Elizabeth, ae 4m. SASE 9 Jul 1853

EVANS, Mrs. __, mother-in-law of Dr. George McCullough,
        Florissant, 8 July ae about 62.   NERA 15 Jul 1849
    Lindal James, infant of Augustin, on Sunday.   MORE 7 Feb 1832

EWING, Sonoma Dale, ae 19m 12, 1 October at the home of
        her grandfather C. S. Ewing.   LEXP 4 Oct 1854

    Children of William L. and Clara, St. Louis:
        George on 6 September ae 5y 5m.   MORE 8 Sep 1853
        Nathaniel L., youngest son, 13 May.   " 14 May 1846

    William G., son of Col. George W. of St. Louis, at
        Monticello IL 25 July ae 2y 9m 2d.   MORE 28 Jul 1847

FACKLER, James H., son of William H. and Pamelia P., in
        Franklin Co. 11 August ae 7m 13d.   MORE 20 Aug 1842

FAGAN, Amanthus, daughter of Thomas and Caroline, 8 Apr.
        in Louisville ae 6y 3m. Liberty MO pc MORE 15 Apr 1848

    Thomas Bouchier, son of James and Sarah, ae 8.   " 8 Jul 1849

FAGG, Maj. John at his home in Pike Co. 12 October
        in his 71st year.   LADB 19 Oct 1846

FARMER, Benjamin, estate, Chariton Co.: sale of grain and
        property by W. W. Farmer, adm.   BRUNS 21 Jan 1854

FARNHAM, children of Augustus, 5th-Green:
        Alwin ae 5 and Ann ae 3 burned in an
        explosion of spirit gas.   MORE 18 May 1846

FARRAR, Dr. Bernard ae 65. (cholera epidemic)   MORE 4 Jul 1849
    Charles T., son of Dr. B. G., Friday night.   " 28 Aug 1832

    Henry "many years a fifer with the St. Louis Greys." " 24 Jul 1849

FARRELL, Benjamin at his home in St. Charles Co. 11 May,   LADB 31 May 1847
          "long a respectable citizen of that
          county." Methodist.

          John W., infant of John, 16 August.   MORE 19 Aug 1840 ·

          William 16 August after a short, painful illness.   NERA 16 Aug 1845

FARRENS, Eli H. in Andrew Co. 1 October ae 19.   JEM 20 Oct 1846

FARRIS, Samuel P., infant of Gen. Robert P. of St. Louis,   MORE 13 Oct 1829
          in Potosi 1 October.

FARWELL, children of Lyman and Eliza Ann, St. Louis:
          Helen Maria 19 April ae 8m; funeral from   MORE 20 Apr 1840
               #37 6th St., near Pine.
          Ellen, only daughter, 23 December ae 17m.   "   23 Dec 1847

FAY, sons of Nahum (Nathan?) and Mary: St. Louis
          Henry Beaumont 17 April; funeral from
               home, 7th St. south of Market.   MORE 18 Apr 1840
               Buried Presbyterian Cem.
          Edward Forbes, ae 7, eldest son, Saturday. "   5 Jan 1841
          George Lathrop 4 July. Boston pc   "   5 Jul "

FELLOWS, Ann Eliza, daughter of H. P. and Eliza, in   SLMD 3 Mar 1855
          Canton 14 February ae 1y 6m.

FELPS, Richard Theodore, son of Richard and Elizabeth,   PWH 21 Oct 1847
          infant, died 13 October.

FENNELL, Emma Margaret, youngest daughter of Capt. Thomas P.,
          3 August of croup ae 3y 1m 6d.   MORE 4 Aug 1846
          Philadelphia pc

FENLEY, Mary Ann, infant of Edgar and Lucy C., in   SLMD 26 May 1855
          Boone Co. 11 May ae 9m.

FENTON, Elizabeth, daughter of George, 6 Nov. in 20th y.   LADB 13 Nov 1848

FERGUSON, Charles Richard, son of John H. and Maria, infant, NERA 4 May 1845
          6th-Cerre. Buried Methodist Cem.

          Charles Webster, son of Charles C. and Harriet,   SLMD 1 Jan 1854
               31 December ae 1y 7m 15d.

          Delia Emma, daughter of William W., 5 April   SLMD 13 Apr 1854
               ae 15y 6m.

FERGUSON or FERQUEAN, __ son of John, of cholera in Palmyra. MORE 28 Jun '33

FERGUYS, James in Weston 29 December of lung congestion.   SLMD 8 Feb 1855

FERRIS, John B., oldest son of Jabez and Elizabeth, in   MORE 14 Sep 1841
          his 14th year.

FICHTENKAM, Isabella, daughter of George and Elizabeth,   MORE 30 Mar 1853
          7th-Marion, 29 March ae 7y 5m 25d.

FIELD, George Baker, son of George B. and Lenora,   MORE 23 Jul 1851
          22 July ae 1y 6m 20d.

          Joseph Matthew, only child of Joseph and Eliza,   NERA 21 Jul 1849
               20 July ae 6y 6m.

33

FIELD, Mrs. Mary A. in Cooper Co. 18 October.   NERA 31 Oct 1845

FIELDS, Fannie Shackleford, infant of Prof. Wm. C. and
          Lucy B., in Columbia 17 April ae 9m.   SLMD 28 Apr 1855

FILLEY, sons of Giles F. and Maria M.:
          Giles Franklin 21 August ae 1y 28d.   MORE 22 Aug 1846
          Eldridge 19 Oct ae 10m 11d on Collins St.   "   20 Oct 1847

FINCH, Caroline Isabella, daughter of William T. and
          Eliza Ann, 20 May ae 19m 5d.   MORE 23 May 1842
      Louise Eveline, only daughter of William T.,
          Saturday ae 4y 5m.   "   6 May 1850

FINE, Julia, daughter of Philip, on Wednesday last.   MOG 25 Apr 1812

FINN, Stephen, 2nd son of Margaret and Stephen, ae 16m.   MORE 10 Jul 1849

FINNEY, Daniel, son of Bernard and Jane, 27 June ae 6y 6m;   MORE 28 May 1850
          lived Spruce betw 13-14.

      Mary Louise, daughter of W., 7 March.   MORE 8 Mar 1833

      Sons of William and Jane, St. Louis:
          James, ae 11m, yesterday.   SCOMB 5 Aug 1836
          Oliver Ormsley yesterday ae 3y1m26d.   SWERE 28 Feb 1848

FISCHER, Joseph R. of consumption, 31 March.   MORE 1 Apr 1850

      Therese Emilie, only daughter of John Heinrich
          and Mary Theresa, Sunday ae 2y 3m 7d.   "   7 May 1850

FISHBACK, George, funeral notice; lived Olive betw 15-16.   MORE 6 Sep 1849

FISHER, Catherine J., youngest daughter of E. and J.,   GLWT 1 May 1851
          29 April.

      Charles Lyman, son of Charles and Sophia, 23 May   SLMD 24 May 1853
          ae 5m 15d. Lived 7th-Clark.

      Franklin, ae 34. Buried Presbyterian Cemetery,   MORE 3 Jul 1849
          funeral from 2nd Presbyterian Church.

      George Stewart on 30 May ae 5y 18d. Minneapolis pc   MORE 5 Jun 1853

      Henry, son of Robert and Sarah H., Olive betw   MORE 12 Oct 1849
          9th-10th, ae 3y 7m.

      James Walter at Glasgow 26 February, only son of   MODE 7 Mar 1848
          E. and J., ae 6y 1m 19d. Scarlet fever.

FITCH, Joseph, son of Nathaniel G. and Margaret, 20 June   MORE 22 Jun 1847
          ae 3m 1d.

FITZGIBBON, William Scovill, son of J. H. and Amelia,   MORE 12 Sep 1853
          10 September ae 2y 1m.

FLAKE, Mary E., infant of William, Thursday last.   LADB 5 Feb 1849

FLEMING, children of Fielding, Palmyra:
          Benjamin Leander 5 October ae 6m.   PWH 7 Oct 1843
          Mary Frances, ae 5, Sunday last.   "   14 "

FLETCHER, Mary Elizabeth, infant of Elias, 19 February.   PWH 25 Feb 1847

FLOYD, Mary Ellen, consort of Judge J. J., at Linnaeus   JEM 20 Oct 1846
                    3 October.

FLYNN, Eliza wife of John, 13th-Olive, 12 Dec. ca 28.   SLMD 14 Dec 1853

FONTAINE, children of Thomas L.:   (St. Louis)
      Mary Jane, oldest daughter, 4 Aug. ae 3y 6m.   MORE 6 Aug 1838
      Wilmer Spence, infant, Wednesday Sept. 12.   "   13 Sep 1838

FORBES, Austin, of A. & I. Forbes, ae about 40. Funeral   SLINT 28 Jan 1850
      from home of Edwin Ellis, 4-- N. 2nd.

      Cornelia, infant of Isaiah and Cornelia, ae 4m,   SLMD 25 Jan 1856
      20 January. Lived 8th betw Locust-St. Chas.

FORD, Ether, son of Dr. Ford, 16 September in Memphis MO   CANE 29 Sep 1853
      ae 14y 1m 26d.

    Sons of Oliver and Sarah K.: (St. Louis)
      Wm. Oliver 18 September ae 3m. Buried   NERA 19 Sep 1845
               Presbyterian Cemetery.
      Wm. K., only child, 26 July ae 13m 17d.   "   26 Jul 1849

FORDER, Mary daughter of Peter 12 July in St. Louis Co.   MORE 15 Jul 1849
      in her 20th year, formerly of Baltimore.

FORESTER, Eliza M. on Tuesday ae 5y 6m; lived on Pine St.   MORE 6 Oct 1841

FORT, Henry, of St. Charles Co., in Jefferson City 25 Mar.   NERA 5 Apr 1845

FORTUNE, Mrs. Anne, 9th-Franklin, 28 September ae 30.   SLMD 29 Sep 1854

      W. B., son of T. L. and Mary, ae 3m 27d.   SASE 20 Aug 1853

FOULKS, Christopher, "old and respected" on 4 Sept.   SLDU 5 Sep 1846
      Ae 75y 9m. Funeral Centenary Methodist.

      Mrs. Mary, wife of John Sr., at Baird's Hotel in   LADB 3 Feb 1851
      Louisiana MO, 30 January.

FOWLER, Robert, son of Robert, Oak betw 2nd-3rd,   MORE 29 Dec 1838
      28 December ae 4y 8m.

FOX, Charles, son of Abraham, Friday last.   MORE 26 Feb 1833

      Conrad, 247 2nd St., 29 April of consumption ae (57?)   "   30 Apr 1850

      John, native of Co. Longford IRE, 13 May in his 37th   NERA 22 May 1849
      year, resident of St. Louis 24 years.

      Thomas Hall, son of Dr. T. H., at the home of his   LEXP 13 Sep 1854
      grandfather Andrew Wood Sr. of Mercer Co.
      KY 6 Sept., of typhoid, ae 6y.

FOXTON, Elizabeth C., consort of William, 15 July at her   NERA 2 Aug 1849
      home in Jefferson Co., of cholera, ae 41.

FOXWORTHY, William, near Williamsburg 30 Dec. at the home   SLMD 9 Jan 1855
      of Joseph Foxworthy, in his 65th y.

FRANCIS, __, infant daughter of Calvin, ae about 1 year.   MORE 9 Aug 1831

      Children of Henry and Rebecca: (St. Louis)
      Mary Lydia, youngest daughter, 13 Sept.   SLDU 16 Sep 1846
               ae 3y 10m.
      George, an infant, yesterday.   MORE 17 Jun 1845

FRANKLIN, Ella B., daughter of Joseph F. and Elizabeth, 27 October ae 5m.　　　MORE 28 Oct 1843

FRAZER, Ebenezer Newton, son of Wm. M., at Monticello ae 6m.　　　BOLT 9 Jul 1842

Charles Henry, youngest son of John and Sarah W. and grandson of Elizabeth O'Connor in Ralls Co. 11 October ae 2y 5m 4d.　　　PWH 19 Oct 1848

William Eugene, son of Joseph and grandson of Mrs. Elizabeth O'Connor in Ralls Co. 10 Sept. ae about 9; mother died 6 years ago.　　　PWH 14 Sep 1848

FREE, Mary Virginia, daughter of Mrs. Mary Free, yesterday.　　　SWERE 2 Aug 1847

FRELEIGH, Charlotte, daughter of J.H.(?) and Susan, 10 Jan. ae 2y 5m; lived 61 Collins. (SLDU gives father as Capt. J.B., 13 Jan.)　　　MORE 11 Jan 1847

Sarah, infant of John H. and S. R., 22 January.　　　MORE 23 Jan 1850

FRICKE, Edward Adolphus, son of George W. and M. Agnes, infant, 9 June.　　　SLMD 12 Jun 1854

FROST, Mrs. Wealthy, on 16 June.　　　NERA 18 Jun 1845

FROTHINGHAM, Abby Elnora, daughter of George H. and Sarah, 20 December ae 11m.　　　SWERE 30 Dec 1844

FRUITT, Mary, daughter of Franklin and Mary, Sunday last ae 1y.　　　JEM 27 Jul 1847

FULKERSON, Polk, infant of William, 22 August.　　　MPSC 23 Aug 1846

FULENWIDER, Charles Welling, son of Judge C. P., in Jackson MO 2 January.　　　MORE 19 Jan 1853

FULTON, Catherine, consort of John and daughter of Aaron and Jane Faris, 8 Dec. ae 38y 6m.　　　MORP 9 Dec 1845

Miss Tabitha in St. Charles 24 July of congestive fever in her 48th year.　　　SLOB 7 Aug 1834

Willie H., son of W. H. and Lavinia, 30 June ae 2y 1m 18d.　　　SLMD 3 Jul 1854

FURGUSON, Emily, infant of William and Lucinda, 3 August at the home of Matthew Ripper.　　　MORE 5 Aug 1853

GAINES, A. in Washington, Franklin Co. 16 August ae 64y 8m, of consumption. Native of VA, served in the War of 1812, stationed at Norfolk.　　　SLMD 1 Sep 1855

Elizabeth Virginia, only daughter of Gen. E.P., in New Orleans 23 May ae 8m 11d.　　　MORE 15 Jun 1841

GALAVAN, Daniel of chronic diarrhoea on 23 July, ae 27. Formerly of Carrighead, Co. Carlow, IRE.　　　NERA 27 Jul 1849

GAMACHE, Charles J. at Carondelet 10 April ae 18m.　　　SLMD 13 Apr 1854

GAMBLE, Archibald Jr. 15 September in his 8th year.　　　MORE 17 Sep 1845

Edward, son of Hamilton R., 8 January.　　　" 11 Jan 1831

GAMBRILL, James Wallace, son of T., 16 August.   MORE 20 Aug 1835
GAMBREL   Lucy Elizabeth, daughter of Thomas, 9 April
                ae 4y 3m 27d.   MORE 11 Apr 1837

GAMEREIL, Lucy S., youngest daughter of James and Mary E.,
           5 August ae 6y 9m 20d.   MORE 6 Aug 1853

GARBER, (C.G.?) of Buchanan Co.   MORE 7 Oct 1850

GARDNER, Elizabeth G., wife of W. G., in Cass Co.
           18 January ae 36.   MORE 2 Mar 1850

GARLAND, William Burwill, son of Hugh and Ann, ae 2y 6m.
              Funeral Christ Church. VA pc   MORE 2 Mar 1853

GARMON, Catherine Josephine, infant of Timothy and
           Catherine, 9 December.   MORE 12 Dec 1842

GARRATY, Caroline A., daughter of J. W., 12 November ae 6. MORE 22 Nov 1831

GARRISON, Cornelius K, son of Oliver and Louisa C., 7 Dec.
           ae 13m 20d. Buried Bissell cemetery.   MORE 8 Dec 1847

              Isabella Harriet, ae 4y 23d. Funeral from home
              of John Blakely, 3rd-Green.   MORE 24 Apr 1849

GASS, Charles Benjamin, son of John and Prudence, 5 July
           ae 17m 13d. Troy NY pc   NERA 6 Jul 1849

GAY, Ann Jane, daughter of John H. and Sophia, 25 July in
           her 13th year.   NERA 25 Jul 1849
     John Jr., of a lingering illness, in his 26th year.   "   6 Aug 1849

GEARHART, William D., son of Isaac of Howard Co., in   MODE 13/11
              Boonville 3 February.   Feb 1847

GEIGER, Hannah 30 June ae 9m. Funeral from the U.S. Arsenal
              to the Catholic Cemetery.   MORE 1 Jul 1848

GEISLER, Amanda, daughter of Peter and Eliza, ae 1y 2m 27d. "   23 Sep 1849

GEITY, Henry of St. Louis near Panama 17 January, en route
           to CA; of fever. Left mother, sister;   MORE 18 Feb 1850
           brother-in-law of Daniel Rawlings.

GENESTELLE, Marie Louise ae 29.   MORE 28 Aug 1849

GENNETT, Mary, formerly of St. Louis, 25 August in
                St. Joseph ae 14.   MORE 4 Sep 1849

GENETTE,   Elizabeth, wife of Gregory, 4 July ae 19.   NERA 6 Jul 1849
   GENETTO   Gregory, formerly of Canada, in his 23d year.   "   4 "   "

GENTRY, James S., son of George W. and Louise, 26 August
              in Shelby Co. in his 8th year.   PWH 2 Sep 1843

           Mary Stevens, daughter of William and Harriet,
           13 July ae 7m 17d.   MORE 14 Jul 1853

           Richard Lee Roy, son of Crain C. and Jane,
              8 June ae 6m 8d.   MORE 9 Jun 1845

GEORGE, Mrs. Elizabeth in Callaway Co. 9 October ae 73.   JEM 20 Oct 1846

GEORGE, Robert, of Monroe Co., 29 October ae 35.   JEM 3 Nov 46

GERARD, Octavia, daughter of Joseph and Margaret, ae 12,   SLDU 25 Feb 47
    24 February. Funeral from Female
    Orphan's Asylum, Biddle betw 9-10.

GERMON, Henry Snyder, son of John S., 25 September   MORE 27 Sep 1847
    ae 4y 9m. Philadelphia pc

GERRARD, Mrs. Messina, near Hannibal, 20 April.   HAJ 25 Apr 1850

GIBSON, Meichel D. Y., son of Charles H. and Louisa,   MORE 18 Jan 1848
    15 January ae 18m 17d.

GIGAIRE, J. B. 23 October ae 75. (MORE 24 Oct says 73.)   NERA 24 Oct 1849

GILBREATH, Theodore Dunklin, infant of Rev. J. N. and   MORE 13 Dec 1849
    Sarah, at Des Peres Inst. 10 Dec. ae 1y 6m.

GILES, William, only son of Wm. S. and Frances, 23 November. SLMD 24 Nov 1853

GILL, sons of John H. and Frances E.; Baltimore pc: MORE 27 Apr 1846
    John, eldest, 14 Apr ae 9, of scarlet fever.
    William L., youngest, date not shown, ", ae 2.

GILMAN, Virginia, daughter of W. S. and Abia S.,   MORE 4 Oct 1845
    3 October ae 7m.

GIST, family of Robert C. of St. Louis:
    Louisa Wood, only daughter, 16 July at the home   MORE 18 Jul 1838
        of Nimrod Dorsey, scalded; ae 2y 7m.
        (Dorsey lived near Alton IL)
    Charles McIntire, only child, in Cincinnati   MORE 23 Jul 1840
        16 July ae 11m.
    (Mrs. Gist - Mary - had died in March.)
    David, Jr., son of Robert and Mary, 21 February   MORE 22 Feb 1847
        of brain congestion ae 3y 1m 6d.

GLADDEN, Elijah of St. Joseph in St. Paul 19 July ae 20.   SJA 23 Aug 1850

GLASCOCK, __, a little daughter of Col. Charles, ae 6,   MORE 9 Oct 1839
    in Ralls Co. about 26 September.

    Emma, infant of George and Lucy Ann, Wed. last.   PWH 9 Mar 1844

GLASSGOW, William Wright, son of William H. and Mary,   MORE 13 Apr 1853
    12 April ae 1y 7m 18d. Buried Bellefontaine.

GLEIM, Edgar Johnson, son of Edgar H., 19 Feb. ae 2y 3m.   MORE 21 Feb 1839

GLOVER, Joseph W. either killed, or died as a result of a   LADB 13 Jun 1846
    duel with Geo. W. Buckner in Palmyra.

    Robert, in Callaway Co., 22 October.   NERA 28 Oct 1845

GODER (GODAIRE?), Eleanor Ladouceur, wife of Baptiste,   MORE 13 Aug 1849
    in her 52d year.

GODLEY, Rachael, estate in Montgomery Co.: letters of   JEFRE 5 Dec 1840
    administration to Hiram Godley, 10 Oct.
    (shown in JEFRE 13 Feb 1841 as Rockhill, not Rachael.)

GODWIN, Charles Alfred, youngest son of Edgar and Ann   SLMD 8 Aug 1854
    Eliza, 2 August in St. Charles ae 17m.

GOLDSMITH, Rachel, daughter of M. H. and R.,
         27 December ae 4y 7m.   MORE 29 Dec 1847

GOLL, B. G. 12 July of brain congestion ae 63.   NERA 14 Jul 1849

GOMES, Charles, youngest son of John and Emily, 12 April
       ae 4y 6m. Lived on Centre St. Boston pc   MORE 13 Apr 1850

GOOCH, Turner found dead near Middletown, Montgomery Co.;
      he had been shot. He was under indictment   LADB 12 Nov 1849
      for the rape of a Mrs. Angell, whose husband
      was arrested. (November 9.)

GOODALL, John, a merchant, ae about 45, died aboard the
      <u>Aleck Scott</u> en route from New Orleans, on   NERA 26 Sep 1849
      24 Sept. Buried Presbyterian Cemetery.

GOODDING, Mary Ann at the home of her father in Macon Co.
        9 March, ae about 18.   SLMD 27 Mar 1856

GOODFELLOW, Eliza, daughter of Robert and Sarah,
        4 December ae 10m.   SLMD 8 Dec 1857

      William B., eldest son of John, drowned while
      returning from Alton Thursday. Funeral   MORE 7 May 1844
      from home of William Finney; buried
      Methodist Cemetery.

GOODRICH, Gardner, youngest son of James G. and Sarah,
       10 September ae 1m.   SLMD 12 Sep 1857

GOODWIN, Anna, only daughter of George W. and Martha A.
      of St. Louis, in Pattersonville LA   NERA 22 Dec 1849
      4 December ae 2.

      Elizabeth H., daughter of John C. and Amanda F., COMB 2 Dec 1847
      in Vermont MO 19 Nov. ae 6y 7d.

GORE, Mrs. __, consort of J.B., a merchant, 4 November.   HAG 19 Nov 1846

GOSHEN, Miss Yandaloo St. de M. 11 October in Lexington. NERA 22 Oct 1845

GOTT, William C., an attorney in Danville, 8 January in
      his 35th year. Formerly of Montgomery SLINT 22 Jan 1850
      Co. MD, late of Montgomery Co. MO.

GOTTSCHALK, Kossuth, son of Charles W. and Johanna,
      5 July ae 5y 7m; lived 65 Carondelet. SLMD 6 Jul 1855

GOUGH, Mary, wife of George B., in Monroe Co. 3 February. SLMD 19 Feb 1855

GRACE, Mary, daughter of Pierce and Ann Elizabeth,
      24 January ae 3m 19d.   MORE 26 Jan 1846
    Thomas Bond, father of Pierce, in his 68th year.   " 15 Sep 1849

GRAHAM, Hugh at the home of his son Robert 19 July in
       his 65th year.   NERA 21 Jul 1849

      Richard, eldest son of Lt. John, USA, 9 May in MORE 7 Jun 1837
      his 5th year, of scarlet fever.

      Richard, youngest son of Maj. R., 10 Aug. ae 16m. MORE 25 Aug 1836

GRANT, Eulala Josephine, daughter of Moses and Eulala,
      15 Dec, ae 5y 7m 3d.   SWERE 20 Dec 1847

GRANT, Lewis S. ae (22? 32?). Funeral from his mother's   MORE 19 Feb 1850
      home, 10-Wash-Carr. Methodist Cemetery.

GRAPEVINE, Frederick Dudley, son of Frederick, ae 18m 19d.   NERA 4 Mar 1848

GRATIOT, Charles Cabanne, youngest son of J. P. B. and
      Adele, scalded to death at Richwoods   MORE 5 Apr 1848
      on 3 April.
      Julia, daughter of J.P.B. and Adele, infant,   MORE 1 May 1843
       died 28 April.
      Adele, daughter of ", 11 April ae 15y 10m.   "   12 Apr 1844

      Emily Isabella, daughter of Paul and Virginia,   MORE 12 Aug 1841
       11 August ae 5. Buried Catholic Cem.

GRAVES, Sarah Elizabeth, infant of Warren and Sarah, 1 Oct.   JEFRE 7 Oct 1843

GRAY, Mary Josephine, daughter of Thomas and Mary, 9 Apr.   MORE 10 Apr 1847
      ae 4y 5d. Buried St. Vincent de Paul.

GREEN, sons of Alonzo and Mary: (St. Louis)
      Alonzo on Thursday ae 3y 3m.   MORE 8 Apr 1844
      Henry Austin, only son; age and date not shown.   "   23 Apr "
       Buried 1st Presbyterian Church Cem.
     (Note: Green was a proprietor of the Virginia Hotel.)

      William, son of Benjamin and Sarah, 14 February in   PWH 1 Mar 1849
       West Ely ae 1y 3m 6d.

      James, son of James and Sarah Ann, 21 August of   SLDU 25 Aug 1846
       summer complaint ae 1y 19d.
      Sarah Ann, consort of James, daughter of Jesse and
       Mary Laverty, late of Philadelphia, now of   MORP 30 Aug 1845
       NY. Lived at 143 (or 148?) Carr St.

      William B., infant of Moses and Mary, in Hannibal.   HANT 22 Jul 1852

      Mary P., daughter of Rev. James and Julia, ae 19m,   FULT 13 Apr 1849
       scalded to death in Fulton 11 April.

      William, son of Joseph H. and Elizabeth Conn;   MORE 2 Jul 1841
       funeral from home of Maj. W. C. Anderson.

      Thomas Parish, son of Elder T. P., 7 January in   MORE 16 Jan 1838
       St. Louis Co. ae 3y 4m.

      Children of William W. and Sarah Ann: (St. Louis)
       Rebecca C., ae 6, on Friday.   MORE 10 Jan 1847
       William W., ae 15, on Saturday.   "   "
       Joseph Conn, infant; funeral from the   SWERE 10 Jul 1843
       home, 5th near Myrtle.

GREENWELL, Catherine, consort of George F., 21 December   SLMD 29 Dec 1853
      near St. Charles at the home of
      Clement Boyce, ae about 25.

GREGG, Capt. Josiah of Missouri, author of "Commerce of   LADB 20 May 1850
      the Prairie" at Clear Lake, CA 25 Feb.

      Oliver, son of Abraham and Nance, 218 N. 5th St.,   MORE 17 Jul 1847
      16 July ae 15m 16d.

GREGORY, James Eberle, son of Dr. S. T. and Margaret W.,
    in Warrenton ae 1y 11m.   MORE 8 Aug 1849

    Mary Byrd, daughter of Dr. E. H. and J. E. of   MORE 13 Jul 1851
      St. Louis, in Cooper Co. 6 July ae 3.

    Sophia, wife of Charles and daughter of the late   NERA 14 Jul 1849
      Elisha Hall of Fredericksburg, 13 July.

GRIFFITH, George Oliver, youngest son of Mary Anna and the   NERA 19 Jul 1849
      late Joseph, 16 July of cholera.

    Daughters of Capt. Thomas H. and Elizabeth:
      Mary Wilson, eldest daughter, 2 November;   MORE 3 Nov 1847
       lived Morgan-5th. Buried Methodist Cem.
      Elizabeth Hawkes, ae 2y 5m 17d, on 12 Nov.   "   13 Nov "
       Funeral from home of Mrs. Wilson, 6-Morgan.

GRIGGS, Josephine H., only daughter of George W. and
      Josephine, 10 February ae 7y 5m. Lived at   MORE 11 Feb 1850
      262 N. 2nd. Buried Catholic Cem.

GRIMES, Emily E., daughter of Maj. G., ae 19y 4m; lived   MORE 31 Oct 1849
      on Ham near Hickory.

GRIMSLEY, children of Thornton: (St. Louis)
    Arabella, infant, 4 August.   MORE 5 Aug 1834
    Margaretta Arabella, youngest daughter, Mon.   "   22 Aug 1837
    James Nimrod, infant, Wed. night.   "   11 Aug 1829
    Thornton, infant, 17 April.   "   18 Apr 1840

GRINSTEAD, Jacob Wimer, infant of Charles, Saturday last.   MORE 13 Feb 1837

GROVE, Martin near Madison, Monroe Co., 15 Dec. ae ca 65.   SLMD 29 Dec 1853

GRUMLEY, William W., son of Wm. and Elizabeth, 11 August
      ae 8y 2m. Buried Catholic Cem.   MORE 12 Aug 1847

GUERETTE, Louis P., son of Peter and Mary Louise, 15 May.   MORE 16 May 1853

GUION, Amelia, daughter of Louis and Amelia, ae 2y 2d.   "   4 Jul 1849

GUITARD, Mrs. Euralia 23 July ae 59. (cholera?)   NERA 24 Jul 1849

GUNDELFINGER, Monroe Berry, son of Christoph and Sarah,
      21 January in Jefferson City ae 2y 4m.   SLMD 1 Feb 1856

GUYON, Hubert W. D., son of Didier H. and Sarah J.,
      25 May ae 11m 12d.   MORE 27 May 1848

    Melina Elizabeth, daughter of Peter and Mary,
      31 October ae about 3y 2m.   SLDU 2 Nov 1846

HACKLEY, Sarah Ann, daughter of William E., 10 Nov. of   MODE 17/15
      typhoid ae 12y 23d.   Nov 1847

HACKSHAW, Esda Augusta, daughter of Enoch L. and Sophie,   LADB 25 Sep 1848
      19 September ae 15m 19d.

HAGAN, William Earl, son of John and Mary, 9 August
      ae 15m 2w.   MORE 10 Aug 1853

HAGGERTY, Andrew, a laborer living near the Sugar Refinery,   SLMD 14 Jul 1857
      found drowned. Left wife, 2 children,
      and brother.

HAGUE, Otho Wallace infant of John and Catherine, 10 March. MORE 11 Mar 1853

HAIGHT, Fletcher, son of Fletcher H. and Mary, 24 April in his 10th year. Lived on 5th St.. MORE 26 Apr 1847

HAINES, Mary, youngest child of Joseph and Elizabeth, 21 May ae 2y 10m. NERA 22 May 1849

John Nixon, youngest son of Sidney P. and Diadamia, 27 September ae 10m. PWH 30 Sep 1843

Sidney P., of lung congestion, 13 July, "a man of strong mind and unflagging enterprise. . his death is a public calamity." HAJ 15 Jul 1847

HALBERT, Henry 12 December in his 22nd y. Louisville pc MORE 13 Dec 1849

HALE, Anna Bullard, infant of Dr. E. and Harriet, 27 Nov. MORE 29 Nov 1848

Francis D., infant of Dr. Edward, 18 May ae 4m. Buried Bellefontaine. " 19 May 1853

Mrs. Elizabeth, formerly of Philadelphia, 4 July of cholera in her 68th year. NERA 6 Jul 1849

Ellen, 2nd daughter of George C. and Hannah, 12 September ae 6y 10m. SLDU 16 Sep 1846

HALL, sons of Charles R. and Louisa Ann: (St. Louis)

Charles H., Saturday evening after a long and painful illness, ae 4y 6m. MORE 12 Dec 1836

Elisha, youngest son, ae 2, precisely 4 weeks after his brother's death. "Insatiate archer, could not one suffice?" MORE 11 Jan 1837

Children of Dr. J. W.: (St. Louis)

Henry Napoleon, infant (mother shown as Henrietta) 10 July. MORE 11 Jul 1843

Josephine Stockton, eldest daughter, 12 April in her 10th year. Lived 6th-Market. NERA 13 Apr 1849

Charles Rush, son of William and Martha, 16 Jan. ae 2y 4m. Funeral from home of Chas. R. Hall. MORE 18 Jan 1849

Elizabeth, wife of Rev. N. H., pastor of Central Church, 26 February in her 54th year. MORE 28 Feb 1850

James McHenry, only child of Parker Lee and Amanda, 13 Feb. ae 6m 29d. Baltimore pc MORE 16 Feb 1849

Martha, at the home of Judge Lewis, 5 February in her 8th year. MODE 18/16 Mar 1846

Mary Ann, wife of __ (paper blurred). Funeral from Doniphan House. MORE 3 Jul 1849

Rulon S. D., only child of S. Kellogg and Massie, 28 April of brain congestion ae 10m 5d. SLMD 1 May 1857

Samuel, son of Rev. N., in Fayette. MIN 24 Aug 1833

HALLAM, Cornelia, wife of Alexander, 7 May ae 23. MOSN 12 May 1838

HAM, Amelia, wife of Peter of St. Louis, in Peoria 19 Apr. in her 30th year. Buried Catholic Cem. MORE 23 Apr 1850

HAM, Tullia Virginia, daughter of Peter N. and Amelia C., 30 July ae 2y 3m. Buried Catholic Cemetery.   MORE 31 Jul 1843

HAMILTON, Frederick A. in Danville 18 July.   NERA 6 Aug 1845

    John C., son of James A. and Diana, formerly of Augusta Co. VA, in Lincoln Co. 6 Dec. ae 27y 4m 18d.   NERA 21 Dec 1849

HAMMOND, George A., son of William and Mary of Jefferson Co., 15 July ae 14m.   MORE 22 Jul 1851

    John, in Herculaneum, 10 June in his 44th year, native of MO, "old, valuable citizen."   SLMD 14-15 Jun 1854

    Joseph A., Sheriff of Jefferson Co., 30 June of cholera.   NERA 6 Jul 1849

    Mary Ann, eldest child of John and Frances E., of Jefferson Co., 25 Feb. ae 7y 2m.   MORE 28 Feb 1845

HANCOCK, George V., youngest son of D. J. and Lucinda, 9 April ae 7m 10d. Funeral 2nd Baptist.   MORE 11 Apr 1853

    Jonny, only son of R. C. and Amelia, 15 May in Fayette ae 14m 24d.   SLMD 9 Jun 1855

HANENKAMP, children of Richard P. and Julia, of Glasgow:
    Charles Frederick, only son, 7 Oct. ae 1y 3m.   BOLT 14 Oct 1843
    Richard Pemberton, 19 August, ae 1y 27d.   " 30 Aug 1845

HANKINS, Alonzo A., son of Joseph and Nancy, 22 Sept. ae 5y 8m 6d.   MORE 23 Sep 1851

HANNA, Mrs. Anne E., daughter of Robert Poage, decd., of Greenup Co. KY, 15 Feb. in 40th year.   SLMD 10 Mar 1855

    David Coulter, son of A. F. and Sarah Ann, Thursday last ae about 2y.   MODE 22 Feb 1848

    Daughters of George and Caledonia:
        Ida Constance on 8 Feb. ae 3y 9m.   MORE 9 Feb 1853
        Zoe Wilkerson on 12 Feb. ae 1y 10m 26d.   " 13 " "

HANNON, James, only son of Patrick and Mary Ann, of 195 Morgan, 17 October ae 4.   SLMD 18 Oct 1855

HAPENNY, Sarah Jane, daughter of T. S. and Rebecca, 18 August ae 7m. Pittsburgh pc   SLMD 19 Aug 1854

HARDEN, Mrs. Sarah in Callaway Co. 28 Sept. ae 73.   JEM 20 Oct 1846

HARDIN, ___, son of Joseph, accidentally killed by the discharge of a shotgun, Monday last.   BOLT 16 Jan 1841

HARDY, Mrs. Jane L., consort of J. R., in Hannibal 26 Jan.   LADB 3 Feb 1851

HARLAN, James M., ae 13, in Canton 20 July.   CANE 3 Aug 1854

HARLOW, Frances, only child of William P. and Frances J., 2 February ae 10m 19d.   MORE 3 Feb 1852

    Nicholas, estate in Chariton Co.: Final Settlement by L. Applegate, P.A.   BRUNS 23 Jun 1855

HARLOW, William, youngest child of Sylvanus and Margaret,   MORE 25 Dec 1848
++   23 Dec. ae ly 9m.   Bangor ME pc

HARRIS, Emily, only daughter of Isaac and Mary, 14 Dec.   BRUNS 23 Dec 1847
         in Bedford, Livingston Co.

      Henry W. at the home of his grandfather, Henry   LEXP 14 May 1845
          Wallace, in Lexington 22 May in his 3rd y.

      Joel B., son of Capt. John H. and Nancy, at the   SLMD 17 Mar 1855
          home of his brother in Boone Co. 21 Feb.
          in his 23d year.

      John Edgar, youngest son of Oliver and Mary C.,   MORE 17 Apr 1848
          15 April ae 21m.

      Peter B., eldest child of Peter B., Mon. last ae 2.   MIN 7 May 1825

      Sarah Ann, daughter of William and Esther, at   SLMD 5 Sep 1854
          Allenton 25 August ae 14.

++ HARPER, Willie G., youngest son of J. G. and Elizabeth C.,   SLMD 5 Jun 1857
         4 June of measles ae 2y 18d. Lived at
         201 Chestnut; buried Bellefontaine.

HARRISON, Chester, son of James, 7 February ae 17m.   SWERE 16 Feb 1846
         Josephine, daughter of James and Maria,   MORE 10 Jul 1848
          6 July ae 18m.

      Elizabeth B., consort of John B. of Tuscumbia,   JEM 27 Nov 1847
          20 Nov. ae 30; short illness.

      S. M., consort of Jason, in Jefferson City   NERA 1 May 1845
          20 March ae 54.

HARRYMAN, Caroline, a little girl, fell from the 3rd floor
         window of Mrs. Gassaway's boarding   MORE 7 Sep 1843
         house on Washington Ave., 25 August,
         and survived only a few minutes.

HARSHAW, family of William and Zaida Ann: (St. Louis)
         John R., only son, 24 November ae 2y 4m.   MORE 26 Nov 1838
         William, ae 2m 13d, on 11 January; lived   MORE 13 Jan 1840
         at 194 7th St.
         Zaida Ann, ae about 4, on 14 February.   "   15 Feb 1853

HART, Aaron B., son of Capt. John and Sarah, 11 January   NERA 13 Jan 1846
         ae 18m.

      Infant of Oliver and Mary, 7th-Pine, died 2 March.   MORE 3 Mar 1848

      T. B. murdered at Palmyra by John Wise, a post office
         clerk in St. Louis. During the cholera   LADB 13 Aug 1849
         epidemic Wise had sent his wife to Palmyra to
         visit relatives; Wise intercepted her letters
         to Hart, stabbed and shot him. Hart was a
         well-known saddler, a medical student, had served
         in Doniphan's Regiment; he was a handsome man,
         dubbed "Lord Byron."

HARTNETT, Mary, daughter of John and Ann Eliza, 12 March   MORE 14 Mar 1853
         ae 7m 21d.

HARTSHORN, Augustus, infant of Augustus and Sarah Jane,   MORE 28 Jun 1842
      27 June. Funeral from home of James K.
      Thompson, Elm St., to Methodist Cemetery.

HARTT, George C., son of Albert G. and Margaretta P.,   COMB 15 Apr 1847
      13 April ae 1y 10m.

HATCHER, children of Thomas E. and Martha Ann: (Palmyra)
      Jane Elizabeth, ae about 2, Thursday last.   PWH 29 Apr 1847
      Thomas E., infant, "yesterday noon."   "   24 Jun "
      William Morgan, ae 7m 20d, on 10 April.   "   13 Apr 1844

HAVENS, Josephine, youngest daughter of Joseph and Eliza,   MORE 6 Oct 1845
      119 S. Main, yesterday.

HAWKINS, Abagail, consort of H. B., 27 July in her 38th y.   NERA 27 Jul 1849
      Ill 4 weeks. Buried Presbyterian Cem.
  __, infant daughter of A. B., Sunday last.   PWH 17 Oct 1840

      Corinna, daughter of James C., 13 February in   PWH 12 Mar 1845
        Shelbyville "a few days short of 13."
        (Tribute in PWH 6 August, same year.)

HAWLEY, Elizabeth, only child of B. F. and L., 28 March   MORE 28 Mar 1850
      of lung inflammation, ae 3y 7m.
      Albany NY pc

HAWPE, Rudolph at Arrow Rock 8 October, ae 50; formerly   MORE 19 Oct 1849
      of VA (Augusta Co.), in MO 27 years.

HAY, Alice, daughter of Dr. J. A. and Elizabeth, 27 March   MORE 31 Mar 1853
      in LaGrange, ae 13m 2d.

HAYDEN, Charles Henry, infant of Benjamin F., Tuesday last.   PWH 7 May 1846

      Margaret E., daughter of Dr. J. R., 16 May   SRJ 6 Jun 1840
        ae 6y 5m 4d.

HAYS, __, son of Major Hays, of Hannibal, set fire to a   LADB 23 Apr 1849
      keg of powder in his father's store and died
      Friday of injuries. (Hannibal Courier)

HEADLEE, Artemisa Jane, wife of Rev. John H., in   MORE 30 May 1850
      St. Francois Co. 20 May.

      Caleb in Greene Co. 7 Aug., "old, respected."   JEM 17 Aug 1847

HEARTLEY, Jacob "respected and much liked" citizen of   SLMD 12 Dec 1854
      Greene Co., 23 November ae about 40.

HEATH, William at the Virginia House, Hannibal, ae   HAG 3 Feb 1848
      about 40, formerly of Louthan Co. VA (sic).

HEATON, Charles Oscar, son of D. J. and Lucinda, 10 Oct.   STGAZ 12 Oct 1853

HEDGES, Hannah, consort of Isaac A., 13 July ae 36.   NERA 14 Jul 1849

      Otey Kemper, son of Rev. C. S., at Jefferson   MORE 10 May 1842
      Barracks ae 4y 1m.

HEIGENBERG, Catherine, wife of Henry, in her 49th year.   MORE 21 Jul 1849

HEISKELL, Dudley, infant of Wade H., Thursday last.   PWH 12 Aug 1847

HELFENSTEIN, Robert C., oldest son of John P. and Mary Ann, in Newton MA 9 March in his 4th year.   MORE 25 Mar 1850

HEMPSTEAD, Edward Jr., infant of Maj. Edward, 18 April.   MOG 25 Apr 1811

    Helen, daughter of Thomas, ae 9m, at the plantation of Stephen Hempstead.   MOG 14 Jun 1816

HENDERSON, Lieut. Bennet H., at Jefferson Barracks, Sunday last.   MORE 10 Jul 1832

    Children of George and Mary: (St. Louis)
    George, only son, ae 1y 5m 6d.   MORE 19 Apr 1850
    Kate McCulloh, ae 15m, on 9 July.   " 10 Jul 1851

    Robert H., near Jackson, Saturday last.   JASO 2 Jan 1838

    Sarah Jane, infant of George and Jane.   MOSN 6 Oct 1838

HENDREN, John William, son of Maj. Samuel O., 7 October ae 4y 7m.   PWH 17 Oct 1840

HENDRICKS, Mrs. Lucy R., 22 June.   NERA 7 Jul 1845

HENING, children of Robert M. and Elizabeth H.:
    Edward C., ae 8y 1m, on 19 January.   MORE 20 Jan 1847
    Henrietta M., 5y 10m, on 20 January.   " 21 Jan "
    (SLDU 22 Jan. shows Henrietta as 4y 10m.)

HENLEY, Octavia, daughter of E. and L., 23 September of brain disease ae 2m 1d. Richmond VA pc   SLMD 26 Sep 1856

HENNING, James G. in St. Francisville 4 April ae 74.   NERA 18 Apr 1845

HENRY, children of Dr. Julian: (St. Louis)
    John Joseph, infant, 29 November.   MORE 1 Dec 1841
    Josephine, infant, 21 October.   MOG 22 Oct 1820

HENWOOD, John, son of John and Elizabeth, 1 Dec. ae 16.   SLMD 3 Dec 1855

HERNDON, Davidson Headley, son of Fleetwood and Martha, in Boone Co. 2 May ae 13.   MORE 10 May 1852

    James Irving, son of Andrew J. and Emily F., 6 Jun ae 4y 15.   MODE 17/8 Jun 1846

    John William, only son of Wm. J. and Rebecca, in Carrollton MO ae 13m. Richmond VA pc   MORE 3 Oct 1842

    Sarah F., ae 68, at the home of A. J. Herndon, her son, in Fayette, 8 March.   SLMD 24 Mar 1855

HERSEY, Mrs. Catherine at Loutre Island 14 July ae 65.   NERA 8 Aug 1849

HESS, Cora, youngest daughter of James and Prudence, 17 November ae 1y 4m 11d.   MORE 19 Nov 1847

HESSER, Fanny W. in Ashley, Pike Co., daughter of Maj. B.F. and Tennessee, 13 January ae 3y 3m 13d. (also in PWH 3 Feb and MORE 26 Jan.)   BGRAD 20 Jan 1844

HEWITT, James Madison, late of Lincoln Co. MO, son of Charles, at Potosi, W.T.   MORE 17 Oct 1845

HIBBARD, William H., youngest son of Nathaniel P. and
           Catherine, 12 February at Virginia Mines MO   MORE 17 Feb 1845
           ae 3y 5m.

HIBBS, Joseph, infant of Henry, 21 September; lived at
           11-Jefferson.   SLMD 22 Sep 1856

    Henry, parents not shown, 13 September ae 7.   SLMD 14 Sep 1857

HIBLER, __, son of Daniel, ae about 12, killed by
           lightning Sunday morning. Others injured.   MORE 30 May 1843

HICKMAN, Elizabeth F., daughter of Thomas and Harriet,
           in Jackson Co. 10 October ae 19.   JEM 27 Oct 1846

    Laura S., at the home of Mrs. Ashley (of
           Columbia?) 13 July.   MORE 15 Jul 1841

    Children of B. F. and Mary E.:
        Louisa Frances 5 October ae 8y 2m when   MORE 9 Oct 1848
           returning to Jefferson City with her
           mother and family after visiting her
           mother's family in KY. Buried Jeff City.
        Stevenson L. 26 January ae 2y 5m. Family   SLMD 28 Feb 1857
           lived on Clark betw 12-13.

    Rowena, wife of Ezra R., at the home of her
           father, Col. Samuel Ralston, in   SLMD 12 Aug 1856
           Independence, 5 August.

HIGBEE, Rebecca, daughter of John, Thursday last ae 11m.   PWH 27 Aug 1845

HIGGINS, Mary, consort of Joseph, 23 October.   JEM 2 Nov 1848

HILES, Newton in Salt River Twp. 29 January ae about 21.   LADB 5 Feb 1849

HILL, Eliza Jane, at the home of her uncle, J. B. Hill,
           yesterday. Buried Presbyterian Cem.   MORE 22 May 1848

    Josephine, infant of Capt. D. B., 24 July.   MORE 29 Jul 1834

    Julia, consort of Samuel A. and daughter of Maj.
           Hiram Sloan, in Cape Girardeau Co. 11 Dec.   SLMD 23 Dec 1853

    Mary A. S., widow of John, 15 April. Funeral from
           the Christian Church.   HAJ 26 Apr 1849

    William T. on 22 June in his 36th year. Left wife,
           2 small children. From Louisville KY   HAJ 27 Jun 1850
           "some years ago."

HINKSON, Elizabeth Frances, wife of Addison, 7 December
           at the home of her father, Lewis Castleman,   NERA 3 Jan 1846
           in Washington Co.; in her 22nd year.

HINTON, David, lately from CA, at the Virginia Hotel; from
           Lafayette Co., where his parents lived.   MORE 10 Jan 1850
           Buried Methodist Cemetery.

    Howard Roberts, son of the Rev. Isaac and Sarah,
           in New Orleans 25 Feb. ae 5y 9m.   MORE 9 Mar 1846

HIRGINS, Tarah C., wife of R. S., 27 June. Bridgeton NJ pc   SLNL 3 Jul 1847

HIRSCHBERG, Sophie, wife of Louis, 154 4th St., 16 June.   MORE 17 Jun 1850

HOBBS, Jacob, in his 66th year.   MORE 3 Sep 1849

HODGES, Lavinia, wife of John D. of St. Louis, 11 May in
     Jefferson City ae 17.   NERA 15 May 1849

HOFFMAN, Hannah, funeral notice; she lived in Carondelet.   MORE 12 May 1849 .

HOGAN, Emma, infant of Mr/Mrs. Edward. Funeral from the
     home of Mr. Penn on 5th St.   SLDU 30 Nov 1846

HOLCOMB, Mrs. Franky, consort of Jacob of Cape Girardeau Co.,
           19 July in her 65th year. She left   CGWE 28 Jul 1848
           2 sons, 1 daughter; was a Baptist.

HOLDEN, Charles Christopher, son of John and Ellen,
        11 August ae 1y 10m.   MORE 12 Aug 1853

     Charlotte Gallison "of this city" 30 June.   MORE 1 Jul 1843

     Children of Edward: (St. Louis)
         Duncan Lamont on 7 January, ae 10m.   MORE 10 Jan 1844
         Charlotte G., in her 8th year.   "   13 Jun 1849

     Edward M. at his home in Perryville 9 May in his
         54th year, leaving an "afflicted family."   MORE 7 Jun 1850

     James C., son of Col. Holden of St. Louis, at the
         home of Maj. Sayers in Mississippi Co.,   MORE 15 Feb 1850
         of "an effusion of blood on the brain."

*? HOLEMS, Howard Leslie, son of Henry and Clara E.,
        7 January in his 5th month.   MORE 10 Jan 1848
HOLLAND, Elizabeth Rebecca, only child of Eliza and
        the late Henry, ae 2y 2m.   MORE 10 Mar 1851
     Capt. Henry K., no data (he died during the
        cholera epidemic).   MORE 12 Jul 1849

HOLLYMAN, Edward, son of Thomas, Friday last ae about 15.   PWH 9 Oct 1845

HOLM, Mrs. Cornelia, of consumption, 3 November ae 26;
     lived on 13th betw Christy-Orange.   MORE 4 Nov 1849

*? HOLMES, Clara E., wife of Henry, living on Brooklyn Ave.
     in north St. Louis, and their daughter   MORE 10 Jul 1849
     Frances L. (during the cholera epidemic).

HOLTON, Henry, 3rd son of Alfred B. and Nancy E., 5y 6m.   MORE 28 May 1840

HOMAN, Frances, only daughter of J. Smith Homan, on
     Sunday, 5 July ae 18m.   MORE 7 Jul 1840

HOMES, Francis King, son of William and Julia of St. Louis,
     14 January at the home of Mrs.   SLMD 17 Jan 1857
     Charles R. Welles, Springfield IL,
     ae 6y 4m.

HOMMANN, John Herbert, son of Rev. Wm., 15 Jan. ae 3y.   JEFRE 22 Jan 1842

HONEY, Rev. John M., Methodist, at Hillsboro ae 33.   MORE 13 Jul 1849

HOOD, Margaret, daughter of Abner and Margaret, 20 June   MORP 21 Jun 1845
         ae 9m 17d.

HOOPER, children of Clark and Mary:
         Lois, in her 3rd year; family lived on 7th St.
             "two doors south of the Dutch Reformed   MORE 9 Sep 1840
             Church." Buried Methodist Cem.
         Hiram Clark, ae 10m, on 26 August. Family lived   MORE 27 Aug 1847
             at 6th-Elm.

HOOTES, Thomas R., youngest child of George F. and Sarah A.,   MORE 12 May 1847
         #8 Pine St., 11 May ae $5\frac{1}{2}$y.

HOOTON, Alexander Campbell, son of E., of cholera in   MORE 12 Jun 1833
         Palmyra during an epidemic.

HOPE, William, youngest son of David C. and Narcissa, in   NERA 17 Oct 1845
         Apple Creek Twp., Cooper Co., 7 October
         ae about 8m.

HOPKINS, James Livingston, son of M. W. and Rachel, ae 8.   SLAM 3 Mar 1845

HORE, William Alexander, son of Wm. and Nancy, ae 10m 3d.   SWERE 3 Feb 1845

HORAN, Mary Eleanor, daughter of Robert, 15 July ae 8m.   MORE 17 Jul 1851
         NY pc

HORINNE, Edward S., son of Wm. and Emily, 19 Jan. ae 1y 19d. MORE 20 Jan "52

HORR, Albert, formerly of Grafton Co. NH, 11 October of   NERA 14 Oct 1845
         typhoid ae 22.

HORRELL, Ellen, consort of Thomas M. and daughter of the   CGWE 26 Jan 1849
         late Thomas Byrne, 20 January.

         Maximilian, in Cape Girardeau Co. 16 May.   NERA 24 May 1845

         Sarah, youngest daughter of Rev. Thomas in her   SLINT 15 Jan 1850
             (?11th?) year.

         Rev. Thomas 22 February in his 62d year. Funeral   MORE 23 Feb 1850
             St. George's, buried Episcopal Cem.

HORTIZ, Mrs. Margaret, 21 October ae 85.   NERA 22 Oct 1845

HORTON, Tabitha, only daughter of Mrs. Mary, 6 March   PWH 9 Mar 1848
         ae about 16.

HOUGH, Francis F., son of D., 22 September.   MORE 27 Sep 1827

HOURI, Elizabeth, daughter of William Gardner Esq.   MORE 23 Jan 1849

HOUSTON, John, 71 8th St., 20 July ae 38.   NERA 20 Jul 1849

         Children of William and Sarah: (St. Louis)
             Virginia Anne, ae 6; lived at 123 Locust. MORE 8 Feb 1845
             William, ae 7, on 6 November.   SWERE 8 Nov 1847

HOUX, Mary V., daughter of Isaiah F. and Frances A., at   BOBS 11 Mar 1851
         the home of Frederick Houx 2 Mar. 2y 2m 2d.

HOW, John, son of John and Malinda, 17 July ae 22m.   SLMD 18 Jul 1856

HOWARD, Amidee, son of Louis and Mary, 4 July ae 18m.   NERA 6 Jul 1849

         John R., brother of R.J., Saturday, of cholera.   MORE 2-3 Jun '50

HOWE, Charles J. P., only child of Dr. Cheney and Jennet, yesterday ae 3y 4m. Louisville pc — MORE 10 Feb 1844

HOWKS, __ and __, son and daughter of D., in Palmyra during a cholera epidemic. — MORE 28 Jun 1833

HOYLE, children of George and Catherine:
    Mary Sophia "last evening" ae 9m 16d. Lived at 4th-Elm. — MORE 2 Jun 1846
    George Crittenden, ae 1y 11m 13d. Buried Episcopal Cemetery. — " 9 May 1849

HOYT, S. C., of smallpox, 3 January. — NERA 7 Jan 1846

HUBBARD, John: a Masonic procession at Bowling Green, by Old Pike Lodge; William Hurley of Hannibal to preach his funeral sermon. — LADB 11 Jun 1849

HUFF, James, son of Joseph and Elizabeth, 5 July of cholera, ae 7. — NERA 6 Jul 1849

HUGHES, children of Harvey J. and Elizabeth, 231 Carr St.:
    James Harvey yesterday ae 2y 6m. — MORE 6 Jun 1846
    Eliza, ae 1m 2d, on 11 June. — " 12 Jun 1848

    John Ignatius, only son of Richard and Mary, 8 Aug. ae 3y 6m. Buried Rock Spring Cemetery. — SLMD 9 Aug 1856

    Mary, wife of Edwin, of cholera, in her 69th y. — MORE 3 Jul 1849

    Mary, daughter of James, yesterday ae about 3. — " 2 Mar 1853

    Kate Merry, daughter of Thomas R. and Sarah, 12 November ae 15m 27d. — SWERE 15 Nov 1847

    Martha Ann, daughter of Roland and Mary Ann, 1 May ae 6y 2m 25d. — BOLT 3 May 1845

HUGHS, Benjamin A. in Howard Co. 6 September. — NERA 22 Sep 1845

HULL, Peggy Douglas, daughter of the late Edward, died at the home of her grandfather, Maj. James Clark, in Lincoln Co., 25 December ae 5y 6m. Charlottesville VA pc — MORE 30 Dec 1839

HUMPHREYS, children of William, 12th-Franklin:
    Mary Ann, Saturday night last, ae 18. Buried Presbyterian Cem. — MORE 21 Feb 1842
    Thomas Humphrey, ae 4m, on 2 September. — " 4 Sep 1843

HUMRICKHAUS, George A., of Ranenkamp & Co., 11 June ae 39. — MORE 13 Jun 1850

HUNT, A. Scott, infant, only child of John F. and Ediliza, Sunday night, January 19th. — MORE 22 Jan 1840

    Horace Ezra, son of Ezra and Maria E., in Bowling Green 10 August ae 4m 9d. — LADB 19 Aug 1850

    John W., son of Robert and Phebe, 17 July ae 1y. — MORE 20 Jul 1847

    Marie Feliciann, infant of Capt. Theodore, Friday. — MORE 3 Sep 1825

HUNTER, Mary Ann, infant of Andrew and Margaret, 23 Sept. — JEFRE 26 Sep 1840

    Mary Jane, daughter of Mrs. A.C., 10 Mar. ae 8y 3m. — MORE 11 Mar 1848

HUNTER, Richard Henry, only son of Joseph, of Benton MO,   JASO 13 Oct 1838
    30 September ae 4y 2m.

HUNTINGDEN, Mary Forbes, only child of George L. and   MORE 31 Mar 1840
    Hannah F., 30 March ae 12m.

HUNTON, Thomas, infant of Logan and Mary Jane, 31 July.   MORE 5 Aug 1840 ·

HUNTSBERRY, __, __, __, 3 children, of cholera in Palmyra.   MORE 28 Jun 1833

HUSSEY, Loretta, youngest child of Mr/Mrs. B., formerly   MORE 16 Jul 1851
    of Holton ME, ae 3y 20d.
    Charles Stetson, at his father's home, 8 May   MORE 10 May 1853
    ae 22. Bangor ME pc

HUSTON, Andrew, at the home of Obey Roberts, 11 February;   MORE 13 Feb 1850
    river men especially invited to funeral.

    Catherine Isabella, infant of James and Jane,   JEM 21 Sep 1847
    Friday last near Jefferson City.

HUTAWA, Edward, 26 Jan.; lived 3rd betw Market-Walnut.   MORE 28 Jan 1847

HUTCHERSON, Charles in St. Charles Co. 29 September.   NERA 7 Oct 1845

HUTCHINSON, Charles Claiborne, eldest son of James A. and   KCEN 24 May 1856
    Catherine F., at the home of E. M.
    McGee, ae 4y 1m 11d. Lynchburgh pc

HUTCHISON, John Y., son of Nathaniel, Tuesday in   WEM 10 Jan 1839
    Boonville ae 2y 4m.

HUTTON, Ellen, daughter of James and Abigail, Gravois Rd.,   MORE 25 Aug 1846
    ae 19m. Funeral from St. John's Church.
    Robert Porter, son of James, 14 August in   SWERE 16 Sep 1844
    St. Louis ae 2y 2m.

HYDE, Cecelia, only child of George and Cecelia,   NERA 19 Jul 1849
    ae 1y 9m 7d.

HYNSON, Augustus R., son of A. R. and Nannie, of summer   SLMD 3 Sep 1857
    complaint, 12 September ae 13m. Memphis
    and Baltimore pc

INGE, children of Chesley B. and Avee V., Virginia Mines MO:
    William Thompson 6 August ae 5m.
    Avee Clemence 20 August ae 5y 7m.   MORE 27 Sep 1845
    Chester Chiles 18 September ae 3y 9m.

INGRAM, Arthur, son of Thomas Jr., infant, Tuesday last.   MORE 21 Aug 1832

    Sidney S. in Greene Co. 7 August.   JEM 17 Aug 1847

IVORY, Jeremiah, of Pittsburgh, father of John C. of   MORE 23 Aug 1849
    St. Louis, in his 56th year.
    Sarah Ann, eldest daughter of John C. and B. M.,   SLMD 21 May 1855
    19 May ae 6y 5m; lived 13th-Pine.

JABINE, Thompson, son of Eliza and Charles, 29 October   MORE 1 Nov 1838
    ae 1y 11m 12d.

JACKS, Miriam Phoebe, wife of Samuel. (cholera?)   MORE 10 Jul 1849

JACKSON, __, infant son of Columbus and Virginia, in   LADB 26 Mar 1849
    Louisiana MO 21 March ae about 2m.

JACKSON, Ann D., eldest daughter of William D. and Mary L.,
           at their home in Bowling Green 3 August   LADB 19 Aug 1850
           of consumption in her 20th year.

        Archibald, ae about 70, in Cuivre Twp. 22 May.   LADB 3 Jun 1850

        Harriet, wife of Thomas and daughter of Robert P.   NERA 12 Nov 1845
           Williams, yesterday ae 25.
        Mary Emily, daughter of Thomas and Harriet, 9 May
           ae 2y 6m. (Sic - did he marry two women   MORE 10 May 1850
           named Harriet?)
        Both funerals from St. Paul's Church.

        John Samuel, son of Samuel, 30 June in this city. MORE 2 Jul 1835

        Laura Jane, infant of James and Elizabeth L., at   BOLT 14 Oct 1843
           Glasgow, ae 1y 4m 19d.

JACOB, Sarah M., daughter of H. S. and M. W., 30 March   SLAM 4 Apr 1845
           ae 8m 3w 3d.

JACOBS, John, in Shelby Co., 22 May.   NERA 31 May 1845

        Robinson, son of the late Robinson and Emma Ritner, SLMD 5 May 1855
           at the home of Mrs. Mary Jacobs, in
           Ray Co., 12 April ae 2y 5m.

JAMES, John, late of St. Louis, at Sutter's Fort, CA of
           cholera 12 September in his 44th year. Native   MORE 27 Dec 1849
           of South Wales. "Kind husband, affectionate father."

        John W., son of C. P. and Eliza.   MORE 24 Feb 1851

        William, in Ste. Genevieve Co., 31 April ae (68?88?) SLMD 26 May 1855

JAMISON, children of David and Meeky, St. Louis:
                   Emmeline Alzonia 29 July ae 20m. Lived   MORE 30 Jul 1842
                      10th betw Walnut-Clark. Methodist Cem.
                   Susan Elizabeth 25 July ae 2y 4m. Lived   "   26 Jul 1847
                      7th betw Spruce-Almond.
           Louisa Bell, daughter of James H. and Louisa G.,   MORE 5 Aug 1847
              at Virginia Mines 29 July ae 7m 27d.

JANUARY, Thomas T., son of Thomas T. and Maria, ae 4y 2m,   MORE 1 Oct 1844
           on Sunday, 29 September.

JAQUES, Adaline, infant daughter of Benjamin T., no date.   MORE 8 Jul 1828

JEFFERSON, Missouri, wife of Robert, 23 November ae 28;   JEM 27 Nov 1849
              daughter of Judge Robert and Jane Ewing.
              Left 4 children.

JEFFERY, James, daughters of, St. Louis:
              Virginia Louise, ae 3y 10m, on 29 July.
              Laura Margaret, ae 15 (18)m, on 30 July.   MORE 1 Aug 1838
                 (MOSN says formerly of Hartford Co. MD)
              Laura Virginia, ae 5y 5m, of whooping cough
                 and scarlet fever. Presbyterian Cem.   MORE 6 May 1844

JEFFREY, Ann Eliza, daughter of Jacob, 293 5th St.,   MORE 29 Jun 1848
              28 June ae 11m. (Her mother died the
              previous January.)

JEFFREYS, Victoria Adelaide, daughter of Coleman,   BRUNS 14 Apr 1849
                29 March ae 8.

JENKINS, __, son of William, drowned at Lexington, ae 2.   MORE 10 Aug 1843

JENKS, Horace B., ae 42; funeral from the home of his   MORE 16 Aug 1849
                brother George, 11th betw Olive-Locust.
        NY & Salem MA pc
        Annie Griswold, daughter of Mary and the late Horace, " 29 Sep 1849
                27 September ae 13m.

JETER, sons of Benjamin F. and Mary Jane:
                Littleton T., infant, Thursday.   BOLT 19 Jun 1841
                Marcellus, infant, 17 August.   "   19 Aug 1843

JETERS, Clara Maria, daughter of Lloyd and Mary,   SLMD 29 Apr 1854
                27 April ae 2y 6m.

JETT, William Van Court, infant of S. C. and N. J.   MORE 19 Jul 1851
                Buried Bellefontaine Cemetery.

JEWETT, William Cornell, son of Wm. G. and Almira; no data. MORE 6 Aug 1849

JOHNSON, __, infant daughter of Samuel and Barbara Ann,   MODE 11 Mar 1846
                ae "nearly 4 months."
        Edwin Alexander, son of Ashton, late of   MORE 15 May 1849
                Petersburg VA, 14 May ae 8y 10m.
        Eliza Branch, infant of Ashton P. and Eliza,   "   8 Jan 1852
                ae 19m 5d. Funeral St. John's Church.

        Joseph Stephen, oldest son of Joseph C. and   SLMD 22 Dec 1853
                Pauline, 20 December.

        Kirtley C., son of David and Sarah, 13 December   SLMD 28 Dec 1854
                in Randolph Co. ae 6.

        Heber, youngest son of Edward A. and Harriet,   MORE 12 Dec 1843
                9 December ae 2y 2m.

        Daughters of French, of Brunswick:
                Margaret, ae about 4, yesterday.   BRUNS 16 Dec 1848
                Harriet M., ae 15m, 8 July.   " 12 Jul 1849

        Elizabeth Courtenay, wife of George, late of   NERA 9 Oct 1849
                Lurgan, IRE, 7 Oct. of consumption.

        George, at his home in Louisiana MO 12 Dec. in   LADB 17 Jan 1848
                his 41st year. Native of KY, to Louisiana
                at an early age. Protracted illness.

        Henrietta, daughter of Rev. Thomas, 20 July   BOLT 26 Jul 1845
                ae 16m.

        John O. on Apple Creek 2 Oct. in his 2nd year.   INP 11 Oct 1823

        Joseph K., eldest son of John M., 4 October   HAJ 11 Oct 1849
                near Hannibal ae 25y 1d.

        Children of Julius D. and Neville, St. Louis:
                Ellen Elizabeth 8 May ae 9m 12d. Buried MORE 10 May 1848
                St. Charles. Lynchburg VA pc
                Charles Neville, infant, no date.   "   13 Sep 1843
        (cont.)

                                53

JOHNSON, children of Julius and Neville, St. Louis, cont.:
    Julius Rosati 9 August, ae 19m 15d.   MORE 10 Aug 1842
        Funeral at St. Charles.

    Sarah Elizabeth, infant of Collins, Friday.   PWH 20 Feb 1841

    William Edwin, son of William and Gabrella,   COMB 28 Jan 1847
        25 January ae 10m 5d.

JOHNS(T)ON, Jane, wife of Samuel, 14 July of cholera.   MORE 15 Jul 1849

JONAS, Ann Elizabeth, daughter of William H. and Nancy T.,   MORE 26 Jun 1841
    ae 3m 15d.

JONES, Admiral W., only child of Hiram and Jane, 5 Jan.   CANE 12 Jan 1854
    ae 2y 4m 8d.

    Benjamin Lewis, infant of Wilson H. and Elizabeth   MORE 29 Feb 1848
        of Montgomery Co., 21 February.

    George Sydney, son of B. F. and Lucinda E.,   MORE 23 Jul 1847
        22 July ae 16m 21d.

    John H. at the home of his father in Manchester,   MORE 9 Nov 1849
        ae 24y 6m.

    Martha B., wife of Rev. Charles, Boatmens' Chaplain   MORE 15 Sep 1849
        of St. Louis, ae 35.

    North, 2nd son of R. H. and Maria, 20 September   JEFRE 25 Sep 1841
        in his 6th year.

    Rice, in Glasgow 23 November.   SLMD 12 Dec 1854
        Mrs. Rice, 30 November.

    Susan, wife of William D., ae 47, on 21 September
        of cholera; left a large family.   JEFRE 5 Oct 1833
        also Mary, daughter of William, ae 7.

    Isaac H., son of Theodore, "this morning."   PWH 1 Jan 1845

    William, in Benton Co., 22 February.   NERA 12 Mar 1846

    William N., son of John and Malinda, 19 April   MORE 25 Apr 1848
        at Bridgeton in his 12th year.

JORDAN, Henry Clay, son of R. S. and Eliza Jane, 7 June   MORE 10 Jun 1849
    ae 10m. Louisville pc

    Robert W. at his father's home in Buffalo Twp.   LADB 17 Mar 1851
        16 March, ae about 20.

JUDD, Emma Ann, youngest child of George and Minerva, of   SLMD 4 Jun 1854
    congestion of the head, 3 June ae 3.

JULIEN, Frances, wife of J. M., 6 March in St. Louis.   NERA 9 Mar 1849

JUSNEL, Anna A., daughter of Jules and Knight, Tuesday.   SWERE 14 Aug 1848

KAIN, Thomas, killed by a blow from Philip Keating at   SLMD 5 Jan 1855
    Keating's home; cause, "jealousy."

KARST, Hypolite at his father's home on 7th St., ae 14.   MORE 7 May 1850
    Joseph Theodore, son of Aloys & Catherine, 11 Jul ae 14m. " 13 Jul'44
    Victor, son of Michael & Louise, 29 Oct. ae 6y 9m.   " 2 Nov 1846

KEEFER, Miss Eliza V. in Canton 8 March ae 24.   SLMD 24 Mar 1855

KEENEY, Mary, estate in Montgomery Co.; Final Settlement   FULT 24 Nov 1848
    by Calvin Jones.

KEITH, Mrs. Sarah at the home of her son-in-law W.N. George   LADB 1 Feb 1847
    in Boone Co. 6 Jan., in her 84th year.

    William Henry, son of Quincy A., 5th-Pine, ae 3y 8m. MORE 12 Dec 1845

KELLEY, Sarah, daughter of Thomas P. and Mary, 9 July   SLMD 16 Jul 1855
                               ae 10m.

KELLOGG, Francis Robert, son of Capt. Edwin, ae 4m 17d.   MORE 12 Jul 1839

    Mary, daughter of Seymour and Margaret, 5 March   MORE 8 Mar 1843
    ae 2y 9m 20d.

KELLY, children of Eugene and Anna T., St. Louis:
    Joseph, infant, 11 December.   SLDU 12 Dec 1846
    Josephine, infant; lived 8th-Pine.   " . . .
    (twins? Josephine also in MORE)

    Margery on 13 September in her 22nd year. Funeral   SLDU 14 Sep 1846
    from her brother John's home, 11-Green.

    Children of William F. and Anna Maria, St. Louis:
    Mary H., only child, 31 March ae 16m 4d.   MORE 1 Apr 1853
       Lived Washington betw 10-11.
    Frederick, ae 16m, 26 March. Funeral from   SLMD 27 Mar 1855
       Samuel Hawkins' home, 6th St.

KEMPER, Laura, daughter of Simeon and Jane, 4 September.   STGAZ 14 Sep '53

KENDALL, Miss Mary, of cholera, 4 July.   NERA 6 Jul 1849

    Mary A., infant of Mr./Mrs. B. N., 4 August.   MORE 6 Aug 1853

KENADY, Unity, ae 63, on 14 August of a paralytic affliction.   LADB 17 Aug 1846
    Winchester KY pc

KENNEDY, Kate, infant of Adam and Margaret, 3 February of   SLMD 4 Feb 1856
    whooping cough ae 9m 2d.

    Sons of S. S. and Mary Barrett, St. Louis:
    Thomas S. ae 1y 2d; funeral Christ Church.   MORE 27 Oct 1849
    Theodosius Barrett, ae 16m 18d.   " 13 Jul 1851

    William B., of cholera, 20 June in his 48th year.   NERA 21 Jun 1849

KENNER, Stepto at his father's home in St. Charles, ae 18.   MORE 6 Sep 1849

KENNERLY, George, infant of Capt. George H., Friday.   MORE 18 Jan 1831

KENNETT, Cynthia, only daughter of Ferdinand and Julia,   MORE 16 Oct 1845
    yesterday ae 3y 3m 18d. Episcopal Cem.

    Florence, daughter of L. M. and Agnes, 16 Sept.   MORE 18 Sep 1849
    ae 4m 8d.

    Children of Mortimer and Mary H., St. Louis:
    Christopher H., 10 October.   MORE 11 Oct 1839
    Edward B. 20 November ae 2y.   " 24 Nov 1837
    Thomas H., youngest child, 28 May.   " 29 May 1847
    Edward B. 13 June ae 4y 5d.   " 14 Jun 1847

KENNEY, Alexander W., in Polk Co., 27 August.   NERA 5 Sep 1845

KENT, Henry T., a merchant of Louisiana MO, in Clarksville   LADB 19 &
                    in his 38th year.   26 Feb 1849

KENYON, Julia on 12 November, ae 13.   SJA 22 Nov 1850

KERR, George Washington, a merchant, 2 October at his home.   MOSN 6 Oct 1838

        Sally Ann, daughter of William and Mary, 24 April   SLMD 5 May 1855
                    in Warsaw.

        Thomas, near Sarcoxie, Newton Co., formerly of   LADB 19 Feb 1849
                    Pike Co., 29 January ae 50.

        William Wallace, son of Thomas and Susan, late of   BGRAD 11 Jun 1842
                    Pike Co., in Dade Co. 21 May ae 9y 8m 23d.

KEYSER, Rosena, wife of A., in Fulton 14 June.   SLMD 21 Jun 1854

KEYTE, Judith Virginia, youngest child of Mrs. Eliza, ae 9.   BRUNS 26 Jul '49

KIDD, Elizabeth, daughter of William, Friday last.   PWH 12 Aug 1847

KIENLEN, children of C. F., St. Louis:
                    Caroline, infant, 21 November.   MORE 1 Dec 1829
                    Louisa, infant, yesterday.   "   15 Jul 1834
                    Gustavus Adolphus, infant, last Sunday.   "   13 Sep 1827

KIMBROUGH, Duke, in Greene Co., 18 July.   JEM 3 Aug 1847

        Mrs. Franklin, at her home about 15 miles north   SLMD 28 Dec 1854
                    of Columbia, 16 December of
                    smallpox, ae about 27.

KINCAID, Mrs. Catherine 25 June ae 71. Funeral from the   MORE 25 Jun 1850
                    home of D. Rokohl.

KING, Cordelia, wife of John, 1 August in her 19th year.   NERA 2 Aug 1849
                    Funeral from the home of James L. Appleby.   MORE   "

        Montgomery James, son of Dr. Henry and Marian E.,   MORE 14 Oct 1847
                    13 October ae 9y 11m.

        Daughters of Wyllys and Mary W., St. Louis:
                    Mary Ursula, infant, ae 1m, yesterday.   MORE 5 Jun 1844
                    Lived on Erskine's Row, Carr St.
                    Eliza Ann, youngest daughter, ae 2y 3m.   "   27 Jun 1844

KINGSBURY, Johanna Sophia, infant of Lieut. C. P. and   MORE 3 Aug 1851
                    M. J., 2 August.

        James William, only son of Noah, 11 April   COP 14 May 1842
                    in Howard Co.

        William Boggs, son of L. L. and Catherine,   GLWT 18 Sep 1851
                    3 September ae 1y 6m 6d.

KINGSLAND, sons of George and Eliza, St. Louis:
                    David, youngest, 2 February ae 21m.   MORE 3 Feb 1852
                    George Henry ae 8y 3m.   "   27 Feb "

KINKEAD, William, son of Andrew, at Creve Coeur settlement   MORE 19 Oct 1830
                    in his 8th year.

KIRBY, C. C. in St. Joseph 23 July. NERA 12 Aug 1845

KIRTLEY, Lucinda, only child of Columbus F. and Virginia, PWH 15 Apr 1847
    Friday last ae about 18m.

KITTS, Susan, wife of David, late of Hannibal, 4 Dec. in Tully. HAJ 4 Jan'49

KLEIN, children of Joseph and Agnes, St. Louis:
    Aubry, ae 9m 7d, Friday last. MORE 26 Sep 1842
    Henry Gay, 2y 5m, 11 November. " 15 Nov 1842
    Harry Fletcher, ae 14m, Tuesday. " 19 Dec 1844
    Julian Reynolds, 15½m, 26 January. " 28 Jan 1847

KLELL, Francis, a German, fell from a window of the California
    Exchange, 7th-Market; a coal miner from SLMD 10 Jan 1855
    Gravois diggings, apparently drunk.

KNABB, George W., son of Peter and Mary Ann, 14-Olive, MORE 6 Sep 1847
    5 Sept. ae 4y. Catholic Cemetery.

KNAPP, daughters of John and Virginia, St. Louis:
    Virginia A., ae 2, on 7 August. MORE 9 Aug 1847
    Mary Eleanor, infant, 15 Feb. SLMD 16 Feb 1854

KNOTT, Sarah Ann, daughter of William and Martha A., of NERA 7 Jul 1845
*   brain inflammation, ae 4y.

KNOX, children of Dr. F., St. Louis: (possibly R.?)
    Eliza, ae 2y 10½m, on 4 September. SLDU 4 Sep 1846
(see Dr. R. below) Franklin, only son, 18 November. MORE 20 Nov 1848

    Milton Huntley, only son of Milton and Mary C., of MORE 5 Oct 1844
    erysipelas, ae 2m.

    Children of Dr. Reuben, St. Louis:
    Jefferson Kilpatrick, youngest son, ae 3y9m. MORE 5 May 1841
    (his mother Olivia had died in 1839)
    Reuben, son of Dr. R. and Eliza, ae 8m 24d, SLAM 4 Apr 1845
    30 March. Raleigh & Newburn NC pc

* KNOWLES, William, son of Edward, Franklin betw 10-11, SLMD 16 Oct 1857
    drowned when returning from a shooting
    expedition to the Illinois side, ae 17.

KNOX, Susan, estate in Chariton Co.: final settlement by BOLT 4 Mar 1843
    John M. Bell.

KRAFT, Barbara, thrown from a wagon near Lafayette Park; SLMD 28 Oct 1857
    husband and child ae 5 mentioned.

KRAIGER, Frederick William, son of Peter and Dinah, 6 Oct. MODE 14 Oct 1846

KRETSCHMER, daughters of Frederick and Mary Ann, St. Louis:
    Ann Regina 16 January; lived Walnut betw 6-7. MORE 17 Jan'44
    Laura Corina 15 Nov. in 7th year. " MORE 16 Nov 1842

KRIBBEN, Henry C., ae 21. MORE 7 Jul 1849

KRING, George Chrisman, infant of Henry W. BOLT 5 Nov 1842

KRUM, Mary Ophelia, daughter of Hon. J. M., Saturday. SWERE 15 Jul 1844
    Lina, daughter of John M. and Mary O., 6 Dec. ae 12. SLMD 7 Dec 1857
    Church of the Messiah. Bellefontaine Cem.

KUNKLE, Mary Elizabeth, daughter of David and Sarah H., in Boonville 13 Nov. in her 4th year.   BOLT 19 Nov 1842

KYLE, Margaret Anne, daughter of Robert, last evening. Lived on Stacker's Row, Broadway.   MORE 2 Jul 1841

KYLER, Mary Eliza, daughter of Alderman George, 198 Wash, of lung disease, ae 3y 8m. Shelbyville IN pc   SLMD 29 & 31 Jul 1857

LA BARGE, Octavia, daughter of Charles and Octavia, 29 Apr. Ae 2y 8m. Funeral from home of Joseph La Barge.   MORE 30 Apr 1853

Thomas P., son of Joseph and Eulalie, 22 Sept. ae 8y 1m.   MORE 23 Sep 1844

LA BEAUME, Theodore, youngest son of Theodore and Eliza, of New Orleans, 12 April.   MORE 20 Apr 1844

LACY, E. B. on 25 February in his 25th year. Quincy pc   MORE 26 Feb 1848

Stephen, son of W. L. and Sophronia F., 3 March at La Grange, ae 5.   SLMD 17 Mar 1855

LADEW, Catherine, wife of Stephen, Sunday ae 65. Funeral from home of son Augustus, 10th-Wash.   SLMD 12 Dec 1853

LAFERTY, Mary, infant of James and Ellen, on Sunday night ae 16m.   MORE 8 Sep 1840

LAFON, Fayette, youngest son of John, in Lewis Co. 24 Sept.   PWH 2 Sep 1847

Thomas, son of Dr. Joseph, Monday last ae about 10.   " 23 Mar 1848

LA GRAVE, Louis Valle, son of Anthony and Mary, 12 May ae 4y 6m.   MORE 13 May 1853

LA GUERRIER, Colastic, youngest daughter of Charles and Constance, 17 March ae 10m.   MORE 18 Mar 1843

LAMBDIN, Alice Ward, infant of Robert B. and Mary A., 27 January ae 9m.   STGAZ 28 Jan 1852

LAMKIN, Lucy Hord, daughter of James C., 22 June in 5th y.   PWH 24 Jun 1843

LAMONT, Jane, daughter of Daniel, died Sunday.   MORE 12 Jul 1836

LAND, Margaret M.: estate in Montgomery Co. Letters of Administration 16 Oct. to Cary T. Gabart.   FULT 30 Oct 1848

LANE, Edward, in Cuivre Twp. 3 October ae 26; left "several children."   LADB 9 Oct 1848

James C., son of Nathan and Julia, 27 Sept. ae 2y11m7d.   MORE 28 Sep 1851

Martin M. at his home in Cole Co. a few days ago, ae about 55. Left wife, large family.   JEM 2 Feb 1847

Victor, infant son of Wm. Carr, Friday last.   MORE 6 Oct 1829

William on 13 Feb. in his 49th year. Methodist.   JEM 16 Feb 1847

LANGLEY, Virginia Missouri, eldest daughter of James F. and Catherine J., 14 Oct. ae 5y 7m.   MORE 16 Oct 1846

LANIUS, William Henry, infant of Rev. J., 22 September.   PWH 24 Sep 1842

LANSING, children of Abram A. and Frances Ann, Palmyra:
        Mary Eleanor, ae 7, Thursday last of croup.   PWH 29 Oct 1846
        Sarah Emma, ae 1y 11d, Friday. Buried in
        the Presbyterian Cemetery.

LATAMORE, James H. in Cuivre Twp. 16 July, ae 23.   LADB 26 July 1847

LATTIMERE, Robert, native of Scotland, in St. Charles Co.   NERA 8 Oct 1845
        31 September.

LAUGHLIN, Alvin, son of M. L. and M. A., at Brownsville   SLMD 5 May 1855
        ae 12m 6d.

LAUMAN, Maria Louisa, daughter of Frederick and Margaret,   SLMD 7 Oct 1857
        6 Oct ae 1y 16d.

LAURIE, Charles L., infant of Joseph N. and Jane C.,   WEM 1 Aug 1839
        ae 1y 3m 5d.

LAVEILLE, family of Joseph C., St. Louis:
        Cornelia, infant, Tuesday night.   MORE 14 Jul 1829
        Josephine, ae 24y 2m, at the home of   MORE 3 Jan 1849
        Lawrason Riggs.

LAW, Edwin, son of Richard H. and Ann, Sunday last   MODE 26/17
        ae 1y 3m.   Aug 1846

    Mrs. Fanny, ae 26, at Providence 4 May.   SLMD 9 Jun 1855

LAWLER, __, a little daughter of Patrick, ae about 2,   MORE 18 Mar 1844
        drowned when her head was caught in a
        bucket of water.

    Michael, brother of William, 1 October ae about 38.   SLMD 2 Oct 1857
        Native of Marysborough, Queens Co. IRE.

LAWLESS, John, son of James and Mary, at Ravenswood in   MORE 19 Jan 1844
        St. Louis Co., 16 January ae 10.

    Children of L. E. and Virginia, St. Louis: MORE 23 Jul 1833
        William Frederick ae 5, on 19 July.
        Louisa Marie ae 9m, also on 19 July.
        Both of cholera.

LAZELERE, Ella, daughter of Alfred and Margaret, 28 July   STGAZ 3 Aug 1853
        ae 21m.

LEACH, Timothy S., of cholera (18?) June. Interred in   HAJ 27 Jun 1840
        family burying ground. Newark pc

LEAGUE, Martha, consort of William R., Wednesday. Left   HAG 9 Sep 1847
        husband and several children.

LEARNED, Howard Bowker, eldest son of Henry and Clarissa   NERA 22 May 1849
        of St. Louis, at Independence, aboard the
        Mary, of cholera, 7 May ae 21y 6m.

LE BLOND, Louis Adolphe, son of Joseph, 10 Sept. ae 3y 5m.   MORE 11 Sep 1840

LE BOUE, Frederick, ae 3y2m; lived 3rd betw Myrtle-Spruce.   MORE 1 Jun 1849

LE BEAU, Virginia, daughter of C. F. and Virginia, 21 May   MORE 22 May 1852
        ae 8m 8d. Buried Rock Spring Cem.

LE COMPTE (HEBERT), Margaret, of cholera. MORE 6 Nov 1832

LEE, Bettie Davis, daughter of William F. and Mary S., SLMD 3 Mar 1855
    21 February in her 8th year.

    Elliott, infant son of John, in St. Louis 21 July. SCOMB 22 Jul 1836

    Jane, daughter of Mrs. Lee, when her clothes caught MOG 15 Sep 1819
        fire; she survived only a few hours. (A Mary
        Ann Lee appears on the tax list for this period.)

    Henry C., son of Henry C. and Mary E., at Clinton, SLMD 5 May 1855
        Monroe Co., 14 April ae 6m 10d.

    John, in St. Charles Co., 4 August. NERA 18 Aug 1845

    William, son of Mr/Mrs., ae 5. (Cholera epidemic?) MORE 5 Aug 1849

LEEPER, __, child of Calvin, died of a rattlesnake bite. BRUNS 20 Sep 1849

LE FAIVRE, Antoine, an old citizen, 19 August in his NERA 20/30
        49th year; long illness. Left a Aug 1849
        large family.

LEGRO, Emily, daughter of David and Martha, 15 Sept. ae 15m. JEFRE 19 Sep'40

LEMOINE, Elizabeth Johnson, daughter of J. D. and MORE 10 Sep 1851
        Elizabeth E., 9 September ae 15m.

LEMON, George W., son of Wm. J., 1 July ae 9m 5d. SASE 9 Jul 1853

    James, the City Register, Sunday ae about 58. MORE 11 Feb 1850
        Funeral from home of B. Rice, 189 Carondelet.

LEONHARD, ___, infant daughter of George and Wilhelmina, MODE 10/8
    30 October. Nov 1847

LEPERE, Peter, son of Martin, 9 July in his 23rd year. NERA 15 Jul 1849

LESLIE, Kate, youngest daughter of Miron and Catherine, SWERE 3 Aug 1846
    last Monday.

LESPERANCE, John B., 23 October ae 51. NERA 24 Oct 1849

LETCHER, Charles Carroll, infant of I. A., yesterday. MORE 16 Jul 1833

    William Campbell, older son of Wm. H. and MORE 2 Sep 1851
        Evalina, in Marshall, ae 23m 6d.

LEVY, Rachel, widow of Abraham, mother of Jeannette Marks, MORE 17 Jul 1849
    in 54th y. Member Ladies Hebrew Benevolent
    Association.

LEWELLIN, Nancy, consort of James K., 30 May ae 21, of MORE 31 May 1850
        consumption. Buried Methodist Cemetery.

LEWIS, Ann Elizabeth, wife of John R. (cholera epidemic?). MORE 10 Jul 1849

    Charles William, only child of Charles and MORE 12 Feb 1839
        Elizabeth, ae 8.

    J. Cooper in Cape Girardeau Co. 9 December, SLMD 21 Dec 1853
        "old and respected."

    Laura Louisa, youngest daughter of G. F. and MORE 18 Mar 1847
        Caroline, 17 March ae 2y 4m.

LEWIS, Mrs. ___, wife of Joseph, in her 78th year. Mother   CGWE 9 Dec 1848
          of 14 children, 13 grew to adulthood.
          Came to MO in 1797.

      Pape W., son of B. W. and Amanda of Glasgow, 22 May   BRUNS 31 May 1849
          in his 5th year.

      John G., youngest son of Thomas, 9 June in his 3rd
          year. (BRUNS 1 July says died at the home   MODE 27 Jun 1848
          of grandparents in Howard Co.)
      Thomas S., son of the late Thomas of Glasgow,
          ae 9y 3m.   MORE 27 Aug 1851

      Thomas Harwood, second son of Charles and Caroline,   MORE 25 Sep 1845
          23 September ae 2y 9m 27d.

      Col. Wm. H. in Lafayette Co. 14 September.   NERA 23 Sep 1845

      William J., son of James and Virginia, of Glasgow,   SLMD 18 Jan 1854
          6 January.

LIEFFREING, Mary H., daughter of V. X. and Julie,   PWH 6 Sep 1849
          Tuesday last ae about 18m.

LIGGETT, Emma Romanza, daughter of C. M., 10 April ae 4y6m. SWERE 17 Apr'48

LIGHTNER, Isaac, died on 30 June. (Cholera epidemic?)   MORE 4 Jul 1849

LIGHTON, Mary Jane, daughter of Alexander J., 31 March   PWH 1 Apr 1843
          ae about 20m.

LINDELL, Miss Sarah 16 February ae about 70; long illness. MORE 18 Feb 1850

LINDSEY, Margaret, infant of G. A. and J. B., 13 June.   MORE 14 Jun 1842
          Lived Washington Ave. betw 3rd-4th.

LINTON, Mrs. Phoebe, late of Arkansas. (Cholera epidemic?) MORE 14 Jul 1849

LISA, Mary (first wife of Manuel) Tuesday morning last.   MOG 13 Feb 1818
     Raymond, son of Manuel, 14 July.   "   25 Jul 1811

LISLE, children of Benjamin and Margaret, Cole Co.:
          Thomas M., age about 4, last week. (Paper torn) JEFRE 13 or 20
             (father shown as General Benjamin)   Nov 1841
          Sophia Louise, ae 7m 8d, 30 July.   "   5 Aug 1843

LITTELL, Julia H., daughter of William T. and Sarah,   MORE 15 Feb 1853
          yesterday ae 2y 2m 6d. "Only daughter."

LITTLE, Thomas J., in Canton, 20 May.   SLMD 9 Jun 1855

LIVESAY, Joseph, infant of Joseph and Amandy, on Sunday   LEXP 30 Jul 1844
          ae 7d. (Mother had died Thursday.)

LIVINGSTON, Mortimer, only son of George H. and Elizabeth, MORE 25 Jan 1853
          ae 5m 11d.

          Dr. James, at his home in Grundy Co., 5 March   SJA 28 Mar 1850
          ae (42? 43?).

LOACH, Emily, only daughter of P. and M., 4 December
          ae 7y 7d. Funeral from home of Charles   MORE 10 Dec 1848
          LaBarge, Green betw 6-7. Catholic Cem.

LOCKE, children of Joseph and Cassandra, St. Louis:
    John Armstead, 2nd son, 15 March ae   MORE 16 Mar 1853
    9y4m 15d; lived 465 Washington.
    Joseph H., only son, 2y 6m.   "   5 May 1853
    Buried Bellefontaine.

    Clara, daughter of Richard N. and Mary Ann,   MORE 2 Sep 1853
    3 August ae 20d.

LOCKHART, J. on 24 June, ae about 6 years.   INP 3 Jul 1824

LOGAN, Greenberry, "a yellow boy," drowned off the Convoy   MORE 4 Aug 1846
    at Grand Tower.

LONERGAN, William, of cholera, 18 July ae about 25.   NERA 10 Jul 1849

LONG, Elizabeth, wife of William L., at Gravois in   MORE 7 Jul 1849
    her 61st year.

    Mary Jane, daughter of Ferman, 5 January in   BGDB 10 Jan 1846
    Culver Twp. ae 9.

    Park B., ae 33, on 18 October.   MORE 20 Oct 1849

    Richard H. at Fort Gibson in his 24th year.   "   5 Mar 1849

LONGDO, Lawrence Henry, son of Lawrence and Laurinda, MORE 23 Jul 1851
    18 July in his 4th year.

LONGUEMARE, Leontine ae 14y 5m. (Cholera epidemic?) MORE 12 Jul 1849

    Children of Charles and Felicite, St. Louis:
    Marie Berthe, ae 11m, 18 May.   MORE 19 May 1848
    Ernest, infant, 21 July.   " 24 Jul 1843

LORING, daughters of Charles E. and Mary, St. Louis:
    Martha D., ae 7y 7m, Thursday.   MORE 2 Mar 1844
    Isabella W., ae 2y 2m, 11 June.   " 12 Jun "

LOUTHAN, sons of Walker, Palmyra:
    William on "Thursday last" (25 August).   PWH 27 Aug 1842
    Infant son ae 3m, yesterday.   " 13 Jan 1848

LOVE, Mrs. Granville near Middleton 31 January ae 66. SLMD 18 Feb 1856

LOVING, Ella Greenhill, daughter of Rev. R. G. and M. E., SLMD 24 Jan 1855
    at Weston 1 January.

LOWDEN, John, of Charleston, Mississippi Co., 17 Sept. MORE 2 Sep 1837
    (from the Charleston Courier)

LOWES, George, native of Yorkshire, ENG. (cholera epidemic?) SWERE 17 Jul'49

LOWREY, Ann L., consort of John, 12 July of bilious   NERA 15 Jul 1849
                 diarrhoea.

LOWRY, Priscilla, only daughter of   MORE 24 Aug 1849
    Samuel and Priscilla, ae 2y 4m 2d.

LOYD, Mrs. E., wife of Jerry, 15 November near Canton. CANE 23 Nov 1854

LUCAS, children of James H., St. Louis:
    Emilie, ae 15m 15d, yesterday.   MORE 2 Jul 1842
    John B. C., ae 17m, yesterday.   " 27 Jun 1844
    Emilie, ae 4m, 14 Feb. Family cemetery. " 15 Feb 1849

LUCK, __, a son of Diggs of Pike Co., ae about 12, shot himself accidentally while hunting in Illinois. — LADB 22 Oct 1849

LUKE, Annie Wallace, daughter of John W. and Kate, of croup, 17 April ae 3y 3m. — SLMD 18 Apr 1857

LUND, Alice Augusta, daughter of Dr. I. C. and J. E., of cholera, 9 June in her 8th year. — SLMD 15 Jun 1854

LUNEY, Jane M., consort of Peter, 15 February in her 25th year. Interred Pittsburgh. — SLNL 19 Feb 1848

LURTON, Cynthia, daughter of Charles and Cynthia, ae 12y 5m. — SCWR 3 Jun 1854

LUSK, Charles Jr. in Benton Co. 16 September. — NERA 27 Sep 1845

LYDICK, daughters of John, in Palmyra:
    Ann Eliza 15 September ae 12y 11m 6d. — PWH 17 Sep 1845
    Amanda Elvira ae 9y 10m 17d. — "
    Lucinda Cassander, infant of John and Ann, 21 April ae 2y 1m. — " 30 Apr 1842

LYLE, children of Alex L. and Caroline, St. Louis:
    Samuel Wilson 14 April in his 14th year. Lived 7th-Walnut. — MORE 15 Apr 1840
    Maria Virginia ae 5y 6m. Lived 165 7th St. — " 3 Jan 1849
    Harrison, ae 8y 6m, on Thursday. — SWERE 14 May "

LYMAN, John M. in Rocheport 12 June. — NERA 24 Jun 1845

LYNCH, Charles Augustus, only son of William L. and Mary J., 7 July ae 1y 11m 18d. — SLMD 8 Jul 1854

    James, son of George and Frances, 21 May. — MORE 22 May 1852

    Janetta, daughter of Robert and Matilda, 19 June ae about 3 years. — MODE 27 Jun 1848

LYON, Louisa, wife of F., in Warren Co. 30 April ae 30y 1m 24d. Daughter of Capt. Garrett, of St. Louis Co. — SLMD 7 Jul 1855

LYONS, Margaret, daughter of J. H. and Catherine, 16 June ae 1y 10m. Buried Catholic Cemetery. — MORE 17 Jun 1848

McADAM, Eliza Jane, consort of Thomas, 20 November of cholera morbus in her 28th year. — NERA 3 Dec 1845

McAFEE, Jane Amanda, daughter of Rev. Robert L., in Columbia Wednesday ae 2 years. — MIN 26 Oct 1833

McALLISTER, Archibald, late of Knoxville KY, in 33rd year. — MORE 17 Jul 1849

McALISTER, Samuel Carson, infant son of Robert and Elizabeth, 27 September. — MORE 29 Sep 1847

McBRIDE, Francis, at the home of James Walters in St. Louis Co., in his 27th year. Philadelphia pc — MORE 3 Jul 1849

McCANN, __, son of Benjamin, ae 3, burned to death in Ralls Co. 7 January. — MORE 20 Jan 1846

McCANN, William, son of William and Sarah,
        15 October ae 2y 3m.   SWERE 18 Oct 1847

McCART, William H. H., son of B. N. and Jane S., 2 June.   STGAZ 8 Jun 1853

McCARTAN, Mrs. Nancy, ae 42, on 25 June; funeral from
          home of George Knapp.   MORE 25 June 1850

McCARTHA, Catherine, ae about 8, burned to death last week
             when her clothes caught fire. Lived   MORE 29 Jan 1838
             with an aunt who was unable to save her.

McCARTHY, Margaret on 2 March ae 5 years.   NERA 4 Mar 1846

McCARTNEY, Samuel son of Samuel and Julie, 30 April of
          bronchitis ae 1m 8d.   MORE 3 May 1848

McCARTY, Ellen Virginia, daughter of David, Monday last.   PWH 16 Sep 1847

      James, in Lexington, 8 November.   JEM 23 Nov 1847

McCAUSLAND, Audley, of typhus, at his father's home on
           Monday last.   MORE 2 Jan 1835

      Laura, infant of John, on Sunday morning.   "   18 Mar 1833

McCLEARY, Francis, of stab wounds received in a fight on
         8th near Wash several evenings ago.   MORE 10 Feb 1850

McCLELLAND, Jane, late of Newry, Co. Down IRE, in 57th y.   MORE 10 Oct 1849

McCLENNY, William S. in St. Charles Co. 24 August.   NERA 27 Aug 1845

McCLOUD, William died in New Orleans 7 March.   SWERE 20 Mar 1848

McCLOY, Charles Henry, son of Mary W. and Capt. John,
          ae 5y 5m 7d.   MORE 31 Mar 1851

McCLURE, Dr. Robert in Dardenne Twp., St. Louis Co.,
         22 September. a Presbyterian.   SLOB 2 Oct 1834
      John S., his son ae 12, on 28 September.   "

McCONNEL, __ a little girl ae 4 or 5 was so badly burned
         when little boys accidentally set her clothes   WEJ 25 Jan 1845
         on fire that she died a little later.

McCORD, Edna, wife of Capt. James, 12 August at their
         home near Clarkvsille in her 33rd year.   NERA 15 Aug 1849
      Nancy Jane, infant of Capt. James, 2 February
         at the Virginia Hotel.   MORE 3 Feb 1840

      Mary, consort of Col. I., at the home of her son-
         in-law W. P. Snell, near Fulton, 17 January   MORE 29 Jan 1850
         in her 53rd year. A native of Harrisburg PA,
         to MO in 1844.

      Sarah Ann, daughter of Reuben C. and Mary Ann,
         10 October ae 1 year.   NERA 13 Oct 1845

      Thomas B., son of James H. and Matilda, 3 February
         ae 3y 6m. Lived 10th-Brooklyn.   SLMD 7 Feb 1856

McCORKELL, Thomas M., ae 27, son-in-law of the late James
         Ramsey of Baltimore, at the home of   MORE 5 Mar 1845
         his cousin Geo. Foster in Londonderry Ire.

McCORMICK, Emily Martha Arsheven, consort of Alexander,   NERA 27 Jun 1849
       26 June of cholera ae 23y 7m (52?) days.

McCOWAN, Joseph, suddenly on 12 November.   HAG 18 Nov 1846

McCOY, Alice, wife of W. of St. Louis, 3 July of cholera at   NERA 6 Aug 1849
       Holmes Hotel, Cincinnati, in her 23rd year.

McCREERY, Charles of St. Louis in Louisville 11 Jan. ae 23.   MORE 12 Jan 1850

McCULLOUGH, Dr. George at his home in Florissant 9 July,   NERA 15 Jul 1849
       ae about 28, formerly of MD; also
       his eldest daughter Virginia in her
       9th year on 10 July. (See EVANS, Mrs.)

       Mrs. Nancy 2 July of consumption.   SLOB 3 Jul 1834

McCUNE, Irene, daughter of John S. and Ruthanna, ae about   MORE 19 Jan 1847
       3 years, on 16 January.

       Joseph P. at his home in Pike Co. <u>6</u> November, ae   LADB 14 Dec 1846
       31. Left wife, 2 children.

McCUTCHEON, Bethial Urie, second son of John and Isabella,   MORE 14 Mar 1853
       13 March ae 4y 6m.

McDEARMAN, James, editor of the St. Charles <u>Chronotype</u>,   SLMD 8 Nov 1853
       Friday last of typhoid ae about 21-22.

McDERMOTT, Catherine, daughter of Francis and Ann,   SLMD 5 Sep 1854
       4 August ae 7m 22d.

       Michael, ae 38, of cholera on 11 June.   NERA 12 Jun 1849

McDONALD, children of John and Esther Ann, St. Louis: MORE 4 May 1852
       Mary Janette 26 April of scarlet fever.
       Josiah Herrick 27 April ".

McDONOUGH, Ferdinand S., son of Capt. James of St. Louis,   NERA 4 Aug 1849
       at the home of Samuel McCullough in
       Meramec Twp. 31 July in his 7th y.

       Maria Louisa, infant of Patrick, Wed. morning.   MORE 23 Aug 1831

McDOWELL, Emma Virginia, daughter of John and Judy,   MORE 12 Mar 1849
       ae 1y 11m 18d.

       James, son of Dr. James and Elizabeth, 27 Sept.   SLMD 29 Sep 1856
       ae 1y 24d. Richmond VA pc

       William Greetham, son of Dr. J.B., drowned in a   MORE 19 Feb 1844
       cistern while playing near his home on
       Market St., ae 4½. (Obit on 20 Feb.)

McEFEE, Mrs. Nancy at Strongtown, Grundy Co. 11 January   SLMD 31 Jan 1855
       of winter fever in her 67th year.

McENTIRE, John, "many years a resident," 20 July ae 59.   NERA 21 Jul 1849

       Julia J., daughter of Joseph and Morgiana R.,   SWERE 16 Feb 1846
       10 Feb. ae 2y 2m. Louisville pc

McEVOY, Catherine Cecelia, daughter of John and Margaret,   MORE 24 Sep 1847
       an infant, 23 Sept. Lived 21 St. Charles.

McEWEN, John Asaph, infant of Robert and Mary,
        10 August ae 6m 20d.   MORE 19 Aug 1843

McFADIN, John Shotwell, son of James M. and Anna T.,
        ae 21m 24d. Buried Louisville.   MORE 25 May 1852

McFARLAND, Augustus William, son of John, ae 3m 12d.   WEM 25 Jul 1839

McFARLANE, James, in his 55th year, 18 June. Friends of
        J. Ragan invited. Catholic Cemetery.   MORE 18 Jun 1850

McGEE, A., son of A. B. H., near Westport, ae about 5.   SLMD 17 Jan 1855

McGILL, Rosalie, youngest child of Theodore L. and Adele,
        22 February ae (13? 18?) m.   MORE 24 Feb 1843

McGINNEY, Rachel, wife of Peter, in her 37th year. Lived
        at Franklin-Wash. (Cholera epidemic?)   MORE 10 Jul 1849

McGINNIS, Archelaus, 14 November in Hannibal, one of its
        oldest citizens.   HAG 18 Nov 1846

        Sons of James C. and Julia, St. Louis:
           Thomas Mortimer 20 Feb. ae 2y 16m. (sic) MORE 23 Feb 1847
           James Richard 27 March ae 1y 4m.   "   29 Mar "
           Family lived on Washington Ave.

McGIRK, Martha C., daughter of A. S., 8 July ae 2y 6m. MIN 16 Jul 1825
        Matthias Haywood son of A. S., on 4 August.   "   5 Aug "

        Elizabeth, estate in Montgomery Co.: Final
           Settlement by David J. Talbot.   FULT 28 Sep 1849

McGOVERN, Patrick, son of the late John, ae 8 years.   SOV 19 Mar 1836

McGOWN, Francis Henry, infant of Henry C. and Mariam, at
        the home of Daniel McGown in St. Charles Co. MORE 10 Apr 1852
        2 April ae 1y 8m 3d.

McGREGOR, Mrs. __, wife of Peter, 18 July of cholera;
        lived on Olive betw 7-8.   MORE 18 Jul 1849
      Peter, at the home of Mrs. Dunn, 6 September. " 7 Sep 1849

McGUIRE, Michael, native of Ireland, 21 March of consumption
        ae about 65. "Respectable citizen."   LADB 26 Mar 1849

McGUNNEGLE, Harry, infant of George K. and Elizabeth.
        Buried Christ Church Cemetery.   MORE 26 Jun 1849

McILROY, Dominic, of Magehan and McIlroy, 31 December of
        lockjaw, "no relatives at his bedside." SLNL 3 Jan 1846

McILVAINE, Martha, sister of Jesse, superintendent of the
        county farm, 29 August. Buried in the   MORP 30 Aug 1845
        Presbyterian Cemetery.

McINTYRE, ___, ae 6, son of Patrick, drowned in the Missouri
        River Saturday last; his father offers a GLWT 30 Jun 1852
        reward to the person finding his body.

        Bevil, formerly of NC, recently of Polk Co., in
           Greene Co. 25 July, ae about 35.   JEM 3 Aug 1847

McIVER, Joseph, infant of Bernard and Rose, 12 August. SLMD 13 Aug 1854

McJILTON, John William, son of James T. and Rachel, 20 Oct. ae 17m 13d. Lived Olive betw 9-10. (His mother died in 1848.)   MORE 21 Oct 1845

      Elvira H., youngest daughter of James and C. H., 27 July ae 5m.   MORE 28 Jul 1851

McKAY, Laura, consort of Dr. Samuel H., at the home of Mrs. Lewis in Lincoln Co. 11 June in her 23rd y. Long illness. Left husband, 2 infant daughters.   LADB 18 Jun 1851

McKEE, Firmin Roy at St. Joseph 18 March, son of Martha and the late Capt., ae 7y 2m 22d.   MORE 3 Apr 1850

      Jane, wife of Henry Sr., 13 July of bilious diarrhoea in her 64th year.   NERA 14 Jul 1849

      Henry Sr. in his 72nd year. Funeral from the home of his son William, 8th-Green.   " 14 Oct 1849

      Josephine, daughter of Henry and Matilda, 31 January ae 8m.   SWERE 5 Feb 1849

      Isabel, daughter of Hiram and Nancy, 7th-Clark, 27 May in her 2nd year.   MORE 29 May 1847

      Mary Catherine, consort of R. B., of consumption, Sunday last; daughter of James Holton of Frankfort Co. (?). (see below)   JEM 16 Feb 1847

      James, son of R. B. of Jefferson City, 9 December in Frankfort KY ae 2y 10m.   " 21 Dec 1847

      William Henry, in his 19th year, 10 Feb. Funeral from home of his br-in-law S. B. Roll.   MORE 11 Feb 1850

McKENNA, Rosannah, daughter of Thomas and Ellen, yesterday ae 3y 6m.   SWERE 7 Aug 1848

McKENNEY, Maj. R. T. at his brother's home in St. Louis on 1 July.   SLOB 3 Jul 1834

      John Gerard, infant of Samuel T., Sunday night.   MORE 11 Aug 1829

McKENNY, Virginia, only daughter of John H. and Mary A., 31 Jan. at Burlington IA ae 2y 3m.   MORE 12 Feb 1842

McKENZIE, Mary, wife of Walter, ae 30. (Cholera epidemic?)   MORE 7 Jul 1849

MacKENZIE, children of Kenneth and Mary, St. Louis:
      Marshall, youngest son, 28 October.   SWERE 1 Nov 1847
      Kenneth, only son, 7 November.   " 15 Nov "
      Mary Marshall, daughter of Kenneth, 23 January. Funeral from Christ Church.   MORE 25 Jan 1853

McKIE, Edith James, wife of Robert and daughter of John James of Baltimore, in her 40th year. Lived Main nr Almond. (Cholera epidemic?)   MORE 4 Jul 1849

McKINNEY, Mrs. Ellen of St. Louis at the home of her br-in-law in New Orleans, of gastritis, 3 Dec.   MOSN 15 Dec 1838

      James, in Monroe Co., 9 Sept. ae about 50.   JEM 21 Sep 1847

      Talitha Caroline, wife of E. D. and eldest dau/ Maj. James P. Campbell 12 Nov. ae 19y 6m at her home nr Springfield.   SPRIG 13 Nov 1848

McKINZIE, Norman, son of Mr. N. of St. Louis, Tues. last.   MOG 21 Mar 1811

McKNIGHT, H. C. of the 3rd Reg. MO Vols "in a distant and
           hostile land." Tribute by LA G. O. E. O.   LADB 17 Jan 1848

      Elizabeth and Andrew, children of Thomas, Friday. MORE 10 May 1824

      Julia S., daughter of John and Sarah, 14 May
          in Hannibal ae 4y.   SLMD 26 May 1855

McLONEY, Mary Catherine, infant of James and __, 8 June   MODE 17/
        ae 3y 1m.   8 Jun 1846

McMULLEN, Mrs. Catherine "of a pulmonary affection" 19 June   NERA 21 Jun 1845
        in her 56th year; formerly of
        Louisville, in St. Louis ca 5y.

McMURRAY, John Denneron, youngest son of John D. of   MORE 2 Apr 1844
      St. Louis, in Allegheny City PA 23 Apr.
      Sarah Ellen, daughter of John D. and Eliza,   " 4 Aug 1845
        3 Aug. ae 9m; lived 48 Chestnut.
      John, "formerly of St. Louis" in Baltimore.   MORE 29 Apr 1846

McNAIR, children of Alexander, St. Louis:
        Benjamin Howard, ae 6, on 5 September.   MOG 13 Sep 1820
        Stella Ann, oldest child, Sunday ae ca 15.   "   "

      Cornelia Ellen, daughter of William, Saturday   BOLT 22 Feb 1845
        last ae 2y 11m.

      Pinky, who died ae 4, a little poem in memory.   SLMD 23 Mar 1855

McNEIL, children of Joseph and Elizabeth, St. Louis:
        Caroline, eldest daughter, 21 December ae   NERA 22 Dec 1845
         4y 7m; lived 9th-Pine.
        Elizabeth, 2nd daughter, 26 Dec. ae 3y 2m.   " 27 Dec "

McNEILL, John W. of California MO in Cincinnati 19 Sept.   JINQ 2 Sep 1841

McPHERSON, Isabella Virginia, infant of Isaac and Ellen   MORE 14 Nov 1848
      of St. Louis, 5 Nov. in Waterloo MO.

      Robert, in Cape Girardeau, 19 June.   NERA 26 Jun 1845

McPIKE, Alcy, relict of William, at her home in Pike Co.   LADB 24 Apr 1848
      21 April; one of earliest settlers.

      Margaret H., consort of Abraham, 10 August in her   LADB 19 Aug 1850
        25th year. Daughter of Youel and Ursula
        Morris of Spotsylvania Co. VA; lost parents
        young. To MO with relatives 1836, lived with
        br-in-law Simeon P. Robinson. Baptized
        Mt. Pisgah Church 1844. Left husband, baby.
        Richmond VA pc

McREA, Henry Atkinson, son of Capt. Samuel, 11 October   MORE 14 Oct 1837
(MACREE)   at Jefferson Barracks ae 4y 5m.
      Children of Maj. Samuel and Mary:
        Samuel, ae 13m, on 2 September.   MORE 24 Sep 1845
        Mary, ae 2y 7m, on Saturday.   " 13 Oct "
        Ann, only daughter, 17 July ae 6m.   NERA 20 Jul 1849
        (Maj. Samuel died before Ann.)

McQUHAE, Capt. Henry T., of consumption, 8 April.   MORE 10 Apr 1850

McVICKER, William Henry, son of Thomas H. and Elizabeth   MORE 21 Oct 1845
      Jane, Park betw Carondelet-7th, yesterday
      ae 9m 15d. Buried Episcopal Cemetery.

McWILLIAMS, Mary Helen, daughter of John L., 28 February in   SLMD 17 Mar 1855
      Cape Girardeau, of consumption, ae 14.

MACK, George Washington Irving, son of N. W., ae 2 or   BORE 12 Dec 1843
      3 years, 1 December.

MACKAY, Frederick Gustave, son of Zeno and Marie, at   MORE 2 Dec 1842
      Gravois 24 November ae 10y 11m.

    Col. Aeneas, Deputy Quartermaster-General, after a   MORE 24 May 1850
      short illness. Buried Jefferson
      Barracks. His children:
      John, youngest son, 8 January ae 5y 11m.   "   10 Jan 1844
      Mary, youngest daughter, 13 Dec. ae 7m.   "   22 Dec 1845
      Grace, ae 19m 17d, on 12 June.   NERA 16 Jun 1849

    Capt. John, at his home near Clarksville, 30 Apr.   LADB 8 May 1848
      in his 58th year. From TN 1815, to
      Pike Co. 1816. Baptist.

MACKEY, John M., only son of James S. of Calumet Twp.,   LADB 24 Sep 1849
      12 September ae 2y 4m 16d.

MADDOCK, Randall M., infant of Wm. L. and   SLMD 3 Mar 1854
      Caroline J., 1 March.

MADDOX, James W., son of Thomas H. and Ann P., 30 July   MORE 5 Aug 1851
      ae 11y 8m.

MAGEE, children of C. R. and Sarah R., of Monticello: CANE 5 Jan 1854
      Lucinda on 23 December ae 8y 4m 8d.
      Louisa Ann on 29 December ae 3y 3m 13d.
      (their only children)

MAGINIS, William McRea, son of Arthur L. and Mary E.,   MORE 4 Aug 1838
      of whooping cough, this morning ae 8m.

MAGUIRE, John H., son of John and Catherine, 26 February   SLMD 27 Feb 1855
      ae 8m.

MAGWIRE, Joseph, son of John and Angeline, 26 June ae   MORE 27 Jun 1845
      1y 6m; lived on Bellefontaine Rd.

MAHAN, ___ daughter of Mr. _, of cholera in Palmyra.   MORE 28 Jun 1833

    Mary, wife of James, and sister of Mrs. Charlotte
      Muldrow, in Palmyra. Born 3 October 1796,   SLOB 7 Aug 1834
      married in 1817. (A long obituary.)

    Mary Grundy, infant of James F. and Julia, 10 Sept.   PWH 16 Sep 1843

MAHEGAN, Mary, wife of D. A., 18 February.   MORE 19 Feb 1850

MAIGNE, Samuel M., son of John C. and Mary Ann, ae 2,   MORE 17 Jun 1844
      yesterday.

MAJORS, James, in St. Charles Co.   NERA 7 Oct 1845

MALLORY, Seneca Thomas, only son of Wm. T. and Sarah,   MODE 15/13
      Tuesday last ae 4y 11m 23d.   Jul 1846

MALONE, Galvin, in his 38th year, 15 June.   MORE 17 Jun 1850

MANN, Ann F., wife of George B., 12 October in her 20th   NERA 14 Oct 1845
          (29th?) year.

      George B., "many years a resident." NY, Boston,   MORE 12 Jul 1849
              NH pc. (cholera epidemic?)

MANNING, Felix, of Perry Co., died 19 March 1853; the   SGPD 9 Apr 1853
          Publ. Adm. takes over his estate.

MANSFIELD, Walter, son of Jude C. and Elizabeth, 23 May   MORE 27 May 1852
          ae 6y 10m.

MANSUR, children of Dr. Mansur of Grape Grove, Ray Co.,
          gr-chn of Maj. A. Basye of Jefferson City:
          Susan Augusta 7 March of congestive
                  scarlet fever, ae 6y 6m 13d.   JEM 13 Apr 1847
          Stephen Warren 15 March ae 13m 5d.

      Lucy Ann, daughter of Charles and Rebecca Abb W.   MORE 9 Aug 1841
          (sic) yesterday. Catholic Cemetery.

MANTZ, Charlie, son of Charles and Caroline, 25 August   SLMD 26 Aug 1854
          of brain inflammation ae 1y 6m. Baltimore,
          Frederick Co. MD, Indianapolis, and San
          Francisco pc. Buried Wesleyan Cemetery.

MARGERUM, John W. in his 25th year, native of Scott Co. KY;   HAJ 7 Sep 1848
          nephew of Thomas S. Miller. Member IOOF,
          Sons of Temperance, Christian Church.

MARKS, Rosa, daughter of Simon and Caroline, 29 May   MORE 31 May 1853
          ae 7m 9d.

MARKWELL, William in Platte City 25 June.   NERA 14 Jul 1845

MARLOW, Lucien, infant of Charles Jr. and Mary Via, 20 Feb. SLMD 22 Feb 1854

MARQUIS, Martha Jane, daughter of D. J. and L. A., of   SLMD 4 Mar 1854
          brain fever, 2 March ae 3y 3m.

MARSH, Margreann, wife of John J., 13 October ae 25y 8m 19d. SLMD 14 Oct 1854
          Weston MO & Rahway NY(?) pc

      Susan, consort of William J., 30 August; long illness. HAJ 7 Sep 1848

MARTIN, Augustus, only child of David L. and Amanda,   SWERE 5 Mar 1849
          26 Feb. ae 9m 6d. Parkersburg VA pc

      George, native of Ireland, in St. Louis 10 years,   MORE 12 Sep 1849
          7 September in his 30th year.

      George W., son of Robert and Susannah, 21 Feb.   BGDB 5 Apr 1845
          in Buffalo Twp. in his 12th year.

      John Henry, eldest son of John T. and Priscilla,   MORE 21 Mar 1844
          yesterday; funeral from home, Walnut
          betw 6-7. Buried Methodist Cemetery.

      Joseph K., in Lafayette Co.   NERA 31 Jul 1845

      Mrs. Mary at her home in St. Louis Co. 16 May ae   MORE 20 May 1850
          88y 2m; in county 54 years, died where
          first settled.

MARTIN, Mrs. Mary, ae 54, on 14 July. (cholera epidemic?) NERA 14 Jul 1849

    Serena J. Leonard, daughter of T. F. and Jane M., MORE 22 Oct 1849
        66 S. 2nd St., in her 14th year.

    Susan Ferguson, infant of Dr. M. and Elizabeth, MORE 19 Nov 1846
        18 November.

MASON, Alice Graham, youngest daughter of Col. R. B. and MORE 19 Feb 1847
        Margaret, ae 4, scalded; Col. Mason was in
        CA with his regiment.

MASSIE, Lucinda, consort of Thomas M., in Cincinnati IL in LADB 9 Jul 1849
        her 24th year; left husband, widowed mother.

    Rebecca Ann, daughter of John C. of Louisiana MO in " 16 Jul "
        Pike Co. IL 13 July of cholera in her 18th
        year; had gone to help relatives.
    Sylvanus, son of John C. of Louisiana, MO, in " 18 Jun "
        Cincinnati IL of cholera, in his 28th year.
        Left wife, 2 small children.
    John C., son of the late Sylvanus and Harriet, " 9 Jul "
        4 Jul ae about 18m.

    ___, son of Theodorick, 10 August ae 9m. PWH 14 Aug 1841

MASTERSON, James, formerly of Mobile AL, 21 July of MORE 22 Jul 1849
        cholera ae 32.

MATHEWS, Catharine, daughter of Jane and Edward, 22 February SLMD 23 Feb 1855
        of consumption, ae 3; lived 7th-Wash.

MATLACK, Margaret Ann, daughter of William L. and Harriet SWERE 26 Aug 1844
        Ann, ae 15m 14d. Philad. & Pittsb. pc

MATTHEWS, Carles (sic) Oscar, son of Francis A. and Nancy MODE 7/5
        of Madison, IN, 26 Sept. ae 11m. Oct 1846

    Elizabeth, infant of P. V. (no other data). JEFRE 24 Aug 1839
    Louisa Ann, infant of P. V. and Anna, 12 July. " 24 Jul 1841

    Mary Frances, of consumption, 9 March ae 15. SLMD 10 Mar 1856
        Lived 7th-Wash. Buried Calvary.

MATTOX, children of Edwin A. and Mary S., St. Louis:
        William Edwin, ae 1y 11m, 30 October. MORE 31 Oct 1840
        Frederick, ae 9m, 27 April. SLMD 28 Apr 1854

MAURO, children of Philip and Elizabeth, St. Louis:
        Mary H., 3rd daughter, 30 January; notice MORE 4 Feb 1840
        deferred because of brother's absence.
        Matilda, no age shown; funeral St. John's Chapel. SWERE 3 Jan 1843

MAXFIELD, Leander Fallan, son of Andrew H. and Mildred SWERE 13 Oct 1845
        Ann, 6 October ae 13m 1d.

MAXWELL, Joseph, 19 September ae 37. Lived Morgan MORE 20 Sep 1849
        betw 4th-5th. Mbr Sons of Temperance.

    Samuel, youngest child of Samuel and Mary, MORE 26 May 1841
        19 May ae 12m 11d.

MAXWELL, Susan, daughter of Mrs. Polly, 3 Jan. ae about 6. PWH 7 Jan 1843

       William Henry, infant of Henry and Louisa, 9 July. MORE 12 Jul 1836

MAYER, Mary Hunetha, daughter of Henry F. and Fanny,   STGAZ 27 Oct 1852
     16 Oct. ae 2m 15d. St. Louis pc

MAYNARD, Daniel, of cholera, 17 July in his 59th year. NERA 20 Jul 1849

MELINE, Ellen, youngest daughter of F. M. of St. Louis,   MORE 10 Apr 1848
     at Louisville 5 April.

MELLINS, Richard Napoleon, son of John H. and Mary,   NERA 25 Jul 1849
     24 July ae 3y 6m.

MENARD, Marie Therese Alsie, infant of Pierre and   MORE 25 Oct 1844
     Catherine, 30 Sept. at home of H.B. Stillman.

MENEE, William O., son of J. F. and Sarah S. of Franklin Co.,,MORE 7 Sep 1842
     ae 6m 11d. Louisville pc

MEPHAM, Adelaide Maria, daughter of Michael and Maria, MORE 22 Aug 1853
     5 August ae 7m 3d.

MEREDITH, Mrs. Sarah, in Jefferson City, ae 44. SLMD 19 Feb 1855

MERIWEATHER, Elizabeth G., wife of George D., at the home SLMD 3 Mar 1855
     of her father in Lincoln Co., ae
     about 28, on 5 February.

MERRELL, George Kellogg, only son of J. S. and Kate K., SLMD 27 Aug 1857
     26 August ae 16m.

MERRICK, __, son of John, ae about 10, drowned in the MORE 30 Oct 1848
     river opposite Market St. Body recovered.

MEYER, Louis, estate in Chariton Co.: final settlement BRUNS 5 Apr 1854
     by Margaret J. Meyer.

MEYERS, Maria Louisa, daughter of the late David, died MORP 6 Mar 1845
     at her mother's home 1 March ae 17y 8d.

MILBURN, William, son of William and Mary V., 15 August MORE 16 Aug 1847
     near Carondelet ae 1y 5m 20d.

MILLAN, __, infant son of Thomas, on Friday last. PWH 10 Sep 1845

MILLER, __, daughter of John G. of Saline Co., Monday last MODE 4 Nov/
     at home of Gen. William Miller, ae 7m.   31 Oct 1846

    Catherine, consort of William, 1 August of   NERA 2 Aug 1849
      "extreme debility" in her 45th year.

    Christopher, formerly of Nelson Co. VA, 7 Jan. at SLMD 31 Jan 1855
      Whitesville, Andrew Co., ae 43.

    Eliza, daughter of J. A. and E. E., 3 May.   LEXA 9 May 1848

    Children of James Y. and Ann Eliza, Howard Co.:
      Sophia, ae 9m, on 16 December.   SLMD 17 Jan 1855
      Caroline Eliza, in her 4th year, 1 Jan.

    Jane, consort of Joseph H., in Greene Co.   JEM 28 Sep 1847
      11 August ae 40.

MILLER, Johanna, consort of William and daughter of the late Matthew Casey Sr., 8 January of consumption. Charlottesville VA pc   SLINT 10 Jan 1850

Clarence, only son of Madison and Margaret, at the home of C. B. Fletcher, Herculaneum, 1 August ae 15m.   MORE 10 Aug 1842 .

Mary B., wife of Thomas S. of Hannibal and daughter of John and Margaret McKamie, formerly of Mercer Co. KY, 30 August in her 37th year. Converted in her 14th year.   HAJ 6 Sep 1849

Moses, in Callaway Co. 22 October, a citizen there nearly 40 years.   JEM 2 Nov 1848

Nancy, consort of Moses, in Clay Co. 10 Oct. ae 52.   " 27 Oct 1846

Liza, youngest daughter of Capt. William B. and Eliza, last evening.   SWERE 22 May 1848

Sinclair K., son of S. K., "this morning" of scarlet fever, ae about 6.   STGAZ 7 Jan 1852

MILLIGAN, Edward, infant son of Louisa F. and Edward, late of Philadelphia, 23 August. (His mother died in 1847.)   MORE 24 Aug 1837

Edward, son of Edward, 22 May ae 7.   SWERE 28 May 1849

William Henry, son of Edward and Maria, of whooping cough, Sunday, ae 16 weeks.   SLMD 29 Jun 1857

MILLS, Mary, daughter of Adam L. of St. Louis, Saturday.   MORE 7 Oct 1828

MILTON, Virginia, daughter of George W. and Ann, 10 September ae 8y 3m.   PWH 17 Sep 1845

MINARD, Henriette Charlotte, daughter of Rev. P. R. and Mary, 21 July of cholera infantum ae 9m.   NERA 23 Jul 1845

MINOR, Edwin C. in St. Charles Co. 21 August, late of Fairfax Co. VA.   MORE 3 Sep 1849

Virginia Ann, daughter of A. J. and the late Mary Ann of St. Louis, 8 December ae 4. Left father and sister.   SJA 13 Dec 1850

Mary Ann, consort of Andrew J., 2 April ae 25.   MORE 3 Apr 1850

MITCHELL, Ann Maria, daughter of Francis and Adeline, 5 July ae 11m. Eastern papers pc   MORE 6 Jul 1844

Andrew Monroe, infant of Alexander and Julia C., Friday last.   MODE 28 Mar 1848

Harriet, daughter of R. P., in Clark Co., 26 August ae 14.   JEM 21 Sep 1847

Levin Ballard, son of W. W. and Rhoda, ae 16m, Saturday last.   MODE 16/14 Sep 1846

MITCHUM, John, a cousin of Samuel Steel, in CA 19 March ae about 29. Born Woodford Co. KY.   SJA 31 May 1850

MOFFAT, James, oldest son of James and Marion, 24 Jan. ae 3y 3m. Buried Presbyterian Cem.   MORE 26 Jan 1848

MONDAY, Mrs. James, daughter of Jesse Raglan of Cass Co., near Sonoma CA 15 November.   SLMD 17 Jan 1855

MONEY, Edward Vanness, son of Edward and Adeline, 27 April ae 9m 11d.   MORE 1 May 1843

MONTAIGNE, Joseph, ae 65, on 4 March.   MORE 6 Mar 1850

MONTGOMERY, Camillus, son of Col. J. J., Wednesday morning last ae about 8.   PWH 12 Aug 1840

     Judge James, in Osceola, 2 December ae 71y 3m 8d. Born in Wythe Co. VA, to MO 1832, first to Saline Co., to Osceola 1838. Held various offices both in VA and MO.   SLMD 21 Dec 1854

MOONEY, Mary Agnes, youngest daughter of Francis A. and Mary, ae 14m. Boston pc   MORE 10 Aug 1851

MOORE, Benjamin, murdered by David Jeffords in Scott Co. about 13 January; governor offers a reward for Jeffords' capture.   MORE 13 Feb 1850

     Edward Stanley, son of John H., in Jefferson City 8 March, of croup, ae 2y 3m.   SLMD 26 Mar 1856

     F. J., estate in Chariton Co.; Letters of Administration to James G. Moore, 5 February.   GLWT 14 Feb 1856

     Elizabeth, relict of James, 21 March ae 76. Staunton VA pc   NERA 31 Mar 1846

     Margaret F., youngest daughter of Capt. D. D., 18 July ae 9y 5m; lived 230 N. 7th.   MORE 19 Jul 1849

     Thomas, eldest son of G. and Elizabeth, ae 5, at Wayne City.   INJN 31 Oct 1844

     William, of Macon Co., died of injuries received in the St. Joseph explosion, was buried at the head of Island #67 on the plantation of W. McNiel. Left wife, child. Member IOOF.   MORE 2 Feb 1850

     William, estate in Chariton Co.: Final settlement by John E. M. Triplett.   BRUNS 13 Dec 1856

MOORS, Julia, youngest daughter of John T., 13 February ae 14m.   MORE 24 Feb 1851

MORDICA, Harry Samuel, infant of Samuel & Mary, 13 January in New Orleans.   MORE 24 Jan 1850

MOREHEAD, John, in Ray Co., 3 October.   NERA 16 Oct 1845

     Laura, daughter of Philip C. and Evaline, 15 Apr.   SLMD 18 Apr 1854

MOREHOUSE, children of Capt. D. B. and Charlotte, St. Louis:
     Joseph, ae about 3y 10m, at the home of J. J. Brown near Galena, 18 January.   MORE 27 Jan 1844
     Legrand, youngest son, 5 Feb. ae 2y 1m 16d.   SWERE 12 Feb 1849

MORELEY, Samuel P. in Buchanan Co. 29 May of smallpox, ae 3y 3m 15d.   MORE 10 Jun 1853

MORONEY, Johanna ae 7m 21d; lived on S. 7th St. MORE 6 Aug 1851

MORRIS, Leroy Washington, son of Ezekiel and Eliza, BRUNS 2 Dec 1848
  20 November ae 6y 10m 2d.

MORRISON, children of Capt. P.(and Irene) St. Louis:
  Irene M. at Jefferson Barracks 29 August MORE 4 Sep 1843
   ae 1y 6m 26d. New Orleans pc
  John L. at Jefferson Barracks 25 May. " 26 May 1847
  Clara S. M. at Jefferson Barracks ae 18y3m15d. " 14 Mar '46
   (last 2 don't show mother's name)

MORRIS, William John, son of David and Emily, 29 May MORE 30 May 1848
  ae 6y 11m. Buried Presbyterian Cem.

MORRISON, children of Alfred W., Secretary of State:
  Miss ___ in Jefferson City 11 January. SLMD 22 Jan 1856
  Susan in Jefferson City 23 May. " 9 Jun 1855
   (mother not shown)
  Sarah Louisa, infant of Alfred W. and MODE 22 Feb 1848
   Minerva, Saturday last ae 13m.

  Mary, wife of William and daughter of Capt. NERA 10 Dec 1849
   Lewis Bissell, in her 21st year.
  William Coleman, son of William and Mary Ann, MORE 23 Jul 1847
   ae 1y 5m.

MORRISS, John Polk, only son of Thomas W. and Elizabeth MODE 18/16
  of Glasgow, 15 February ae 5m. Mar 1846

MORROW, Mrs. ___ and ___, son of Samuel, both of BRUNS 24 May 1849
  cholera. (From the Statesman, Columbia.)

MOSELEY, Samuel Pyson, son of Robert and Mary A., STGAZ 1 Jun 1853
  29 May ae 3y 3m 13d.

MOSS, Francis, estate in Chariton Co.: final settlement BRUNS 23 Jun 1855
  by Lisbon Applegate, Publ. Administrator.

MOTHERSHEAD, Margaret H., youngest daughter of Charles, BEA 4 Aug 1831
  of Boone Co., at Glen Finlass, Jefferson Co.

MOWRY, Minerva E., granddaughter of Judge Wm. Dunning, STGAZ 11 Aug 1848
  ae 11m.

MULBERRY, Jacob L., estate in Montgomery Co.: final LADB 31 Dec 1849
  settlement by Shelton B. Farthing.

MULFORD, Charles Frazer, youngest child of John P. and SWERE 28 May 1849
  Ruth H., 20 May.

MULHALL, John, ae 26, yesterday. NERA 24 Apr 1849

MULL, Elijah C., oldest son of William, 29 April MORE 1 May 1834
  ae 11y 8m 12d.

MULLEN, William son of Patrick and Margaret, 12 March SWERE 19 Mar 1849
  ae 8y 9m.

MULLIGAN, Alice Jane, daughter of John and Missouri, MORE 6 May 1847
  5 May ae 6y 8m.

MULLIKIN, Maria Louisa, infant of Charles (no data). MORE 8 Jul 1828
  Mary Eliza, daughter of Charles, 14 June. " 18 Jun 1833

MULLINS, ___, a gambler, at Keytesville Saturday night. BRUNS 14 Jun 1849

MUNDY, Juliann, wife of Ezra, 250 Washington Ave., ae 45. MORE 5 Nov 1849
      Buried Wesleyan. New Brunswick NJ pc

MUNROE, Rebecca, consort of William, 19 May of apoplexy MORE 20 May 1850
      ae 53.

MURPHY, Anna, only daughter of W. S. and Aletta, at SLMD 17 Mar 1855
      Weston 23 February ae 3y 23d.

      Mrs. Elizabeth, in her 70th year, 21 March at the NERA 22 Mar 1849
      home of her son Stephen, opposite
      Mound Market.

MURRAY, Florence Bell, youngest daughter of R. W. and SLMD 21 Dec 1854
      Sarah, in Boonville 2 December.

      Gabriel, son of Andrew, 5 May ae 3. Buried MORE 6 May 1852
      Rock Spring Cemetery.
      Thomas G., son of Andrew and Catherine, 18 Nov. " 20 Nov 1847
      ae 2y 11m. Lived 14th nr Christy.

MURRELL, Alice, wife of Lemuel, 19 November in Warsaw of SLMD 12 Dec 1854
      typhoid, ae 49.

MUSICK, William Gilpen, son of William and Precilla of NERA 25 Mar 1846
      Gravois Settlement, 22 March ae 6y 8m.

MYERS, Barbary, estate in Scott Co.: Final Settlement SMAD 2 Mar 1838
      by John Moore.

      Laura Emmons, daughter of Frederick M. and Eliza C., MORE 18 Jul 1844
      yesterday ae 11½m.

NEELY, Alexander in Cape Girardeau Co. 10 March. NERA 21 Mar 1846

NEILL, Polly C., estate in Montgomery Co.: Letters of FULT 15 Sep 1848
      Administration to Benj. F. Sharp 22 Aug.

      Susan C., wife of John, 31 May in her 21st year. NERA 5 Jun 1849

NELSON, Miss Elizabeth, ae 78, at the home of Judge SLMD 4 Jan 1855
      H. Roberts, Monticello, 20 December.
      John Dargan, son of Thomas and Elijah (sic) MORE 20 Aug 1847
      19 August ae 4m 28d.

      Maria Emeline, daughter of A. R. and F. M., 26 Oct.
      near California, Moniteau Co. ae 2y 7m. MORE 30 Oct 1849
      Parkersburg, Winchester, Warrenton VA pc

NETHERTON, Florence Harrison, daughter of Col. G. H. and JEM 27 Oct 1846
      Ann Eliza, 24 Oct. ae 1y 2m 27d.

NEWBERRY, Albert, formerly of Bloomfield CT, 24 July of NERA 25 Jul 1849
      bilious dysentery.

NEWKIRK, C. C. in Andrew Co. 10 March, ae 23. SLMD 27 Mar 1856

      Thomas C., son of Thomas and Sarah, 22 May SWERE 29 May 1848
      ae 1y 10m.

NEWMAN, Jonas, ae 54. (cholera epidemic?) MORE 4 Jul 1849

NEWMAN, daughters of Michael and Margaret, St. Louis:
     Mary Jane Frances on 7 October. Jefferson City
      (MO) and Harrisonburg VA pc   SWERE 18 Oct '47
     Julia A. H., eldest daughter, 4 February.   MORE 5 Feb 1849
      Funeral 4th St. Methodist.

     Virginia Hartley, daughter of Arthur R. and
      Margaret A., 19 August in Charleston MO   MORE 31 Aug 1846
      ae 3y 8m 2d.

     William Ethan, son of Dr. T. W. and Julia, of SLMD 6 Nov 1857
      16 St. Charles St., 5 November ae 17m 21d.

NEWTON, Lewis in Randolph Co. 7 December in his 61st y.   SLMD 29 Dec 1853

NICHOLDS, Martha, 3rd daughter of Capt. J. F., Wednesday   MODE 5/3
     last in Glasgow, ae about 8.   May 1847

NICOL, Daniel Lorimer, son of James and Grace, 29 April   MORE 1 May 1848
     ae 5m.

     William, of inflammation of the brain, 10 January MORE 12 Jan 1850
      ae 4y 5m. Funeral from his mother's home,
      7th below Spruce. Buried Presbyterian cem.

     William H., Surgeon, of the 6th Reg. Inf., 5 March MORE 8 Mar 1831
      at Jefferson Barrack ae 40. Native of NY.

NICOLET, Maria Jane, consort of Henry L. and daughter of NERA 15 Jul 1849
     Joseph Stout, 13 July of cholera.

NICHOLSON, Peter, a Scotchman ae 23, "a man of intelligence" MORE 5 Jun 1849
     fell from the revenue cutter, drowned.

NISBET, William T., second son of William and Mary S.,   MORE 14 Sep 1853
     13 September in his 25th year.

NOBLE, John K.: funeral from his home, Chambers   MORE 10 Jul 1849
     betw Broadway-9th. (cholera epidemic?)

NODIE, Minerva S., wife of Col. J., in Andrew Co. ae 19,   JEM 15 Dec 1846
     on 21 November.

NOLAN, Mrs. Margaret, in St. Charles, 22 December.   SLMD 29 Dec 1853

NOLLAU, Theophilus, son of Rev. Lewis E., 20 June of   SLMD 23 Jun 1854
     flux, ae 5.

NOONAN, Mary Josephine, daughter of Cornelius and   SWERE 1 Nov 1847
     Catherine, 30 October.

     Michael, son of C. and M., 31 December.   MORE 1 Jan 1853

NORCOM, Alice, youngest daughter of William R. and   MORE 3 Apr 1847
     Harriet J., in New Orleans, ae 9.

NORRIS, Edward Taylor, son of W. W., 18 December at   SLMD 4 Jan 1855
     (Belair?) ae 4y 20d.

     Ella C., youngest daughter of Sarah and the late MORE 18 Feb 1850
     Charles A., on Friday.

     Sarah J., consort of William and daughter of Kinsey
     Stone of Bourbon Co. KY near Platte City SLMD 28 Apr 1855
     8 Apr. in 44th y.

NOYES, Edward, son of John P. and Eliza, ae 1 year.   MORE 11 Aug 1840
        Baltimore MD & Portland ME pc

NUGENT, Francis 17 June in his 19th year. Funeral from his   MORE 18 Jun 1849
        father's home, 7th-O'Fallon.

NUNN,N. G. at his mother's home in Cape Girardeau Co.   SLMD 23 Dec 1853
        19 December, of consumption, in his 27th y.

OAKLEY, Sarah Catherine, daughter of Timothy, Wednesday   MORE 2 Dec 1836
        in her 3rd year; lived at 134 First St.

O'BANNON, John R., only son of Joseph P. N., ae 3 weeks. INP ca 1 July 1825

OBESHAW (AUBUCHON), Augustin, in Florissant, in 22nd y.   MORE 16 Oct 1849

O'BRIEN, Mary Ann, daughter of Hugh, 2 June.   MORE 16 Jun 1837

O'CONNELL, Cornelius, formerly of Macroonia, Co. Cork,   SLMD 18 Jul 1857
        17 July of brain congestion, ae 60;lived
        Wash St. betw 5-6. Buried Calvary.
        New York & Boston pc

        Daniel, son of Simon and Mary, 12 January   SLMD 13 Jan 1855
        ae 2y 8m 16d; lived Broadway opposite Wash.

O'FALLON, Constance, eldest daughter of Maj. Benjamin.   MORE 21 Aug 1832

O'FLAHERTY, Marie, infant of Thomas and Eliza, 20 Jan.   MORE 22 Jan 1853

OGDEN, John Thomas, son of Hiram and Harriet, ae 3y 3m.   SLMD 17 Feb 1855

    Mary, wife of James, 16 September ae 27.   MORP 19 Sep 1845

    Mary Elizabeth, infant of James C. and Juliet T.,   MODE 12/10
        yesterday morning ae 1 year.   Aug 1846

OLIVER, William, only son of William C., 25 August in
        Ste. Genevieve ae 2y 2m. Grandson   MORP 8 Sep 1845
        of C. Detchemendy.

OLNEY, Mrs. Martha P., wife of William H., late of
        Galena IL, 11 May of dropsy ae 38.   MORE 14 May 1850

O'MEARA, Catherine, youngest daughter of Patrick and
        Mary, 19 April.   MORE 21 Apr 1852

ORME, Francis, infant(sic) of Archibald, 12 July ae 3y 8m.   MORE 19 Jul 1831

ORNDORF, Mary, daughter of Joseph and Jane, 26 September   SLMD 27 Sep 1853
        ae 12; lived Broadway nr Sturgeon's Mkt.

OSBORN, children of James M. and Eulalia, St. Louis:
        Charles Edward, ae 13y 9½m, 17 December.   MORE 19 Dec 1844
        Mary Sophie, ae 15m, 26 July.   "   27 Jul "
        Sarah Euphemia, only daughter, 9 Oct. ae 3y 2m 8d. " 11 Oct "

OSBORNE, Benjamin, in Benton Co., 25 September.   NERA 11 Oct 1845

O'SULLIVAN, Herbert, only child of Thomas S. and Mary A.,   SLMD 16 Jun 1854
        Wed. of brain congestion ae 5y 4m 9d.

OTTE, Dr. William, in Moniteau Co., 18 October.   NERA 20 Oct 1845

OUTCALT, Eliza White, youngest dau/Geo. W. & Frances, in   MODE 25 Feb 1846
        Rocheport 10 Feb. in 3rd y. Formerly of
        Zanesville OH.

OWEN, Mary Sarah, daughter of Richard, 10 January.
Funeral from Mrs. Powell's home, 21-Morgan.   SWERE 19 Jan 1846

PADDLEFORD, sons of H. and Phebe, St. Louis:
Frank, ae 16m, 2 June near Carondelet.   MORE 3 Jun 1848
William Perkins, ae 1y 11m, on 1 November.   "   3 Nov 1842

PAGE, Daniel Dearborn, infant of Daniel D., Saturday last. MORE 21 Feb 1832

Thomas Jr., ae 5; lived on Walnut betw 6-7.   MORE 7 Feb 1846

PAINTER, Susan, widow of John, 23 January ae about 80.
Left 4 sons, 3 daughters.   CGWE 26 Jan 1849

PALLEN, Susan Cochran, infant of M. M. and Janet.   MORE 24 Aug 1849

PALMER, Emma, daughter of Thomas and Letitia, in Columbia
10 March ae 18m 10d.   SLMD 24 Mar 1855

Morris Landis, infant of David and Sarah, in
St. Joseph on 8 August.   MORE 19 Aug 1851

PAMMER, Herman, ae 6, drowned near Hermann 24 July.
Youngest son of Caroline, a widow, who   MORE 31 Jul 1841
will pay for his burial, or for moving, if
body found. He wore a "dark striped summer
frock coat and pants" with "gilt buttons."

PAPIN, George L., son of Joseph and Sophie, ae 14m. MORE 4 Jul 1849

Joseph, ae 70y 3m. Buried St. Vincent's Cemetery.   "   22 Apr 1850

PARISH, John, estate in Wayne Co.: petition to sell
slaves, by David V. Parish.   CGWE 17 Nov 1848

PARK, Ann C., at the home of her mother, Mrs. Eleanor Park,
of Union, Franklin Co., 3 March in her   MOAR 12 Mar 1840
20th year, of consumption.

Jane Abbe, daughter of Mathew and Jeannette, 5th-
Washington, 13 February ae 2y 3m.   SLMD 14 Feb 1856

PARKER, ___, child of Mr. __, of cholera in Palmyra. MORE 28 Jun 1833

Charles Edward, son of Thomas and Elizabeth,
18 May ae 8m 22d.   MORE 20 May 1848

Laura Jane, daughter of N. W. and Elizabeth,
10 March ae 1y 9m.   MORE 11 Mar 1846

PARKS, Ethelred H., estate in Chariton Co.: final
settlement by Peterson B. Parks.   BRUNS 29 Sep 1855
James Gallaher, son of Robert H. and Mary G.,
27 October ae 1y 10m.   SCNT 9 Nov 1850

Peterson, estate in Chariton Co.: final settlement
by Peterson B. Parks   BRUNS 10 Feb 1855

PARR, Rev. S. S., on Monday last; Baptist, member IOOF
and Sons of Temperance.   HAG 5 Aug 1847

PARRISH, ___, daughter of Benjamin, 15 September.   FARW 22 Sep 1836

Hiram O., in Green Co. 28 September, "worthy
and esteemed."   JEM 5 Oct 1847

PARRY, William Alexander, youngest son of John and Isabella, 8 February.   SLMD 10 Feb 1854

PARSONS, Mary M., infant of the late David C. M., in Ashley Thursday ae 14m 17d.   BGRAD 28 Sep 1844

    Elijah, estate in Montgomery Co.: Letters of Administration to Sarah M. Parsons, Wm. H. Parsons, A. B. Moss, 8 November.   LADB 23 Dec 1850

    Virginia, infant of C. M. and Dorcas T., in Ashley 16 August.   BGRAD 27 Aug 1842

PATCH, Clara Jennings, daughter of William Y. and Clarissa W., ae 1y 11m.   MORE 19 Aug 1847

PATCHEN, Sarah Roxana, daughter of John and Ann, 24 July ae 2y 4m 8d.   STGAZ 27 Jul 1853

PATE, William Edward, infant of David and Martha M., at Waverly, Lafayette Co.   SLMD 3 Mar 1855

PATRICK, ___, son of J., drowned Saturday.   MORE 14 Jul 1846

PATTERSON, Julia Henry, infant of Henry L, ae 11m 12d.   MORE 6 Oct 1841

    Mary, infant of Nathaniel and Winifred, ae 18m, 24 June. Lived Olive betw 4-5.   MORE 25 Jun 1841

    Miss Minerva in Greene Co. 5 September ae 17.   JEM 21 Sep 1847

    Rowena Elizabeth, 4th daughter of Charles and Susan B., 12 January ae 2y 9m 14d.   LEXP 14 Jan 1845

    John S., lately of Franklin Co. PA; funeral from home of John S. McCracken.   MORE 27 Sep 1843

    William, a former state legislator, in Jackson Co.   NERA 9 Oct 1845

PATTON, Ann, estate in Montgomery Co.: final settlement by Jacob Patton.   FULT 24 Nov 1848

    Children of James and Mary, of Independence:
        James Boyers on 9 September.   INJN 17 Oct 1844
        Louise Caroline, in 14th year, 2 Jan.   SLMD 22 Jan 1855

    Samuel, son of Nicholas, ae 1y 11m 17d. Buried Rock Spring Cemetery.   MORE 6 Feb 1853

PAUL, Eulalie Henriette, daughter of Col. Rene, Saturday.   MORE 14 Apr 1834

PAXTON, Tabitha Dorcas, daughter of R. D. and (Coansau?) in Boonville 30 April ae 3y 8m 3d.   MODE 12/10 May 1847

PAYNE, Isaiah, estate in Chariton Co.: letters of adm. to Mrs. Rebecca Payne, 16 February.   BRUNS 25 Mar 1854
    Final Settlement by same.   GLWT 18 Dec 1856

PEAKE, children of Samuel H. and Elizabeth C., St. Louis:
    Ann, infant, yesterday. Lived 5-Locust.   MORE 17 Jun 1846
    James Beale, only son, 22 May ae 17m.   SWERE 29 May 1848
    Henry, aboard the Old Hickory, 4 April, ae not shown.   MORE 10 Apr 1848

PEAKE, Amanda Ellen, daughter of James L, 10 September   PWH 16 Sep 1843
      ae 1y 6m.

PEASE, Louise J., only child of the late James, of heart   SLDU 10 Feb 1847
      disease, Monday ae 4y 2m.

    Joseph Leon, son of Joseph S., 21 April ae 13m.   MORE 23 Apr 1838

PECK, Rosina Hinclay, daughter of E. S. and R. C., late of   MORE 18 Sep 1850
      St. Louis, in Marysville CA 7 July
      in her 8th year.

PEDESCLAUX, Octavus at St. Louis Univ. in his 19th year.   MORE 29 Oct 1849

PEERS, Cornelia C., daughter of V. J. and Julia, 28 Oct.   MORE 30 Oct 1844
      of congestive fever. Lived on Walnut St.

    Edward, son of Gen. Peers of Troy, drowned in   SWERE 19 Aug 1844
      Chouteau's Pond.

PENDERGAST, Garrett, late of Tipperary, 2 Aug. ae 27.   NERA 7 Aug 1849

PENDLETON, Fanny Fraker, daughter of D. F. and Susan,   MORE 17 May 1851
      ae 9m 27d.

PENIX, John on 14 October in his 22nd year.   LADB 18 Oct 1847

PENN, Lawson, son of Dr. George and Sarah Bella, 4th &   NERA 28 Jul 1849
      Vine, of cholera ae 13.   (MORE ")

    Louisa, eldest daughter of the late Shadrach, Jr.   MORE 11 Jun 1851
      Buried Wesleyan Cem.
    William, youngest son of the late Shadrach,   "   27 Jan 1852
      21 January near Troy IL.

PENROSE, Harriet, infant of Maj. Penrose, 18 February.   MOG 8 Mar 1810

PEPPER, Elizabeth, consort of Nelson, 14 July ae 53.   NERA 16 Jul 1849

PERKINS, Alice Sherwood, daughter of Luther and Rosanna,   NERA 14 Jul 1849
      10 July ae 6y 6m.

    Charles E., of Cap-au-Grey, 28 March of lung   LADB 7 Jun 1847
      inflammation, from inhaling gas.

    Wilgus, son of E. P. and Sarah, 13 July ae 1y 15d.   MORE 14 Jul 1846
      Lived 119 N. 5th. Boston pc

PERRY, Frederick B., only son of Wm. W. C. and Isabella B.,   SLMD 25 Aug 1857
      24 August ae 17m 4d. Cincinnati pc

    Mary B., youngest daughter of Thomas W. and Mary,
      on Delavan Prairie (Greene Co.?)
      24 February ae 1y 11m.   also   SLMD 24 Mar 1855
    Thomas W., of typhoid, 8 March ae 32y 1m 5d.

    Moses, in Audrain Co., 11 November ae 23.   JEM 1 Dec 1846

    William Grattan, son of R. P. and Margaretta,   NERA 30 Jul 1849
      30 July ae 21m 8d.

PERRYMAN, Eliza Jane, only child of Hon. D. E. of the MO
      Legislature, 9 December at the home   MORE 4 Jan 1845
      of Robert Blackwell in Washington Co.
      ae 3y 9m.

PETERS, Catherine Conyngham, daughter of Ralph and Ann M., 17 June ae 2y 8m. — MORE 18 Jun 1850

PETZOLD, Margaret S., wife of John, yesterday of a burst blood vessel in her 51st year. Buried in "cemetery on Gravois Road." Lived Congress St. — SLMD 13 Feb 1855

PEUGNET, Hortense, daughter of Louis and Theresa, ae 1y. — MORE 1 Jul 1845

PEYTON, Jane Y., infant of F. S. of Boonville, 30 June. — MODE 11 Jul 1848

PHARR, John, in Pike Co., 18 July. — NERA 29 Jul 1845

PHELPS, Benjamin at Valverdo NM 18 Nov. ae about 27. — MORE 15 Mar 1847

    Lucy Jane, daughter Hon. John S. and Mary, 27 September ae about 3. — COMB 8 Oct 1847

    Susan A., consort of Joseph A., 10 May near Independence. — SLMD 9 Jun 1855

PHILIBERT, George, son of Augustus and Mary, 153 Green St., 19 May ae 1y 1m. — MORE 20 May 1850

PHILLIPS, Alfred J. 17 October in Louisiana MO, ae 20. — LADB 23 Oct 1848

    Nathan Heald, only child of Walter and Zerniah of Rock Island IL, near St. Charles ae 5. — MORE 12 Jan 1837

    Thomas Lee, son of E. J. and Martha, 7 September ae 2y 5m. Bedford VA pc — MORE 8 Sep 1851

    William Stanton, infant of William B. and Sarah, Saturday morning last. — PWH 9 Sep 1847

PHILLIPSON, Martha Snead, wife of (J. H.?) and daughter of George W. Morton of Boonville, 28 Jan. ae 22. — SLMD 17 Feb 1855

PICKENS, Sally A., wife of James A. of Louisiana MO, at the home of James Vennable 16 Sept. of consumption ae 21y 1d. Left a son. — LADB 20 Sep 1847

    Sarah Augusta, infant of James and Helen S., 23 September ae 9m 17d. — " 24 Sep 1850

PIKE, children of James and Mary "on the road from Iowa to Texas:" John ae 3, Nicholas ae 5, Sarah an infant. — MORE 26 Jun 1852

PILKINGTON, Anna, daughter of Samuel B. and Elizabeth, 27 July ae 2y 7m. — MORE 28 Jul 1853
    Lily, 5 July ae 11m 5d. Lived 8th-Barry. — SLMD 6 Jul 1854

PIPPIN, Howell, estate in Chariton Co.: Final Settlement by Lisbon Applegate, Publ. Adm. — BRUNS 1 Sep 1855

PITTS, __, consort of James, in Hannibal Monday last. — HAJ 8 Nov 1849

    Dr. George R., eminent physician, in St. Charles Co. / many years/ 8 September. — NERA 10 Sep 1845

PLANT, Frances Louisa, wife of Wm. M., of cholera ae 24. — MORE 17-19 Jun 1850
    Henry Barnard, son of Wm. and Fanny, ae 22m 15d. — " 26 Sep 1849

PLANT, Henry, late of Northampton MA, of cholera, ae 25.　　MORE 19 Jun 1850

PLATT, A. Switzer, son of J. M. and Laura E., 15 January.　　MORE 17 Jan 1849

POCOCKE, Margaret Ann, daughter of William H. and
　　　　　　Caroline, 28 February ae 7m.　　MORE 3 Mar 1846

POETTER, Adolphus J., son of George and Louisa, 6 March.　　SLMD 9 Mar 1854

POGUE, Franklin A., "a respectable young mechanic" of
　　　　　　Ashley, Pike Co., killed Wed. last;　　LADB 14 May 1849
　　　　　　holding a horse which reared and dragged
　　　　　　him. Member Sons of Temperance.

POINDEXTER, Margaret Leonora, only daughter of Theodore
　　　　　　and Ann, ae 2y 3m 14d.　　MORE 2 Aug 1853

POLK, John W., son of John (of the MO Senate) at their home
　　　　　　in Madison Co. 15 January in his 19th year.　　JEM 26 Jan 1847

POLLOCK, Mary Louisa, daughter of David and Virginia,
　　　　　　1 September ae 10m.　　JEFRE 5 Sep 1840

POMEROY, sons of Augustus D. and Janette, St. Louis:
　　　　　　Henry Bates, ae 1y 2m, 17 Jan. of
　　　　　　　　scarlet fever.　　MORE 18 Jan 1849
　　　　　　John, ae 3y. Funeral from home of
　　　　　　　　Mrs. Dennison, 124 N. 4th.　　"　3 Jan　"

　　　　　　Mrs. Chester, killed in the collapse of the 2nd-
　　　　　　　　floor hall at the Laclede Saloon, where　　MORE 2 May 1850
　　　　　　　　pupils from Purkitt's Female Seminary
POND see POUD　　were having a party. Mrs. Beaky also died.

POOR, John T. at the home of Maj. Campbell in Greene Co.
　　　　　　on 24 July.　　JEM 3 Aug 1847

POPE, Nathaniel at the home of his son-in-law Thomas Yeatman
　　　　　　22 January in his 66th year; Judge of IL　　MORE 23 Jan 1850
*　　　　　　District Ct. Buried O'Fallon Cemetery.

POSTAL, Frances, daughter of William and (Lusa?) 20 July.　　NERA 22 Jul 1849

* PORTER, Jane Jacoby, daughter of Henry and Elizabeth, in
　　　　　　Pike Co. 26 September ae 8. Jeff City pc　　SRJ 2 Oct 1841

　　　　　　Luther, son of Joseph and Susannah, 22 September
　　　　　　　　in Bridgeton ae 10y.　　MORE 29 Sep 1851

POUD (POND?), Mary Auguste, daughter of Charles H. and
　　　　　　Hannah, 7 Dec. ae 2y 6m. Boston, Bangor pc　　MORE 8 Dec 1847

POWELL, Ann, wife of Samuel, in Livingston Co. 19 November.　　JEM 14 Dec 1847

POWERS, John Herbert, son of W. V. and Emiline,
　　　　　　19 December ae 10m.　　SLMD 21 Dec 1853

PRATTE, children of Bernard Jr., St. Louis:
　　　　　　Therese, infant.　　MORE 15 Jul 1828
　　　　　　Emily, infant, 2 February.　　"　7 Feb 1832
　　　　　　Sylvester, son of Bernard and Louise, ae 6m. "　19 Sep 1838
　　　　　Emily, widow of Gen. Bernard, 23 November ae 68.　　MORE 26 Nov 1844

83

PRATT, daughters of Col. Warner Pratt, Knox Co.:
    Amma Hill at her father's home in Edina
        14 August ae 5y 16d.   CANE 25 Aug 1853
      Ellen, only child, 13 August ae 1y 9m 9d.   "   23 Aug 1854

PRESTON, Fanny Louisa, youngest daughter of John B. and
      Lucy Ann, 30 May ae 4y 3m.   MORE 31 May 1850

PRICE, Araminta Franklin, daughter of H. C. and A. L.,
    in Monroe Co. 9 October ae 1y 7d.   HAJ 21 Oct 1852

      Caroline Virginia, only daughter of Capt. E.,
        ae 4y 8m 12d.   MORE 23 Dec 1834

      Erasmus Darwin Sappington, son of William and M.E.,
        at Arrow Rock 23 July in his 2nd year.   MORE 30 Jul 1846

      James S., son of Major J. D. "living on the Bluffs"
        Friday ae 9 or 10.   BRUNS 3 Feb 1848

      Napoleon M., only son of Thomas L. and Lydia,
        19 September ae 10.   JEFRE 25 Sep 1841

      Susan Louise, only child of William W. and
        Henrietta, 8 April ae 18m 12d.   SLMD 10 Apr 1854

      Susan Martha, daughter of Gen. Y. W. and Mrs. P.L.,
        20 January ae about 10.   BOLT 27 Jan 1844

      Sarah (Hillier or Tillier), youngest daughter of
        Clement Biddle Penrose, 15 December.   MOG 20 Dec 1820

PRIEST, John Goodbridge, son of John C. and Virginia,
      27 August ae 2y 8m.   MORE 28 Aug 1851

PRIMEAU, Helen Pelagie, daughter of Lewis and Amanda,
      10 March ae 19m.   SWERE 13 Mar 1848

PRITCHARD, Hector, native of OH, resident of Hannibal
      18m; a Methodist.   HAJ 11 Oct 1849

PRITCHETT, Charles, son of W. H. and Sarah M., 8 September
      ae 10m 12d.   MORE 9 Sep 1845

      Mary Elizabeth, daughter of Jesse and Mary, at
        Carondelet Saturday ae 5m.   MORE 8 Sep 1841

PULLIAM, John R., estate in Chariton Co.: Final Settlement
      by Richard S. Hyde.   BRUNS 18 Feb 1854

      James Elliott, at his father's home, 9 January.   PWH 20 Jan 1844

PULLIS, infant son of Christian and Amelia, 9 June ae 4m17d. MORE 10 Jun '53

PURDY, Frances, infant of James, Saturday last.   MORE 5 Jul 1831

PYLE, William R., youngest son of Ebenezer and Chesandra,
      28 July ae 13m 27d.   NERA 7 Aug 1849

QUERY, Mrs. __, wife of Newton of Cape Girardeau, en route
or QUEERY?   to Perry Co. to visit her children, paused
        to light her pipe at a brush fire; her   SLMD 11 Mar 1854
        clothes were ignited by burning leaves,
        husband couldn't save her. 17 February.

RABORG, Catherine, youngest daughter of Franklin and   NERA 16 Feb 1846
        Malinda, 13 February ae 10m 23d.

RACKLIFFE, Henry Fassett, only son of Charles and Mary,   PWH 16 Jan 1844
        of Shelbyville, Saturday night last.

RAGLAND, Maria Elizabeth, consort of John K., 2 March in   SLMD 24 Mar 1855
        Cooper Co.; dau/Dr. Buckner of Fayette.

RAINES, Nancy Jane, eldest daughter of James and   SPAD 13 Apr 1847
        Elizabeth, 8 April.

RAMSEY, Theron Baldwin, son of John and Mary, 27 July   MORE 28 Jul 1851
        ae 2y 3m.

RANDOLPH, Anne Lyman, daughter of B. H. and Sarah, infant.   MORE 6 Apr 1840
    Lucy, daughter of B. Harrison and Sarah, ae   NERA 31 Oct 1845
        19m; lived Elm-4th.

        Capt. William S. of Randolph & Gorman in 42d y.   MORE 14 May 1850
        Lived Market betw 8-9; wife, sev'l chn.
        (LADB 20 May says formerly of the Lucy
        Bertram, died 13 May of cholera.)

RANEY, Capt. Augustus W. of the Osage Co. Inf. in Jefferson   JEM 13 Oct 1846
        City Saturday last in his 24th y.

RANKIN, Mary Adeline, daughter of Charles and Sarah, at   NERA 6 Aug 1849
        Herculaneum, 1 August ae 1m 22d.

    Mary Clementine, only child of Louis and Cecelia,   NERA 20 Jul 1849
        at Hillsboro ae 1y 8m.

    Robert, "long a resident," at Planters' House;   SLINT 1 Jan 1850
        buried Episcopal Cemetery.

    William Glasgow, eldest son of Charles S., ae 5.   MORE 11 Mar 1846

RANNEY, John Shackford, son of Nathan, 5 April.   MORE 6 Apr 1839
    Nathan William, son of Nathan and Amelia J., in   " 18 Jun 1845
        his 6th year, yesterday.

RANSOM, Elvira, wife of George M. and daughter of David   MORE 10 Jul 1849
        Kennon of Plattsburg NY, ae 35.

RANSON, Francis, son of Walter and Sarah Ann, 13 May   SWERE 14 May 1849
        ae 2y 7m.

    Robert, ae (43? 45?), 27 June. Jacksonville pc   NERA 28 Jun 1849

    William D., eldest son of R. and E., 14 June of   " 16 Jun "
        cholera in his 16th year.

RAWLINGS, children of Daniel and Josephine, St. Louis:
        Daniel A., ae 2y, 15 May.   SLMD 16 May 1854
        Mary Tyler, youngest daughter, 17 May ae 4.   " 18 "

RAYMOND, Charles, son of Capt. Thomas J. and Elizabeth,   MORE 3 Apr 1846
        ae 1y, at the home of James Watson.

REA, children of Horsley and Pamelia J., Cole Co.:
        Thompson E., infant, 2 March.   JEFRE 6 Mar 1841
        Juliett Ann, youngest, and 4th child lost.   " 9 Oct 1841

READING, George, at his home in St. Francisville, Clark Co.
4 August in his 85th year. Formerly of   LADB 25 Aug 1846
Pike Co. (18 years); Revolutionary soldier
in KY. Presbyterian elder 40 years.

RECORDON, Emile, son of Charles and Catherine, Sat. ae 16m. MORE 21 Jul 1840

REDMAN, Benjamin Rezin, son of Rev. William W. and Mary,   MORE 16 Nov 1844
9 November ae 7m 11d.

Chukesberry, ae 65y 3m 15d, at his home on   MORE 8 Dec 1849
Bellefontaine Rd. 7 December.

Rev. W. W. at his home near Danville 31 Oct. in his
50th year, of heart palpitations. A   LADB 12 Nov 1849
minister more than 29 years.

REED, Andrew, ae about 70, on 3 February; his wife had   JEM 9 Feb 1847
died a few weeks before.

Joseph Hiram Hazlett, son of Nathaniel and Mary A.M.,   SLMD 16 May 1855
ae 7m 4d; lived 9th-Mound.

Parthenia, wife of William H.,18th-Biddle, 12 Oct.   SLMD 13 Oct 1854

Samuel, ae 76, 11 October in Boone Co.   JEM 20 Oct 1846

Silas, son of Dr. Silas, 6 February.   SWERE 15 Feb 1847

REESE, Ida Sue, daughter of Addison and Margaret,   CANE 9 Feb 1854
4 February ae 10m.

REID, Maria N., wife of John, ae 29. (cholera epidemic?)   MORE 17 Jul 1849

REILY, children of John P., St. Louis:
Julie Dunn, infant, Wednesday.   MORE 6 Sep 1833
(John P.'s father died same day)
Henry, infant, Friday last.   "   22 Nov 1831
John H., infant, Sunday.   "   21 Sep 1830

Mary Alice, daughter of Philip and Octavia,   SLMD 7 Aug 1855
6 August ae 12m; lived on S. 4th.

RENICK, Harold, infant of Robert M. and Anna, 16 June   NERA 16 Jun 1849
ae 9m. Baltimore pc

RENSHAW, children of William, St. Louis:
Edward, infant, Sunday morning.   MORE 11 Aug 1829
Henry Clay, youngest son, Tuesday last.   "   21 Feb 1832
Virginia, yesterday. (date might be 1838)   "   19 Feb 1837
Charles T., ae 22, yesterday.   "   2 Nov 1843
William Hunter, son of William and Emily,   "   21 Oct 1851
20 Oct. ae 11m 21d.

REYBURN, Thomas, estate in Chariton Co.: Final Settlement   BRUNS 1 Sep 1855
by Lisbon Applegate, Publ. Adm.

REYNOLDS, Samuel Chandler, son of Samuel and Adeline,   MORE 30 Jul 1844
19 July ae 19m.

RHOTON, George, son of the late George, 20 June ae 14m.   SLMD 22 Jun 1854

RICE, Abram H., estate in Chariton Co.: Letters of Adm.   BRUNS 27 Dec 1856
to L. Applegate, Publ. Adm., 15 December.

RICE, Rev. D. E. Y., in Cape Girardeau, 2 June in his 41st year, of chronic diarrhoea. SLMD 23 Jun 1854

James Clay, son of Samuel and M. J., at Neosho 2 March ae 1y 7m. SPAD 7 Mar 1846

RICHARDS, Frances Sydney, infant of Hugh, last Friday. MORE 11 Oct 1827

Margaret, wife of Josiah W. and daughter of the late Nathaniel Phillips, formerly of Boston. Ae 37. Lived 12th-Clark. MORE 3 Oct 1849

Milton B. and his daughter Louisa, ae 2y 4m. (probably cholera victims) MORE 4 Jul 1849

William, son of William and Mary, 18 March ae 1y 7d. Detroit & St. Clair MI pc MORE 20 Mar 1848

RICHARDSON, Asa, Lt. 6th US Inf., at Jefferson Barracks. MORE 21 Apr 1835

Elizabeth S., daughter of Joseph and Emily, 18 October ae 4y 11m 3d. LADB 23 Oct 1848

RICHART, Elizabeth, daughter of A. L. and Jane C., of Canton, 19 June at Fairfield IA ae 6m 23d. CANP 23 Jun 1848

RICHEY, Mrs. Lucinda, late of St. Louis, in Atlas IL 26 August in her 43rd year. MORE 10 Sep 1833

RICHMOND, Aurelia, consort of Joshua, 24 November of consumption. HAG 26 Nov 1846

Capt. Ezra at his home near Hannibal 10 Nov. Native of MA, raised in RI, settled in KY. Volunter in War of 1812. " 18/26 Nov 1846

RICKARD, Thomas J.: funeral from home of his br-in-law William Chappell. (cholera epidemic?) MORE 18 Jul 1849

RIDDLE, Mary Elizabeth, wife of Alexander, 13 February in her 30th year. MORE 14 Feb 1850

Richard Alexander, son of Alexander and Sarah A., 13 July ae 4m. Connecticut pc. (Sarah had died 5 weeks before) MORE 15 Jul 1844

Harriet Wade, daughter of Col. Alexander, 20 July ae 3y 9m. Lived Collins-Biddle. MORE 21 Jul 1846

RIDDLESBARGER, sons of Jesse and Mary, Boones Lick area:
William Patton, infant, Thursday. BOLT 19 Mar 1842
John Perry, infant, 30 August. " 6 Sep 1845

Jesse T., son of J. and Susan L., 21 July. KCEN 9 Aug 1856

Mary William Chiffonette, dau/Mr. & Mrs. Madison Riddlesbarger, 6 Apr. in 3rd y. " 11 Apr 1857

RIDGELY, Hannah Mary, eldest child of F. L., Wednesday. MORE 22 Nov 1833

Josephine, infant of Franklin L. and Eleanor, 15 September ae 1y 11m. " 18 Sep 1837

Thomas Howard, late of St. Louis, at his father's home in Baltimore. " 9 Apr 1838

RIDINGS, Fayette Newton, son of Joseph and Rosana, 1 Mar.   SLMD 24 Mar 1856
    in Randolph Co., of pneumonia, in his 18th y.

RIGDON, Emma, infant of Charles and Ann, 31 July.   SLMD 2 Aug 1855

RIGGINS, James in Clark Twp., Cole Co., 10 October in   JEM 26 Oct 1848
    his 73rd year.

RINGELING, Lizzie, only daughter of Francis and Eliza,   MORE 19 Sep 1853
    ae 5y 10m.

RISK, Frances, daughter of T. F. and Amanda, 19 October   MORE 21 Oct 1851
    ae 16m 10d.
    Mary, only child of T. F., 10 April ae 6y 9m 24d.   "   11 Apr 1855
       Funeral from the Convent of the Sacred Heart.

RITCHEY, Thomas M. at his home near Brown's Ferry,   SLMD 26 Oct 1853
    Meramec Twp., 25 Oct. in (52? 53?)d y.

RIZER, Eleanora, daughter of the late Daniel L. and   MORE 19 Jan 1850
    Prudence, 18 January; lived 92 Elm St.

ROBB, Julia Emmons, infant of Findley and Caroline C. of   SLMD 23 Mar 1854
    St. Louis, in St. Charles 17 March.

ROBBINS, sons of E. H. and Elizabeth, St. Louis:
    Charles Henry, youngest son, ae 5, on 5 Oct.   SWERE 6 Oct 1845
    Chestly, only son, ae 5y 2m, 2 October.   MORE 4 "
    (possibly the same child?)

    Florence Catherine, infant of James S. and   LADB 10 Jun 1850
    Catherine, in Bowling Green ae 3m 11d.

    Mary Augusta, consort of Samuel, daughter of   MORE 10 Jul 1849
    James Longest of Louisville, ae 25.

ROBERTS, Mrs. Rachael of Bridgeport, Monroe Co., 19 May   SLMD 9 Jun 1855
    in Eddyville ae 26.

    W., of Taney Co., 7 June on the Little Blue   MORE 10 Jul 1850
    River ae 9m.

ROBARDS, Mary S., daughter of William and Dorcas,   COP 2 Dec 1846
    22 November in her 23rd year.

ROBERTS, children of T. H. and M., St. Louis:
    Mary Alice, infant, 19 Feb. Louisville pc   SLMD 20 Feb 1854
    William F., ae 3m, on 21 September.   "   22 Sep 1857

ROBERTSON, Melissa Jane, daughter of Judge, 17 July in   JEM 3 Aug 1847
    Greene Co. ae about 14.
    Judge B., member of the Legislature from Greene   "
    Co. last term, 19 July.

ROBIDOUX, Joseph Franklin, son of Isadore, Saturday last.   STGAZ 19 Feb 1847

ROBINSON, Arbella, daughter of John and Mary A.,   LADB 9 Oct 1848
    3 October ae 1y 1m 28d.

    Mrs. James, formerly of MD, at the home of   SLMD 28 Dec 1854
    R. Porter, Monroe Co., Thursday last.

    John B., only son of Wm., Saturday ae 22m.   INP 2_ Sep 1823

ROBINSON, Joseph R., son of Joseph and Eliza, 7 January. MORE 9 Jan 1849
        Friends of Capt. Richard Phillips invited to
        funeral, 264 Morgan. Buried Catholic Cemetery.

        Virginia Augusta, daughter of William and C. A., MORE 5 Aug 1854
            4 August ae 5y 6m. Lived Main-Pine.

        William Harrison, native of Lincoln Co., resident
            of Pike Co. from early boyhood, in his LADB 19 Feb 1849
            28th year. Survived by parents.

ROCHE, M. Michael, son of William and Mary, 3 October MORE 4 Oct 1841
            ae 13m 10d. Lived 45 N. 5th.

ROCHESTER, Mary Rebecca, daughter of Col. A. and Martha SLMD 17 Dec 1857
            Fisher, in Jackson Co. 29 November
            ae 5y 10m 26d.

RODERMAN, children of Charles and Celestina, St. Louis:
        Charles M., oldest child, 8 May ae 11y 4m 22d. MORE 10 May 1847
        Caroline Theresa 12 May ae 7y 3m 21d.   "   13   "
        Adolph, youngest child, ae 2y 8m 2d.   "   19   "
        Interred family cemetery, St. Louis Co.

RODGERS, Eliza, daughter of Samuel and Eliza D., 10th &
            Morgan, ae 2y 11m 17d. Pittsburgh pc MORE 2 Apr 1853

        Emma Jane, youngest daughter of William H. and
            Jane, drowned 1 August ae 17m 8d. SASE 6 Aug 1853

        William A.: funeral from his home, Franklin
            betw 6th-7th. (cholera epidemic?) MORE 7 Jul 1849

RODGERSON, James W., son of David and Maria Eliza, 5 June MORP 10 Jun 1845
            ae 21m 15d. New Orleans pc

RODNEY, Matilda, consort of Michael, in Cape Girardeau Co. CGWE 2 Mar 1849
            2 March; left children and grandchildren.

ROGERS, Mrs. Mary Ann, in her 67th year, on 29 June. JEM 6 Jul 1847
            She was a Methodist.

        Mary Gertrude, only daughter of James A. and
            Frances M., ae 10y 4m. Louisville pc MORE 24 Dec 1847

        William A., son of Thomas N. and S. M., 8 May in
            Columbia ae 10m 26d. SLMD 26 May 1855

ROHRER, Emma S., wife of Dr. J. W., of cholera, 5 July. NERA 6 Jul 1849

ROKOHL, Henry Kinkead, ae 6y 6m 27d, on 5 September. MORE 6 Sep 1853

ROSE, Charles W., "old and esteemed" boot-and-shoemaker of SLMD 15 Jun 1855
        DeKalb, Buchanan Co., 3 May in Weston of cholera.

      Children of Hugh and Elizabeth, St. Louis:
        Anna Maria 30 Jan. of scarlet fever ae 11y 3m 17d. MORE 31 Jan 1848
        Wm. Henry 28 Jan. ae 6y 1m 18d. Buried Catholic
          Cemetery. Halifax NS pc
        Hugh on 5 February ae 1y 5m 28d. SWERE 7 Feb 1848
        Thomas Alexander 30 June ae 1y 9m. Lived 8th & MORE 1 Jul 1841
  (cont.)   Washington. Boston & Halifax pc

ROSE, Charles Edward, son of the late Hugh and Elizabeth, ae 2y 4m 19d.　　MORE 5 Aug 1851

ROSS, Richard, son of Thomas, Monday ae about 18m.　　PWH 24 Jun 1847

Mary Woart, formerly of Newburyport MA, Thursday last at her father's home in St. Charles.　　MOSN 28 Jul 1838

ROSSELL, Mrs. Anna, ae (53?) Saturday last. Quincy pc　　MORE 16 Apr 1850

ROWE, George McCloud, son of John S. and Elizabeth D., 13 April at High Hill ae 8m 2d.　　SLMD 28 Apr 1855

Children of Joseph, St. Louis:
Martha, ae 3, on 25 July.　　MORE 27 Jul 1839
Walter on 14 September ae 11m.　　"　15 Sep 1853
Children of Joseph and Margaret E., St. Louis:
Robert Abrahams, youngest son, ae 2y 3m.　　"　21 Oct 1847
Samuel Harold, ae 8m 16d, at the home of Capt. William Boyce.　　NERA 22 May 1849

ROWEN, Archibald H., on 30 July.　　HAJ 3 Aug 1848

ROWLEY, Orlando R., ae 10m 21d, last Thursday.　　MODE 29/27 Sep 1847

ROY, Mrs. Charity near Hannibal 19 January at a "good old age." Old Style Presbyterian.　　HAG 11 Feb 1847
(HAJ same date gives name as Charlotte.)

Lucy Maria, daughter of Joseph C. and Mary A., 24 July ae 14½m.　　PWH 6 Aug 1845

RUCKER, John A. F., son of Dr. A. and Leah, 7 Aug. ae 20m.　　GLWT 14 Aug 1851

RUDD, Mary, widow of Theron, ae 62. NY pc (cholera?)　　MORE 8 Jul 1849

RUFFIN, Maj., of Cincinnati, at the home of his son-in-law Maj. Hopkins, St. Louis, ae 60.　　SLOB 29 Jul 1834

RULE, Orville G., son of Alexander Scott and Virginia, ae 1y 11m.　　MORE 17 May 1851

RUNYAN, Enoch Robinson, son of R. G. and Elizabeth, 4 May ae 10m 20d. Nashville & Frankfort pc　　GLWT 8 May 1851

RUNYON, Kitty, eldest daughter of B. H. and Mary R., ae 6y 10m. Nashville pc　　MORE 13 Jan 1851

RUSSELL, daughters of John, St. Louis:
Laura Ann, eldest daughter, at Bluff Dale, Greene Co. IL, "lately."　　MORE 18 May 1830
Julia Augusta at Bonhomme 5 September.　　"　11 Sep 1822

James at Oak Hill, his home in St. Louis Co., 3 May in his 65th year. Native of VA, to Cape Girardeau Co. 30 years ago. Edited the Independent Patriot. Member of the Legislature from St. Charles Co., to St. Louis Co. 1827.　　MORE 4 May 1850

Lizzie F., daughter of Dr. J. G. and S. M., in Lafayette Co. 24 December ae 1y 4d.　　SLMD 17 Jan 1855

Mary, consort of H. P. of Arcadia, Madison Co., at her father's home in Hartford CT 1 November of chronic bronchitis.　　NERA 28 Nov 1849

RUSSELL, Eliza Eleanor, daughter of Col. Thomas, ae 6m 5d. WEM 25 Jul 1839

RUST, John Godfrey, only son of John C. and Helen, of
        scarlet fever, 28 February. MORE 1 Mar 1853

RUTGERS, Johanna, widow of Arend, 8 December at her home
        on S. 7th in her 93rd year. MORE 10 Dec 1849

RUTHERFORD, children of Archibald S. and Cornelia, St. Louis:
        Cornelia Stevenson at the family home
          on Walsh Row, 13 July. Presbyterian cem. MORE 14 Jul 1847
        George Shakford, ae 6m 8d. "   18 Jan 1849
        Walter, in Cincinnati, 23 May. "   26 May 1850

        Children of Thomas S. and Lucille, St. Louis:
        Albert Tison, youngest child, 19 March
          ae 18m. Buried Episcopal Cemetery. MORE 20 Mar 1847
        Kate, ae 2y 5m, 24 December. NERA 24 Dec 1849
        Ann Stevenson, youngest child, 31 Dec. SLMD 1 Jan 1856
          ae 10m. Lived 16-Olive.

RUTLEDGE, Mrs. Jane, in her 64th year, 29 Nov. Funeral
        from home of her dau/Mrs. Rutherford. SLMD 30 Nov 1853

RYAN, Annastacea, in her 21st year, 26 June. (cholera?) NERA 27 Jun 1849

    James, estate in Chariton Co.: Final Settlement
        by James H. Ryan. BRUNS 9 Aug 1856

    James Cornelius, son of Jeremiah and Honora, 21 Feb.
        ae 2y 11m. Lived Orange betw 12-13. SLMD 23 Feb 1856

    Margaret, consort of David; lived 5th betw Carr-Wash. SLMD 13 Feb 1855

    Mary Cora, daughter of Moses and Martha, 2 February. SWERE 8 Feb 1847

    Children of Thomas and Anna E., St. Louis:
        Laura Alice, ae 2y 9m, yesterday. MORE 22 Sep 1845
        Mary Louise, ae 4y 1m 13d, 18 April. "   19 Apr 1853
          Buried St. Vincent's.
        Fanny Eugenia, ae 3y, 24 April. "   25   "
        Andrew Edmond, ae 2y 4m, 11 September. "   12 Sep 1849
          Lived at 195 Locust.

RYCHLICAL, Josephine N., infant of J. E., 22 March. MORE 23 Mar 1849

RYLAND, Joseph Erasmus, son of John F., Thursday ae 5. MIN 3 Apr 1829

SACHS, Caroline, wife of F., Saturday last ae 19. JEM 10 Aug 1847

SAGE, Edith S., only daughter of Cornwall and Sarah,
        27 January ae 2. SLMD 29 Jan 1855

ST. CLAIR, John, estate in Chariton Co.: Final Settlement
        by Charles Wheelabarger. BRUNS 25 Oct 1856

ST. CYR, William H., son of P. H. and Maria, yesterday
        ae 22m 16d. MORE 2 Aug 1844

ST. MICHEL, Emilie, daughter of Aspasie and Edward of
        Montreal, 22 June ae 13m 29d. Funeral MORE 23 Jun 1841
        from father's home, 3rd St.

SALISBURY, Belcher Douglas, only son of Philander and   MORE 13 Dec 1847
           Mary, ae 3y 2m. Buried Bissell Cem.

SAMPLE, Charles, son of Charles and Jane, 21 July ae 13m.
           Lived 9th betw Pine-Chestnut. Buried   MORE 22 Jul 1843
           Presbyterian Cemetery.

SAMUELS, Sarah Emma, daughter of Edgecomb, 3 October in   JEM 13 Oct 1846
           Cooper Co. ae 16.

       Jeannette, wife of Marks, in her 32nd year.   SWERE 17 Jul 1849
           (cholera? see Rachel Levy.)

SANDBURG, children of Peter G. and Sarah R., St. Louis:
           Almira Jane Augustine, 8y 4m 8d. NY pc   MORE 19 Jun 1849
           Mary Ann Rosaltha, 21 June ae 7y 5m.   "   23   "
           William Sandberg ae 2y 6m. Lived on   "   28 Feb   "
           Washington betw 8-9.

SANDERS, Ann George, infant of Velarius and Maria,   BGRAD 23 Sep 1843
           19 September ae 5m 20d.

       Nancy A. J., daughter of Harold and Naoma, at   LADB 4 Sep 1848
           their home in Warrenton 21 August in her
           18th year, of gastro-enteritis.

       Thomas H., at his father's home in Jefferson Co.,   SLMD 5 May 1855
           7 April ae 22.

SANDERSON, George W., son of Elias, 30 July.   SWERE 2 Aug 1847

SANDIDGE, James, son of the late Pulliam, killed by a   SLMD 2 Nov 1854
           falling tree. (Trenton Pioneer 26 Oct.)
           Left mother, several brothers.

SANDS, Sarah, daughter of S. G. and Ann M., yesterday   SWERE 12 Jun 1848
           ae 7m 15d.

SANFORD, Catherine, consort of Wyatt, 5 September in   JEM 21 Sep 1847
           Greene Co. ae 26.

SARPY, Eugene, infant of J. B., Thursday night last.   MORE 22 Sep 1829

      Martha Jane, tribute following funeral, no data.   "   15 Mar 1844

SASS, children of Richard Freeman and Charlotte Augusta,
           St. Louis:
           Edward Harrison, ae 9m 13d, 9 September.   MORE 11 Sep 1843
           Charleston SC & Boston pc
           George Frost, only son, 28 Dec. ae 3y4m18d.   "   29 Dec 1847
           Buried Episcopal Cemetery.

SAUCIER, Francis Sr., ae about 81, at Portage des Sioux   SCMO 8 Aug 1821
           6 August; one of the first settlers,
           founder of that village.

SAUNDERS, __ son of Lewis, of Shelby Co., ae 5, trapped in   SLMD 11 Apr 1853
           a field his father was burning.

SAWGRAIN (SAUGRAIN?), Alfred, in his 46th year. (cholera?)   MORE 15 Jul 1849

SCHAFFER, Charles, murdered (reputedly by Matthias, George,   MORE 13 Feb 1850
           and Jacob Mossbacher and Adam Done).

SCHAUMBURG, Amelia, youngest daughter of Charles W. and Orleana, 4 March ae 3y 6m. SWERE 6 Mar 1848

SCHEIBEL, Henry A., son of George and Mary, 31 Aug. ae 4m. MORE 1 Sep 1853

SCHMIDT, ___ drowned "at our landing" Sunday while bathing. BRUNS 25 May 1848

SCHNEBLEY, Anna Mary, daughter of Joseph R. and Sarah, Tuesday last ae about 8. PWH 8 Nov 1849

SCHNEIDER, Hannah, wife of Charles and daughter of Henry H. Carter of Philadelphia, 10 March ae 46. NERA 12 Mar 1846

Mary Ellen, daughter of Frances and Susan, in Hannibal 13 May. SLMD 26 May 1855

SCHOLTER, Cecelia, body exhumed at city cemetery; thought murdered by husband Albert, both had been drinking. Lived 5m out on Olive Plank Road. Buried 2 January; apparently beaten. SLMD 10/11 Jan 1855

SCHOOLFIELD, Mrs. Sarah, wife of Nathan, formerly of Lynchburg VA, 10 January in her 51st year, at Columbia. LADB 27 Jan 1851

SCHURST, Augustus Purcelle, son of Augustus and Sarah, ae 2. MORE 24 Jun '44

SCOLLAY, Leonard G., son of Leonard and Elizabeth, 13 June ae 18m. Lived Olive betw 5-6. SLMD 14 Jun 1855

SCOTT, Adelaide, only daughter of John R. and Catherine L., Tuesday 17 December ae 4y 1m. MORE 18 Dec 1844

Clarence, son of James W. and Leanna, 130 Carr St., 1 April ae 7m. MORE 3 Apr 1847

Enoch, of cholera, 12 July ae 56; shown with Pauline, 11 July of cholera, ae 18. NERA 15 Jul 1849

Hardin, son of Wm. C. and Mary D., 15 Oct. ae 7½m. MORE 16 Oct 1847

Marietta, daughter of John and Eliza J., 5 May ae 6y 7m. SWERE 15 May 1848

William Poston, son of William P. and Martha, ae 1y 10m 5d. MORE 22 May 1852

SCRUGGS, Ivan in Cole Co. 16 October, "worthy and respected." Baptist. JEM 3 Nov 1846

SCUDDER, Dr. Charles, late of Monmouth NJ, several years in St. Louis, 14 Dec. in 57th y. NERA 15 Dec 1849

Mary, daughter of William and Margaret of Birmingham, in Perryville 16 Oct. ae 1y 2w. SGPD 29 Oct 1853

SEARCEY, John Edward, son of Edward and Judith P., 5 December ae 2y 10m. STGAZ 11 Dec 1846

SEARS, Edward Jordan, son of Joseph and Ann M., 17 Aug. ae 11m 5d. MODE 26/ 17 Aug 1846

Frances Ellen, daughter of S. G. and Isabella, 2 May ae 11m. MORE 3 May 1853

SEBASTIN, George 21 May ae 37 after a short illness. NERA 25 May 1849

SEBREE, Elizabeth, widow of Uriel, 21 October. (from
    the Howard Co. <u>Banner</u>) SLMD 2 Nov 1854

SEE, William F., son of George W. and Louisa A., 16 Sept.
    ae 9m 10d. KCEN 20 Sep 1856

SELLARS, Archibald, estate in Oregon Co.: final settlement
    by Isaac Perkins. SPRIM 31 Jul 1856

SELMES, Mary D., wife of T. R.; born NY City 3 Jan 1813,
    to Hannibal with husband 1843; joined HAJ 12 Jul 1849
    Methodist Church 1842. Left husband,
    daughter, son-in-law.

SETTLE, James Brotherton, son of Thomas G. and Matilda,
    4 June ae 6y 6m 1d. MORE 5 Jun 1852

   Margaret, wife of William, 2 August in Ralls Co.
    of bilious fever in her 47th year. HAJ 12 Aug 1847

SEXTON, George Edward, son of James M. and Ann, in Glasgow
    17 September ae 6m. BOLT 14 Oct 1843

SEYMOUR, Lewis Marcus, only child of Emory and Lizzie, ae 2. MORE 4 Mar 1851

SHACKELFORD, E. D., estate in Chariton Co.: final
    settlement by N. J. McAshan. BRUNS 10 Jun 1854

   Mrs. Franc<u>i</u>s or Frances (two items) 27 Sept. HAG 2 Sep 1847
    in Hannibal <u>in</u> 67th year. HAJ "

SHAFFNER, Eliza Rebecca, daughter of Mr/Mrs. A. C.,
    #61 St. Charles, ae 18m. MORE 14 Mar 1846

   Margaret Emma, youngest daughter of George and
    Elvira, 6 January ae 9m 15d. MORE 7 Jan 1846

SHANDS, __, youngest daughter of Joseph G. and Clara
    Walton, 5 July ae 18m 14d. MORE 6 Jul 1844

SHANNON, George C., son of John and Eleanor A., 25 August
    ae 13m 5d. MORE 5 Sep 1838

   James Alexander, son of John H. of Marion Co.,
    15 June. PWH 24 Jun 1847

SHARE, Charles, son of Richard and Ann, 11 July ae 15m 17d. MORE 14 Jul 1845

SHARP, Hamilton, at Mockelumne Diggins 16 June ae 22. MORE 26 Sep 1849

SHAW, Catherine, consort of Andrew, 18 September ae 52.
    Lived Morgan near 7th. (NERA 19 Sept. MORP 19 Sep 1845
    says died 17th, in 57th year.)

   James, formerly of St. Charles. at Herkimer NY on
    27 May, ae about 33. MORE 30 Jun 1829

   James A., son of the late William, 6 January at the
    home of James Bilbro in Lincoln Co., LADB 21 Jan 1850
    ae about 18.

   John B., in 30th year, of paralysis, 12 August; left
    wife, 4 children. LADB 23 Aug 1847

SHAW, Ridgely, son of Lyman, yesterday morning.   MORE 17 Nov 1835
 Octavia, daughter of Lyman and Octavia, of
   St. Louis, in Baltimore 6 March; infant.   " 14 Mar 1838
 Ridgely, son of the late Lyman, 29 January ae 3y.   " 31 Jan 1848

 Martha, infant of William Jr., in Pike Co. 23 March.   LADB 1 Apr 1850

 Mary A., wife of Joel K., in Louisiana MO 4 Sept.   " 16 Sep 1850
   Ae (24?y 10m 10d?). Left infant.

 Mary A., wife of William, 21 Feb. near Savannah ae 22. SLMD 10 Mar '55

SHECKLEY, Mrs. Susan E., of consumption, 15 April ae 62.   SLMD 17 Apr 1855

SHELTON, ___, a child of Mr. Shelton of Charles, was given
   a bottle of whiskey by a Negro, drank too   MORE 13 Nov 1841
   much, and died.

  Ellen Virginia, infant daughter of John G., Sunday. MORE 23 Jul '33

  Helen Gertrude, infant of J. W. and M. W.,
    4 May ae 8m.   SLMD 5 May 1854

  Lelia, youngest daughter of John G. and Mary,
    ae 15m. Funeral from Mrs. Burd's home. MORE 13 Aug 1851

  Mrs. ___, wife of Pines, in St. Charles Co.
    8 September.   NERA 10 Sep 1845

SHEPPARD, Capt. Augustus at Jefferson Barracks 22 January.   MORE 23 Jan 1849

SHEPHERD, John C. at Cuivre Sunday, ae about 6.   BGRAD 21 Sep 1844

 ++ John Cormick, youngest son of J. C. and Frances,
   ae 17m; lived Pine betw 14-15.   MORE 6 Sep 1849

  Sarah Elizabeth, infant of John H. and Elizabeth
   of Bowling Green, on Sunday.   BGDB 4 Oct 1845

 ++ William Nimmo,
   son of John C. and Frances K., ae 20d.   MORE 23 Dec 1844

SHEPHERDSON, Thompson, 17 July; funeral from home of
   Louis Dozier.   MORE 18 Jul 1853

SHERMAN, Sylva J., consort of Rev. D. T. of the MO
   Methodist Conference, 28 April.   LADB 1 May 1848

SHERRICK, George W., son of George W. and Lucy, 27 Dec.
   ae 9m 18d. Lived S, 7th St.   SLMD 29 Dec 1854

SHIELDS, Mary Jane, daughter of Gen. William, of Pettis
   Co., 1 March in her 5th year.   MODE 21 Mar 1848

SHIPP, Miss Jane in Springfield MO 6 March.   SLMD 24 Mar 1855

 Capt. Edward, USA, 22 April of consumption.   MOG 3 May 1817

SHIRLEY, Henry and George, sons of Ephraim and Charlotte,
   2 January ae 7 weeks.   MORE 4 Jan 1851

 George Thomas, infant of James A., in Fayette
   last Saturday.   MIN 1 Jan 1830

SHOBE, Daniel, in Warren Co., 17 September.   NERA 22 Sep 1845

SHOEMAKER, Helen, wife of William, in her 28th year.
    Fannie Jane, their daughter, ae 21d.   MORE 3 Jul 1849
        The family lived at Carondelet & Ann.

SHORE, children of Dr. John and Martha P., St. Louis:
    Edward B., eldest son, 4 February of scarlet   MORE 5 Feb 1847
      fever. Lived Walnut betw 6-7. Ae 4y.
    Thomas, ae 2y 10m 9d. Funeral from the home   " 26 Mar 1847
      of Thomas Shore, 5th-Carr.
    Eliza, ae 11m 25d.   " 10 Jun 1849

    Thomas, ae 26. (cholera epidemic?)   " 10 Jul 1849

SHORTRIDGE, William in Callaway Co. 21 October ae 71.   JEM 3 Nov 1846

SHREVE, Florence, youngest daughter of H. M. and Lydia,   MORE 10 Jan 1851
      8 January ae 18m.

SHRYOCK, Samuel H., ae 19, en route to CA.   MORE 3 Oct 1849

SIGERSON, Delia, daughter of John and Philomena, ae 16m.   MORE 12 May 1849

    Mary, wife of William, 11 December in her 40th   SLMD 12 Dec 1853
      year; suddenly, of pneumonia.

SIGNAIGO, James B., son of James and Margaret,   SWERE 31 Jul 1848
      29 July ae 1y 3m.

SILL, S. M., formerly of Ontario Co. NY, many years a   NERA 15 Jul 1849
      resident of St. Louis, 22 June ae 49.

SILTON, Emma Virginia, daughter of Isaac C. and M. J.,   SWERE 13 Mar 1848
      12 March ae 1y 1m 7d.

SILVERS, sons of Dr. G. H. and Martha A., St. Louis:
    William Henry, infant, Wed. last ae 1m 1d.   SWERE 22 Dec 1845
    Edward F., ae 2y 6m, 12 June at 100 4th St.   MORE 13 Jun 1849

SILVERTOOTH, Shelton J., infant of John and Sarah Jane,   HANT 28 Aug 1852
      25 August ae 2m 12d.

SIMMONDS, Mary V. of Franklin Co. 15 June on the upper   MORE 7 Oct 1850
      crossing of the South Platte, ae 2½y.

SIMMONS, Albert, son of Zachariah T. and Louisa, 26 Apr.   MORE 27 Apr 1846
      in his 10th y. Lived 8th nr Olive.

    Anna Elizabeth, daughter of Dr. R. P. and Ellen,   MORE 3 Jun 1853
      1 June ae 11m 15d.

    Children of C. C. and Julia B., St. Louis:
      William P. on 13 April; funeral from home   MORE 14 Apr 1853
      of Elkanah English. Episcopal Cemetery.
      Mary Louisa, ae 11m 12d, on 6 July.   SLMD 7 Jul 1854

    David accidentally shot by his son, ae about 17,   LADB 31 Jan 1848
      while turkey hunting near Marshall.

    Jennie, daughter of William O., of Hannibal,   SLMD 8 Feb 1855
      29 January in her 4th year.

SIMONDS, Francis, son of John, ae 20, Saturday last in   MORE 11 Sep 1822
      St. Louis.

SIMONDS, children of John, Jr., of St. Louis:
      Francis Henry, infant, ae 13m.   MORE 9 Feb 1830
      George, on Tuesday last.   " 26 Jan 1839

     Col. Nathaniel 7 April at Troy, ae about 75; to
           MO about 1800, official in many   JEM 23 Apr 1850
           territorial and state governments.

     William in Clarksville 16 January, "valued citizen." LADB 5 Feb '49

SIMPSON, Catherine B., daughter of Joseph S. and Eliza,   MORE 8 May 1844
         7 May ae 9m 20d. Lived Spruce St.

     Children of Dr. Robert, St. Louis:
         Sarah G., infant, Tuesday last.   MOG 23 Oct 1818
         Joanna, infant, Friday last.   MORE 21 Sep 1830

SINCLAIR, Eliza, daughter of the late Charles, 12 May   SLMD 26 May 1855
         in Boone Co. ae 20.

SITTON, Isaac, son of Isaac and Martha, 44 Collins St.,   MORE 22 Apr 1850
         21 April ae 9m 10d.

SKAGGS, James, only son of Willis and Elizabeth, 20 Feb. LEXP 22 Feb 1854

SKIDMORE, Philip Wolcott, son of John W., ae 18. Lived   MORE 2 Dec 1843
         3rd-Lombard. Presbyterian Cem.

SKILLMAN, children of Wm. D. and Elvira T., St. Louis:
      William Davis, ae 7y 4m 6d, on 29 July.   MORE 30 Jul 1847
      John Thomas, ae 2y. Lived #55 4th St.   SWERE 22 Jan 1849
         Lexington & Frankfort KY pc

SKINNER, Benjamin A., infant of William, 17 July.   MORE 19 Jul 1831

     Calvin L., in his 19th year, 9 June.   SLMD 12 Jun 1854

     Sarah Ruth, daughter of Alfred and Nancy,   MORE 19 Apr 1838
         17 April ae about 8.

SLAID, Edward in St. Charles Co. 14 September.   NERA 23 Sep 1845

SLATER, James, estate in Chariton Co.: letters of adm. BRUNS 6 Jan 1855
         to J. C. Hutchinson 23 November 1854.

SLAYBACK, children of Alexander L. and Maria, Lexington:
      Emma Claribel 19 August ae about 8.   PWH 7 Sep 1848
      Alexander the same day, both of cholera.

SLEVIN, John Dominic, son of Bernard and Catherine,   SLMD 26 Jul 1854
         25 July ae 1y 19d.

     Maria, daughter of Patrick and Elizabeth, 4 May SLMD 5 May 1855
         ae 10m 24d. Funeral Charles Slevin's home.

SLOAN, children of Edwin C. and Mary, St. Louis:
      Margaret Elizabeth, ae 4y 4m, on 21 August. MORE 24 Aug 1847
      Edwin Morton, ae 5y 9m. Funeral from home   " 2 Sep "
         of George Morton, Spruce St.

SMALL, Ella G., only daughter of James F. and Maria C., SLMD 9 Jul 1857
         8 July of brain inflammation ae 21m.
         Lived 11th St. betw Market-Clark.

SMALL, Martha Ellen, eldest daughter of David, of St. Louis County, 17 May in her 19th year. SLOB 29 May 1834

SMALLWOOD, Benjamin F., son of H., 16 May ae 8y 6m 15d. STGAZ 28 May 1847

SMILY, George, a German, killed on the Alton road while hauling apples for Mr. Bangs; thrown from a wagon, run over. Left wife, 3 chn. (from St. Charles Patriot.) LADB 12 Oct 1846

SMITH, ___, little daughter of Thomas, living 6 miles from Louisiana, drowned in a creek 23 May. LADB 30 May 1846

++ Albert Hamilton, youngest son of Wm. C. and Eliza Jane, 12 February ae 5m 22d. Lived 8th near Olive. Philadelphia pc MORE 13 Feb 1849

Andrew Mitchell, son of Capt. Henry W. and Susan, 31 July ae 13m. SLMD 2 Aug 1855

Annie, only daughter of Capt. A. J. and Ann M, at the home of her gr-father Simpson, ae 4. NERA 14 Aug 1849

Augustin, in Lafayette Co., 13 September. NERA 23 Sep 1845

Charlotte M., wife of S. A., at Saugerties NY 25 December ae 29. SLINT 8-9 Jan 1850

SMITH cont
David M., supposed name of man drowned in Osage R. near Warsaw; probably from Van Buren Co. IA. Had letters from G. C. and John Smith, thought brothers, of Laurel Co. KY; also mentioned William, living near Springfield MO. WEM 10 Oct 1839

Ezilda, infant of Capt. Thomas F., Monday last. MORE 14 Dec 1830

Francis C., of F. C. and E. H. Smith, at Dubuque. NERA 15 Dec 1849

Harriet Frances, youngest daughter of James and Isabella, ae 13m 14d, of scarlet fever. Funeral from home of S. H. Robbins. NERA 26 Feb 1846

++ Henry Countiss, youngest son of W. C. and Eliza J., 28 December ae 1y 6m 7d. SLMD 29 Dec 1855

Henry O., at Richard Hardin's home; from the east, no relatives known. BEA 25 Jul 1829

James M., ae 35, in Pike Co. 3 May. LADB 7 May 1851

John A., in CA about 1 December; resolution from Perseverance Lodge 92 AF & AM. LADB 17 Mar 1851

John H., estate in Chariton Co.: Letters of Adm. to Mahulda Smith, 26 August. GLWT 5 Oct 1854

Malvina, wife of R. E., formerly of Quincy IL, 28 February in her 34th year at 185 5th St. MORE 1 Mar 1850

Martha Louise, only daughter of Benjamin F., in 5th year, on Saturday. MODE 22/20 Sep 1847

Mrs. Mary, wife of William of Pike Co., 25 November in her 32d year. Presbyterian, left 4 little chn. LADB 17 Dec 1849

SMITH, Mary Ellsworth, daughter of Dalzell and Mary, MORE 22 Aug 1840,
        yesterday ae 6m.

    Mr. Posey, of St. Joseph, at Rough and Ready CA LADB 13 Jan 1851
        25 October 1850.

    Margaret Harvey, infant of Robert Y. and Mary Jane, LADB 11 Jun 1851
        31 May in Calumet Twp ae 7m 26d.

    Martha, infant of Col. S. D. and Sarah E., Wednesday. PWH 21 Oct 1843

    Orsina Christine, daughter of Thomas W. and Charlotte
        of Granville, 31 December ae 3y 2d. MORE 16 Jan '41
        Virginia Free Press pc

    Tilghman C. son of Capt. John and Lurency,
        109 7th St., on 7 November. SLMD 8 Bov 1853

    William Henry, infant of William and Ann, 13 May MORE 14 May 1840
        ae 13m. Buried O'Fallon Cemetery.

SMYTH, Mary, consort of Col. Peter, 12 February ae 45. MORP 13 Feb 1845

SNEDECOR, Rev. Parker, at Potosi, 13 July ae 28. Methodist SLOB 7 Aug 1834
        Church South; widow, 2 children.

SNELL, Miss ___, daughter of Maj. Willis W. of Callaway Co., LADB 25 Apr 1846
        hanged herself because of poor health.

SNOW, __ son of Mrs. Snow of Salt Creek, ae 9 or 10, BRUNS 9 Mar 1848
        thrown from a horse and killed.

    Levi, estate in Chariton Co.: Final Settlement by BRUNS 6 Jan 1855
        Lisbon Applegate, Publ. Adm.

    Anna M., wife of R. B. of St. Louis, in NY City MORE 25 Aug &
        while visiting friends, in her 22nd year. 10 Sep 1849
        Funeral at St. Paul's; Presbyterian Cem.

SOMERVILLE, daughters of Dr. John A. and Varilla, St. Louis:
        Ann Eliza L. in Waterloo, Monroe Co. IL MORE 24 Oct 1838
        18 October ae 2m 22d.
        Varrella Richerson, infant. Lynchburgh pc. " 1 Apr 1840
        Mary Thomas, 20 May at home of Wm. H. Jones. SWERE 25 May 1846

SORDERBECK, George, inquest: German, tallow-chandler,
        ae 47, lived at Lowell; had fallen SLMD 26 Jan 1855
        from wagon, died suddenly at home.

SOULARD, children of Benjamin and Rose, St. Louis:
        M. Julia Rose, yesterday, ae 15m 21d. MORE 22 Dec 1840
        Charles Cerre, ae 2y 15d, 27 May. " 29 May 1847
        George Lucien, ae 1y 6m 15d, yesterday. SWERE 7 Aug 1848

SPALDING, sons of Josiah, St. Louis:
        George L., infant, last Monday. MORE 18 Jul 1825
        Frederick, ae 3y 7m, yesterday. " 7 Feb 1840

SPANN, William J., tribute by Sons of Temperance, SPRIG 23 Apr 1849
        Greenfield MO. Wife mentioned.

SPARHAWK, James Goshen, son of Capt. G. W. and M. I., MORE 6 Nov 1845
        ae 2y. Lived 8th betw Green-Washington.
        Presbyterian Cem.

SPAUNHERST, Adamantine Henry, infant of Henry I. and
        Clementine, ae 1y 9d.   MORE 11 Aug 1853

SPEARS, Virginia, at her father's home west of Chouteau's
        Pond, 13 March ae 13.   SLNL 30 Mar 1847

SPEED, John J., at Herculaneum, 7 September.   MOAR 11 Sep 1835

SPENCER, Eliza Ann, only child of Henry and Sophia, #33
        3rd St., 29 August ae 1y 3d.   SWERE 4 Sep 1848

      James, infant of James P., on Saturday last.   MORE 7 Sep 1830

SPRIGG, Genifer at his home in St. Louis 29 May, ae
        about 60. Buried Episcopal Cem.   MORE 30 May 1850

* SPENCER, Lucy, a slave of Dr. M. C. Spencer, age nearly
        100; was divided out in estatesfour times; BRUNS 23 Sep 1848
        could remember Indians in eastern VA.

SPRINGER, George B., only son of G. A., 10th-Carr,
        18 Oct. ae 3y 10m. (also in MORE)   SLDU 20 Oct 1846

SPROULE, Joseph Sr. in Monroe Co. 27 July, ae about 68. JEM 10 Aug 1847

STAGG, children of Edward and Harriet, St. Louis:
        John Daggett, only child, ae 1y 6m 11d.   MORE 13 Oct 1843
        Ferdinand, ae 5y 10½m, on Saturday.   "   13 Feb 1853

      Richard Tenbroeck, eldest son of John and Louisa
      Caroline, yesterday in his 10th year.   MORE 6 Apr 1843

STAILEY, John on October 7 in his 44th year.   NERA 11 Oct 1845

STALLCUP, James in Taney Co. 2 February.   NERA 25 Feb 1846

STANSBURY, Mary Emily, daughter of George L. and
        Lucretia, Saturday last ae 5y 14m.   MORE 17 Oct 1846

STAPLES, James William, infant of John and Lavinia, Wed. BRUNS 28 Oct 1848

STARKWITHER, Charles Noble, son of J. N. and Harriet, of
        cholera infantum, 21 June ae 3m.   MORE 22 Jun 1850

STARNES, children of Nathan and Virginia, St. Louis:
        Virginia, ae 16m, and Charles, ae 6y.   MORE 13 Aug 1849

STEARNS, Timothy Adams, son of J. D. and M. A., in Little
        Osage, Bates Co., 15 Sept. ae 9m 13d. MA pc MORE 25 Sep 1848

STEEL, Samuel C. of Andrew Co. in CA (13? 18?) March of
        bilious fever. Born Jessamine Co. KY, to CA SJA 31 Mar 1850
        a year ago. (see his cousin John Mitchum.)

STEGER, Mary Elizabeth, daughter of J. S. and Ann, ae 5y. MORE 11 May 1849

STEIGERS, Elizabeth K., daughter of Francis J. and Sarah,
        12 January ae 1y 2m.   SWERE 20 Jan 1845

STEINFELD, Julia, only child of John and Maria Louisa, of
        Boonville, 22 August ae 1y 4d.   MODE 6 Sep 1848

STEINS, Catherine wife of Jacob, nee Paus, 10 November
        in her 58th year.   SLMD 12 Nov 1857

STEMMONS, Stephen "aged and esteemed" near Ashley 23 Jan. LADB 5 Feb 1849

STEPHENS, L. R. at Rushville 9 January of pneumonia, ae 25. SLMD 24 Jan 1855

STEPHENSON, Archibald C. and Eliza J., estates in
     Chariton Co.: final settlement, Jesse Brooks. GLWT 5 Oct 1854

     Edward W., son of F. W., 20 December of
          consumption in his 24th year. MORE 24 Dec 1849

STETTINIUS, Adeline Maxwell, wife of Joseph, 27 May of
          cholera ae 23. MORE 28 May 1850

STEVENS, Charlotte, infant of T. B., Saturday last. MORE 28 Jun 1831

     Maria, daughter of Oliver, formerly of Mercer PA, MORE 29 Nov 1838
          24 November ae 2y 2m.

     Martha Olivia daughter of George N. and Martha F., SWERE 3 Dec 1848
          Monday ae 3y 6m.

STEVENS, children of Simeon and Clara (Clarissa), St. Louis:
     Alice Chamberlain, only daughter, 26 November. MORE 27 Nov 1848
     Ella Melissa, only daughter.   " 26 Aug 1847
          (residence, 14th St. south of Market)
     George Henry, ae 3y 9m, 21 April. Lived 5th
          near Market. Presbyterian Cemetery. MORE 22 Apr 1842
          Cincinnati & VT pc
     Charles William, only son, yesterday. Funeral
          from home of George Stevens. MORE 23 Mar 1843
     Edwin Greenleaf, infant, yesterday. 14th St.
          south of Market. MORE 12 Aug 1844

     Simeon, of brain congestion, 12 Jul ae 38. NERA 15 Jul 1849

STEVENSON, John, estate in Chariton Co.: Letters of Adm.
     to Samuel E. Stevenson, 2 June, 1856. BRUNS 28 Feb 1857

     <u>?</u> (possibly Richard) Killed in a fight at
          the Union Hotel. MORE 1 May 1843

STEWART, Margaret, daughter of John and Catherine, 20 July. MORE 21 Jul 1843

     Joshua, estate in St. Clair Co.: letters of adm.
          to Mary Ann Stewart, 13 August. OSIN 9 Jul 1853

     Eliza Gemmill, daughter of Robert (editor of the
          Missouri <u>Courier</u>) Thursday last. PWH 17 Oct 1840

     Thomas, native of Ireland, "a stranger in the
          country," 13 November. SRJ 21 Nov 1840

STIBBS, Elizabeth, consort of Christopher, 6 November, MORP 6 Nov 1845
     in her 68th year.

     Ellen Eliza, infant of John, Thursday morning. MORE 17 May 1839

STILES, Mary Frances, daughter of George and Mary,
          28 June ae 3y 3m. Louisville pc MORE 30 Jun 1845

     Mary Ellen, infant of Simeon and Rebecca. BOLT 8 Jan 1841

STILL, Mrs. ___ in Montgomery Co. 27 May in her 27th year. SLMD 9 Jun 1855

STILLWELL, Mary P., consort of Brison, 9 May in her 24th y. HAJ 17 May 1849
     Eliza Simpson, dau/Brison and Margaret, 14 Dec   " 16 Dec 1852
     ae 7m 2d.

STILLMAN, Malina, daughter of Capt. H. B. and Malina,
        formerly of Peoria, 6 May, ae 14m.   MORE 9 May 1848
      Therese Marguerite, daughter of Capt. Henry B.
        and Melanie, yesterday, ae 10m 18d.   MORE 3 Mar 1852

STINE, Emily, youngest daughter of J. R.; funeral from
        the home of Judge Bowlin.   MORE 22 Oct 1841

      Mary Ann Garret, daughter of Jacob R., 1 September. SWERE 9 Sep 1844

STOCKDALE, James Edwin, son of James and Harriet, 5 Aug. SWERE 9 Aug 1847

STOLTS, Robert, son of Capt. Mathias, 29 September.   MORE 30 Sep 1851

STONE, Caleb S., son of Caleb S. and Ann, in Columbia
        30 May ae 10.   SLMD 5 Jun 1854

      James Madison, son of S. B. and Rebecca, 4 March
        in St. Clair Co. in his 9th year.   SLMD 10 Mar 1855

STORRS, Asahel, ae 32, at New Franklin 3 March.   MIN 24 Mar 1832

STOTLER, Christopher in Cape Girardeau Co. 7 October. NERA 18 Oct 1845

STOUT, Jenny Thompson, daughter of B. F. and Delia,
        ae 3y 5m. Bridgeport pc   MORE 25 Jul 1853

      Julia, daughter of Moses, Friday ae 15m.   COMB 11 Jul 1836

STRAMCKE, William Ferdinand, son of Samuel B. and Anna A.,
        near Lexington 15 Nov. ae 5m.   LEXP 19 Nov 1844

STRACZER, Mary Ann, daughter of Mrs. Mary Conroy, ae
        about 6, Thursday morning.   PWH 12 Mar 1845

STRANGE, Mrs. Mary at her home on Bellefontaine Rd.
        24 May. Buried Bissell Cem.   NERA 25 May 1849

STRATTON, William H. in Bates Co. 23 September.   JEM 13 Oct 1846

STREET, Thomas Clifton, son of Joseph and Eliza, 23 Sept.
        ae 1y 4m 3d. Baltimore pc   MORE 28 Sep 1848

STRIKER, Ellsworth S., at the home of John Smith, on
        Broadway, 27 Dec. Methodist Cemetery. MORE 28 Dec 1839

STRINGFELLOW, daughters of Gen. Benjamin F. and Catherine:
        Mary Waters in Chariton Co. 25 July ae 17m. JEM 10 Aug'47
        Eliza, ae 7m 24d, on 5 September.   " 12 Sep'48

STRODE, Marie Adaline, daughter of William F. and Jane,
        22 December ae 2y 3m 7d.   SWERE 30 Dec 1844

STRONG, H. P. of Ohio in 21st year; brother in Hannibal. HAJ 11 Nov 1847

STROTHER, Emma, daughter of J. W. and M. A., 18 September
        ae 3m 5d. Funeral/home of James Pagaud. MORE 19 Sep 1848

      Mary Eliza, daughter of R.M., of cholera, 25 June. NERA 27 Jun 1849

STROUP, George, formerly of DE, in his 61st year.
        Lived 4th betw Cerre-Gratiot.   MORE 16 Aug 1849

STUART, Ann, consort of Charles W., in Marion, Cole Co.,
        11 May (sic) ae about 25.   JEM 11 May 1847

SUBLETTE, children of Solomon and Frances, St. Louis:
        Solomon Perry, ae 16m 6d.   MORE 28 Apr 1851
        Willie Hugh, ae 1y 4m 20d, on 2 November.   SLMD 3 Nov 1857

SULLIVAN, children of C. D. and Anna J., St. Louis:
        Mary Cornelia, ae 16m 2d, on 4 July.   MORE 6 Jul 1848
        Joseph Daniel, ae 11m 18d; lived 12 N. 6th. "   1 Jun 1849

SUMMERS, Mrs. ___, died in a cholera epidemic in Palmyra. MORE 28 Jun 1833

      John Henry, infant of Berkley S. and Rebecca,   PWH 15 Mar 1849
          8 March.

      George Wright, youngest child of Major G. V., MORE 3 Dec 1846
          at Jefferson Barracks 17 November.

SUMNER, Joseph J., of Florida, at the home of Joseph
        Sumner near Portage des Sioux, 17 Mar. MORE 17 Apr 1834
        "Had determined to visit his parents,
        sisters and brothers in the county,
        with Maj. Hall and his consort."

SUTTON, Francis H., son of Joseph T. and Sarah M.,   MORE 21 Sep 1847
        20 Sept. ae 12y 11m. Lived on
        Franklin betw 12-13.

SWARTWOUT, daughters of Capt. Henry, U. S. Army:
        Helen, at Jefferson Barracks, 3 Aug. ae 2y5m. MORE 9 Aug 1843
        Margaret Elizabeth, ", eldest daughter, 6y2m. "   8 Jan 1844

SWARTS, William Alburtis, son of James H. and Louisa T., MORE 29 Jul 1851
        28 July ae 17m.

SWEARINGEN, William, son of Richard S. and Arabella,   MORE 19 Mar 1847
        183 5th St., 18 March in his 3rd y.

SWITZER, Mary Jane, only child of William N. and Mary MORE 4 Apr 1849
        Jane, ae 10m 10d. Episcopal Cem.

SWITZLER, James Jennings, son of A. G. and Mary Jane, MORE 27 May 1853
        26 May ae 4y 6m. Buried Bellefontaine.

SYLVESTER, John James, only child of John and Mary Louisa, SLMD 11 Dec 1855
        9 Dec. ae 7y 25d; lived 3-Walnut.

SYMMINGTON, children of Capt. John, St. Louis:
        Elizabeth, youngest daughter, ae 10m, at   MORE 30 Jul 1835
        St. Louis Arsenal 19 July.
        Mercer, infant, yesterday at St. Louis   "   12 Sep 1837
        Arsenal. Buried city cemetery.

TAGGART, Mrs. Mahala, daughter of Squire Green, suddenly
        3 January at a dancing party in   SLMD 15 Jan 1856
        Green's Bottom. She had sat down
        to rest, was found dead. (from the
        St. Charles Reveille)

TALBOTT, Louisa P., wife of John S. and daughter of John NERA 18 Apr 1849
        Hall, this morning, ae 22y 2m.

TAMM, Margaret Elizabeth, eldest child of David and MORE 26 Jan 1839
(TATUM?)   Sophie, 24 January.

TANEY, Col. Michael at Potosi 15 January ae 77,
        brother of Chief Justice Taney.   SLNL 22 Jan 1848

TANNER, children of Edward (Edwin) and Ann, St. Louis:
      William Carr Lane, ae 5½m, 4 October.   SWERE 7 Oct 1844
      Montgomery Blair, youngest child, ae 17m 23d,   "   13 Oct 1845
         on 9 October.

    Chauncey, son of James and Harriet, 13 Mar. ae 2y1m. MORE 14 Mar '53

TARGEE, children of Thomas B. and Sarah Ann, St. Louis:
      Isabel, infant, 20 June.   MORP 21 Jun 1845
      Letitia Scott, ae 5y 4m, on 13 October.   SWERE 18 Oct 1847
      Charles, ae 3w 2d, on 12 June.   "   19 Jun 1848
      (above might be in MORE instead of SWERE)
      Clara Stevens, infant, 29 May.   MORE 30 May 1849

TATUM, children of David and Sophie, St. Louis:
      Margaret Elizabeth, oldest child, 3 Aug. ae 4y2m. MOAR 31 Jan 1839
      Alice, ae 3y 6m, on 3 August.   MORE 4 Aug 1853

    Martha, of Jackson Co., ae about 18, burned when a   SLMD 13 Feb 1854
      bedspread on the floor, on which she was
      sleeping, caught fire; a number of girls
      were spending the night at her home, near
      Blue Spring.

TAYLOR, Adaline M., daughter of Thomas and Sarah, 3 March SWERE 6 Mar 1848
      ae 11. Buried Episcopal Cem.

    Anna, daughter of Edward D. 18 July of cholera;   NERA 19 Jul 1849
    Edward Jr., her brother, 17 July in his 6th year.

    Arthur Chouteau, son of George B. and Theresa L.,   SLMD 6 Feb 1855
      of pneumonia, Monday, ae 4m 2d.

    Catherine Jane, daughter of B. F. and Mary Ann,   SLMD 5 Mar 1857
      4 March ae 1y 6m 8d.

    James, son of Isaac and Mary, yesterday, ae ca 4. SWERE 20 Dec 1847
    Kate, infant of Isaac W. and Mary C., Olive St.   MORE 26 Oct 1849

    Elder Jeremiah, in Fabius Twp., Marion Co.,   HAJ 1 Jun 1848
      21 May in his 76th year.

    Lawson, Judge of the Co. Court, in Stoddard Co.   NERA 12 May 1845
      25 April.

    George W., son of Moses, in his 37th year.   MORE 15 Jan 1848

    Children of N. P., St. Louis:
      Sophie Crush in her 9th year; buried North   MORE 4 Apr 1838
        St. Louis Cemetery.
      Julia Wash, ae 4y 8m; mother shown as Matilda. "   13 Apr 1844
        Episcopal Cemetery.
      James Christy, youngest son, 11 October ae 8. SWERE 13 Oct 1845
        (mother shown as Matilda N.)

    Mary Elizabeth, daughter of Thomas, Sunday last.   PWH 12 Aug 1847
    Thomas Anderson, son of Thomas and Sarah,   "   28 Sep 1848
      27 September ae 2y 6m.

TAYLOR, Thomas Woodruff, infant of Robert W., Saturday last. MORE 8 Jan 1839

    Sarah Caroline, infant of William J. and Nancy B.,   STGAZ 4 Dec 1846
        ae 8m 13d, on 29 November.

TESSON, Charles Amede, youngest son of Edward and Lucie,   MORE 24 Aug 1847
        23 August ae 19m.

    Children of Michael Honore, St. Louis:
        Juliette, of croup, on Wednesday last, the
          2nd child lost to the same ailment within   MOG 24 Jul 1818
          a few days.
        Francis ae 6, on 12 December, and Zelie,   MORE 20 Dec 1827
          ae 8, on 16 December.

TEVIS, TIVIS, Susan, infant of S.P., burned when her   BOBS 6 May 1851
        cousin set fire to the prairie.

THARP, Charlotte Mary Amanda, only child of Thomas and   MORP 21 Aug 1845
        Bithema, 20 August ae 1y 8m.

THATCHER, Mary Jane, youngest daughter of J. C. and M.,   SLMD 20 Aug 1853
        in Kirksville 28 July.

THAYER, Mary A., ae 14y 2m, on 23 November.   SJA 29 Nov 1850

THOMAS, __, daughter of Mrs., of cholera in Palmyra.   MORE 28 Jun 1833

    Arthur B., only son of Martin, Tues. ae 1y 14d.   MORE 26 Oct 1837

    Elizabeth, consort of Isaac, in Lebanon OH   MORE 16 Aug 1849
        in her 54th year.

    Henry Allen, only child of John J. and Charlotte,
        ae 6, on 11 October. Funeral from   MORE 12 Aug 1847
        Augustus Brewer home, 63 St. Charles.

    Isaac P.,late Justice of the Peace, Thursday of   MORE 15 Feb 1850
        consumption.

    Children of James S., St. Louis:
        Ariadne, ae 22m 16d, yesterday. (Mother   MORE 14 Oct 1841
          shown as Susan W.)
        Samuel Stevens, ae 19m, on 27 July.   "   29 Jul 1834
        William Edwin 19 Dec. (Susan as mother.)   "   20 Dec 1847

    Marie Antoinette, daughter of F. W. and Mary F.,   MORE 20 Apr 1843
        Myrtle-6th St., ae 1y 3d.

    Margaret Bass, infant of Robert, in Columbia.   MIN 14 Sep 1833

    Samuel, only son of Samuel and Ann, 20 July   SLMD 22 Jul 1856
        ae 1y 9m 24d. NY pc

THOMPSON, Anne eldest daughter of John B. and Anne   NERA 7 Aug 1849
        26 July of consumption, ae 17.

  * Charles Clay, son of R. W. and Lucinda, 26 March   MORE 27 Mar 1848
 *see Eliza, p106/ ae 4y 2m 14d. Maysville KY pc

    Caroline Augusta, only daughter of E. A., ae 1m.   MORE 14 Jun 1842

    Godfrey Pattison, son of W. W., ae 1y 11m, from   MORE 23 Feb 1851
        injuries received in a
        ferryboat explosion.

THOMPSON, Helen Clara, only daughter of F. W., 6th-Myrtle, SLMD 20 Nov 1854
        19 June ae 5y 10m 28d. Christ Ch. Cemetery.

    James A., #80 Myrtle, 10 April in his 31st y. NERA 11 Apr 1845

    Children of John S. and Marion, St. Louis:
        John, ae 1y 11m, 15 July. Lived Morgan MORE 16 Jul 1841
        betw 5-6. Presbyterian Cemetery.
        John, ae 4m, 19 Feb. Presbyterian Cem. "   21 Feb 1846

    Mary Bright, daughter of James R. and Adaline H., MORE 5 Oct 1844
        ae 3m, in Thompsonville NJ 22 September.
        (Parents shown as residents of St. Louis.)

    Merriwether Charles, son of Merriwether and SJA 12 Jul 1850
        Emma C., 9 July ae 21m 21d.

  * Eliza Jane, daughter of R. W. and Lucinda H.,
  * see Charles/ of scarlet fever in her 6th year. MORE 3 Apr 1846
    p 105   Lived 120 Walnut. Catholic Cem.
        Maysville KY pc

    Robert, 9th betw Franklin-Morgan, yesterday in MORE 20 Jul 1844
        (52nd or 32d) y. NY pc

    Stewart, native of Newtown, __mevaddy, Co. Derry, MORE 7 Jun 1850
        ae 36.

    Thomas Edward Dudley, son of Dr. J. B. and E. A., SLMD 17 Mar 1855
        in Bates Co. 17 Feb. ae 1m.

THORBURN, Marshall, son of John, #8 No. Main, MORE 24 Apr 1839
        yesterday ae about 15m.

THORINGTON, Henry, son of John and Emma, 3 March SWERE 9 Mar 1846
        ae 2y 10m.

THORNBURGH, Charles, son of Robert and Julia Ann, SLMD 26 Jun 1854
        24 June ae 2y.

    Thomas E., son of Josiah and Nancy, MORE 12 Jan 1852
        9 January ae 4½y.

    Helen Frances, daughter of William and Fanny, MORE 22 Mar 1853
        ae 23m 5d. Funeral/J. Jones home.

THORNTON, Josephine, youngest daughter of John F. and MORE 6 Aug 1853
        Elizabeth, 5 August.

THORNHILL, Helen Samantha, daughter of the late C. B., SLMD 18 Feb 1856
        at her mother's home 11 February; was
        ill only a few hours.

THROW, Mrs. M., in St. Charles, 13 April. NERA 16 Apr 1845

THURMAN, William Sr., in his 74th year, 10 May of cholera MORE 14 May 1850
        morbus; from Lynchburg VA 3y ago.

THURMOND, Fanny Bell, infant of George W. and Frances Ann, LADB 15 Jul 1850
        13 July ae 9m 2d.

    Thomas, in his 66th year, at his son's home LADB 15 Nov 1847
        9 Nov. From VA in fall of (1831?34?).

TICE, Orestes Augustus, eldest son of John H. and Marion,   SLMD 16 Feb 1854
   Wed. ae 11y 7m 17d. Bellefontaine Cem.

  Peter, father of J. H. of St. Louis in Fulton Co. PA "   11 May 1854
   29 April ae 72.

TIERNAN, Nicholas 26 June in his 42d year. (cholera?)   NERA 27 Jun 1849

TIFFANY, daughters of P. Dexter and Hannah, St. Louis:
   Clara Skinner, ae 11m 11d, 8 April.   MORE 9 Apr 1853
   Mary, ae 9m, 30 Oct. Lived 5th-Olive.   "   31 Oct 1846

TILDEN, Richard Samuel, only son of Richard S. and   MORE or 1 Oct
      Anna E., ae 10m. Lived 8-Chestn. SWERE?   1847
  Richard Swift, only son of Hannah and the late   MORE 23 Apr 1853
    Richard, ae 3y 5m 22d.

TILFORD, Ruth H., consort of Samuel, in her 60th y.   MORE 24 Aug 1849
   Pittsburgh & Philadelphia pc

TILLMAN, Elizabeth Middlesworth, daughter of R. W. and E.   MORE 29 Aug 1853
   27 August ae 1 year less 1 day.
  John H., son of John and Louisa, 7 August   GLWT 14 Aug 1851
   ae 2y 7m 7d.

TILTEN, Henry Clay, son of David and A. C., 28 December   MORE 30 Dec 1844
  ae 7m 5d. Funeral from Boston House.

TIMON, James, 15 March ae 81. Formerly of Baltimore, a   MORE 18 Feb 1850
  resident of St. Louis 33 years.

TISDALE, ___, little son of James D. of Wild Goose Ferry,   LADB 26 Jul 1847
  drowned trying to retrieve a paddle lost
  from a canoe; a slave of Tisdale also
  drowned trying to rescue the child.

  Lewellen, son of D. S. and Mary, in Hannibal,   SLMD 26 May 1855
   11 May ae 9.

TISON, Mary L., daughter of Hypolite and Margaretta,   MORE 21 Feb 1849
   near Manchester 16 February ae 5w.

TITCOMB, William K. ae 28. (cholera epidemic?)   MORE 15 Jul 1849

TITUS, Henry Clay Jeter, youngest son of Lloyd and Mary,   MORE 28 Jul 1851
   26 July ae 15m.

TODD, Benjamin L., at his home in Calumet Twp., Pike Co.   LADB 6 Nov 1848
   23 October; one of its oldest and
   most respected citizens.

  Mary Catherine, youngest daughter of S. A. and B. W., SLMD 25 Mar 1856
   in Weston 1 March ae 1y 9m 20d.

  Children of Roger North, Columbia:
   David, ae 7, last Sunday.
   Matilda Jane, youngest daughter, a few   MIN 12 Jun 1830
   days previously.

TOMLINSON, William, in Randolph Co., 12 December of dropsy   SLMD 29 Dec 1853
   of the heart in his 71st year.
   Formerly of Scott Co. KY.

TOMPKINS, children of William and Mary J., St. Louis:
        Francis, infant, 26 Aug. Lived 11th St.   MORE 27 Aug 1846
        Sally, infant, 14 May.   "   15 May 1848

TOMPSON, Lida, daughter of James, Saturday last at the
        home of Sanders H. Bartlett, ae 4.   LADB 5 Feb 1849

TONCRAY, Emma Virginia, daughter of F. I. and Harriet,
        212 Broadway, 26 August ae 6m 16d.   MORE 27 Aug 1847

TONEY, Victoria Walthall, daughter of Col. George T. and   SPRIG 6 May 1849
        Sarah C., 17 March at their home in
        Lawrence Co. ae (11? 14?)y 2m.

TOOLEY, children of John W. and Mary P., St. Louis (they
                lived on Pine betw 8-9.)
        Oscar on 12 September ae 7m.   SLMD 16 Sep 1854
        Fanny Forbes, suddenly, ae 5, 19 November.
        Laura White, ae 2½, after much suffering,". SLMD 20 Nov 1857
        Both of scarlet fever.

TOWER, Flora, infant of George F. and Julia of St. Louis   SLMD 29 Aug 1857
        in Dubuque 28 Aug. Bellefontaine Cem.

TOWN, Julia Ann, infant of Ephraim, no date.   MORE 8 Jul 1828
    Eliza, dau/Ephraim of St. Louis, in St. Charles   SLOB 1 May 1834
        Monday in her 18th year.

TOWNSEND, children of James B. and Adelaide, St. Louis:
        Adelaide Achsah, ae 9m 5d, 23 January.   MORE 28 Jan 1846
        Florence Mary in Louisville 12 March.   " 19 Mar 1849

        Isadora, infant of Samuel and Margaret,   MORE 18 Dec 1840
        Wednesday 16 Dec. ae 1m 3d.
TOWNSLEY, W. P. C.,of Boonville, 27 December in   SLMD 4 Feb 1856
        San Francisco ae 54.

TRACY, Henry, ae 74, in Norwich CT 21 May; left a large   SWERE 8 Jun 1846
        inheritance to his children, one being
        Alfred of St. Louis.

    Margaret, infant of Charles and Sophia.   MORE 25 Jul 1853

    Mary Ann, daughter of Alfred, yesterday ae 18m.   MORE 6 Oct 1837
        Buried city graveyard.

    William Thomas, son of Edward, yesterday.   MORE 4 Sep 1839

TROWBRIDGE, Daniel Webster, son of Daniel and Martha,   MORE 4 Oct 1841
        6th near Pine, yesterday ae 14m.

TRUE, Jacob, formerly of VT, 14 July of dysentery ae 42.   NERA 15 Jul 1849
    Charles, only son of Jacob and Abbey, 25 June   "   27 Jun "
        ae 4y 8m 20d. VT & NH pc

TUCKER, daughters of Charles L. and Mary W., St. Louis:
        Alice Loveland, ae 3½y, on 20 August.   MORE 22 Aug 1844
        Anna Louisa, age not shown, 12 December.   SLDU 8 Jan 1847

TUFTS, Henry Miller, youngest son of A. and Sarah, on   MORE 23 Aug 1837
        Monday evening last.

TURNER, Ann Eliza, daughter of Henry S. and Julia, ae 2y4m. MORE 13 Jun 1853

Rev. Edward, in Platte City, 28 Sept. ae 80. NERA 18 Oct 1845

Humphrey, infant of Winslow and Emily P., 24 Aug. in Plattsburg ae about 13m. STGAZ 4 Aug 1852

James C., in Greene Co., 2 November ae 42. JEM 16 Nov 1848

Kate Elizabeth, infant of J.B. and M.R., 11 Jan. MORE 13 Jan 1853

Laura, youngest daughter of Howard and Sarah, 27 Sept. ae 2y 7m. SWERE 7 Oct 1844

William, infant of S. A. and Elizabeth, 29 April. SWERE 30 Apr 1849

TURPIN, Champion, estate in Chariton Co.: Letters of Adm. to John Sportsman, 11 June. BRUNS 16 Jun 1855

David William, son of John, formerly of Boston, Tuesday evening ae 4y 4m. MORE 6 Feb 1838

TUTTLE, Charles Freeman, son of David C. and Martha, Wednesday; "nearly 3." NERA 29 Oct 1849

Beverly, infant son of David W., Monday last. MOG 1 Sep 1819

Dudley Cartland, son of B. C. and M. B., 25 Dec. ae ly 10m 6d. MORE 28 Dec 1846

TWICHELL, children of John W. and Frances E., St. Louis:
Alfred Tracy, infant, in Rushville 16 Mar. MORE 28 Mar 1840
John Clifford, ae 2, on Wednesday. Lived on 11th betw Walnut-Clark. " 1 Nov 1843
Eliza Taylor, ae 7m. " 18 Jul 1849
(note: mother of first child not shown)

TWICHEL, Mary, consort of Thomas, 24 September of consumption ae 28. NERA 26 Sep 1845

TWYMAN, __, son of Dr. Lee Twyman of St. Charles, ae about 12, hanged himself last Tuesday. MORE 18 Jan 1845

TYRE, Thomas, estate in Chariton Co.: Letters of Adm. to W. G. Butler, 16 December. GLWT 21 Dec 1854

UNDERHILL, Frank William, son of Edward and Mary, of cholera, ae 6y 2m. NERA 15 Jul 1849

USHER, Samuel, estate in Chariton Co.: Final Settlement by A. Sportsman BRUNS 26 Aug 1854

VALLE, Amedee, eldest son of Amedee and Mary L., ae 4y 2m. MORE 8 Nov 1847

Eliza, consort of C. C. and daughter of Maj. Amos Bruce, at Ste. Genevieve, 21 June ae 17. MORE 25 Jun 1850

VAN CARSTEN, Julia, murdered; her father, Peter, was tried and acquitted. MORE 22 Oct 1848

VAN COURT, Alexander, pastor of Central Presbyterian Church, ae 32. (cholera epidemic) MORE 23 Jul 1849

Benjamin, living at 100 Collins St., 5 January ae 67. MORE 6 Jan 1850

VANDERSLICE, Willie "the interesting mute child"; funeral from father's home, 14th near Carr.   SLMD 26 Sep 1857

VANOVER, Elizabeth, wife of Capt. William; long illness.   JEM 18 Dec 1849

VAN STUDDIFORD, Alexander, son of Dr. W. S. and Margaret, 128 N. 5th, 5 January ae 2y 4m.   SLMD 6 Jan 1857

VAN ZANDT, William, only child of Dr. William, 15 Jan. ae 5. Episcopal Cemetery.   NERA 16 Jan 1846

VENABLE, Thomas, at his home on Locust St. 19 July ae 44.   NERA 25 Jul 1849

VINEYARD, Helen Richmond, youngest daughter of B. W. and Mary M., at Pleasant Ridge, 7 Jan.   SLMD 24 Jan 1855

VIOLETT, John J., only son of Edwin and Harriet, ae 22m 9d. Pittsburgh & Alexandria VA pc   MORE 3 Jul 1851

VIVIAN, Margaret, consort of James. Funeral from home of John Henwood. Died 12 October.   SLMD 13 Oct 1856

VONEYE, ___ infant, in Cooper Co.; her mother, supposedly deranged, cut the child's throat with a razor.   WEM 4 Apr 1839

VON PHUL, Thomas, son of Henry and Rosalie, 25 July ae 6y5m. MORE 26 Jul '48

VOORHIS, Mary Azilia, daughter of R. P. and L. C., 21 April ae 3y.   SWERE 23 Apr 1849

VORIES, Henry, infant of H. M., 29 August.   STGAZ 14 Sep 1853

WADE, Jessie Briscoe, only daughter of William, 6 July ae 7; lived 42 St. Charles.   SLMD 7 Jul 1855

     Children of William and Jane E., St. Louis:
         George Stille, youngest son, 6 May ae 21m.   SLMD 7 May 1855
           Lived 42 St. Charles. Bellefontaine Cem.
         Willie, youngest son, at Jacksonville IL.   " 18 Aug '57
           Lived 32 St. Charles.

     Note: Jessie Ann, wife of William, died in 1849.   MORE 4 Jul '49

WAGNER, Lavinia, wife of Hugh K., 12 July of cholera.   NERA 14 Jul 1849
     (MORE 13 July shows her as Virginia, gives home as Stoddard near Hickory.)

WAHRENDORFF, children of Charles, St. Louis:
         Augustus Joseph, infant, Sunday last ae 2. MORE 27 Jul 1826
         Frederica Louisa, infant, Sunday last.   " 24 May 1831

WAINEY, Charlotte Anna, only daughter of Charles D. and Ellen, 12 May ae 2y 4m.   SLMD 14 May 1857

WAINWRIGHT, John, ae 34y 1m 12d. (cholera epidemic?)   MORE 15 Jul 1849

WALKER, Betsy, daughter of John K., Sunday last.   MORE 8 Jan 1833

     Emma Jane, daughter of Reuben and Elizabeth, ae 13m 1d. Coydon IN pc   MORE 11 Oct 1851

     Col. John, at Sibley, 8 March.   NERA 2 Apr 1845

     Sarah, daughter of Lieut B., USA, 14 October at Jefferson Barracks, ae 2y.   MORE 20 Oct 1829

WALLACE, Mary Albina, wife of Edward, 23 Jan. in 24th y.　　SLMD 24 Jan 1854

　　　William, at the home of his son Dr. H. B. in
　　　　　　　Marshall, 10 January of congestive　　　MORE 2 Feb 1850
　　　　　　　fever, in his 63rd y.

WALSH, Patrick, at Carondelet, 27 Feb. in his 68th year.　　MORE 28 Feb 1850

　　　Children of Patrick, St. Louis:
　　　　　Julia, ae 7, on 5 March. Funeral from father's
　　　　　　　home on Olive St. Catholic Cem.　　　MORE 7 Mar 1837
　　　　　John, infant of Patrick, 3 days after being　　MORE 1 Dec 1823
　　　　　　　accidentally shot by his brother.
**　　　　Peter A., son of Patrick, ae 35.　　　　"　　4 Sep 1849

WALTER, Margaret Cornelia, daughter of James and Martha C.　COMB 18 Feb 1847
**　　　　　　　(no other data given).

WALSH, William, infant of Joseph W., yesterday ae 1y.　　MORE 13 Nov 1839
　　　　Lived Pine St. betw Main-2nd.

WALTMAN, Martha, daughter of A. C. and Lucretia, in　　CANP 27 Apr 1849
　　　　LaGrange 1 April ae 1y 7d.

WALTON, Judge Henry at his home on St. Charles Rock Rd.　MORE 19 Apr 1850
　　　　18 April ae 63.

　　　Lewis, ae 4, eldest son of Samuel B. and Elizabeth,　MORE 8 Aug 1844
　　　　　at their home near Owens' Station 6 Aug.

WANTON, William R., formerly of Louisville, resident of　NERA 6 Sep 1849
　　　　St. Louis 3 years, on 5 September.

WARD, Amy Elizabeth, youngest child of Capt. James and　SLMD 27 Sep 1854
　　　　Ann, 6th-O'Fallon, 23 Sept. ae 2y 5d.

　　　Mrs. Mary A., nee Millis, 2 September ae 29y 10m.　SJA 6 Sep 1850
　　　　　Born Saratoga Co. NY, to Mishawaka IN 1830.
　　　　　Married 1837 (husband from South Bend). To
　　　　　St. Joe 1850. Presbyterian, but had been
　　　　　Methodist. Left children, including son
　　　　　born 15 August. Died of chronic diarrhoea.

　　　William, a veteran of the Revolution, at the home of
　　　　　James Moore in Femme Osage, 16 August.　MORE 9 Sep 1837
　　　　　Emigrated from Ireland at ae 18, died in his
　　　　　82d year. Sheriff and J.P. in PA.

WARDS, Daniel F., originally from VA, late of St. Clair　MORE 20 Jun 1840
　　　　Co. IL, ae 26. (hospital list)

WARE, Adelaide Melinda, youngest daughter of Lorenzo D.　MORE 7 Aug 1837
　　　　and Melinda J., 6 August ae 13m.

WARNE, Sarah Louisa, infant of Thomas and Pamela J.,　MORE 8 Apr 1844
　　　　yesterday ae 7m.

WARNER, Minerva F., at the home of her son F. F. in　MORE 29 Jan 1850
　　　　Weston, ae 45. Presbyterian.

WARREN, Mrs. Betsey, consort of Richard S. of Ralls Co.,　HAJ 18 Mar 1847
　　　　6 March in her 42d year. Left husband,
　　　　several children.

WARREN, Gerard Archer, youngest son of Edward and Mary D.,   SWERE 14 May 1849
          11 May ae 4y 8m 13d. Richmond & Petersburg pc

WASH, Julia, daughter of Robert and Eliza, 17 December   MORE 27 Dec 1847
          ae 2y 6m.

WASHBURN, Hines in Pike Co. 13 April.   NERA 20 May 1845

WASHINGTON, Rosalie, daughter of Dr. James, 20 June   NERA 21 Jun 1849
          ae about 3.
          Augustus B., son of Dr. James and Mary, 4 Dec.   SLMD 7 Dec 1853

WATERS, George Washington, only son of Freeman and Cordelia,
          6 April in Jefferson Co. of scarlet fever,   MORE 10 Apr 1848
          ae 4y 8m.

          Children of James L. and Mary, St. Louis:
          Bertie, daughter, 23 January ae 11m.   MORE 24 Jan 1851
          Rosanna, ae 2m 15d, on 16 July.   SLMD 16 Jul 1856

          Stephen, formerly of Baltimore, in his 74th year.   MORP 19 Aug 1845
          Lived on 7th St.; in St. Louis 9 years.

          Dr. Thomas, near Keytesville, 4 April ae about 36.   LADB 18 Apr 1846
          Formerly of Bowling Green. Warrenton VA &
          Washington DC pc

WATHEN, Maria Jane, 3rd daughter of J. R., 17 March in   MORE 1 Apr 1851
          Cape Girardeau.

WATSON, Alexander, a veteran of the Revolution, in   JEM 27 Oct 1846
          Benton Co. 16 August ae 78.

          Edward Jarvis, infant of Maj. Benjamin, 27 June   MORE 5 Jul 1827
          at Cantonment Adams, ae 9m.

          Feltman, at the home of his uncle R. D. Watson, of   SLMD 9 Dec 1853
          St. Louis Co., ae 28. Lived Orange betw
          13th-14th. Buried St. Vincent's.

          Henry Howard, infant of A. D. and Martha, Friday.   MORE 3 Jan 1839

          Children of John S. and Mary R., St. Louis:
          Eliza Reynolds, ae 13m. Lived Walnut betw 5-6. MORE 20 Jul 1844
          Gertrude, ae 8m, on 23 August. Lived Christy   "   25 Aug 1847
          near 18th. Buried Episcopal Cem.

          Isabella, youngest daughter of W. and Sarah,   SLMD 26 Jul 1854
          23 July ae 5w 3d. Mt. Vernon IL pc

          Ralph, only son of Gen. Ralph and Julie, 2 May   LEXA 9 May 1848
          ae 3y 6m.

          Samuel, a veteran of the Revolution, at his home   MOSN 17 Feb 1838
          near Louisiana MO, ae 81.

WATTS, children of Benjamin and Eveline, Boonslick area:
          Armide, 4 November. (shown as grand-   JEM 17 Nov 1846
          daughter of Hampton Boon)
          Sarah Louisa, infant, 17 September.   BOLT 21 Sep 1844

          Elizabeth, daughter of Col. Henry, formerly of   BGRAD 20 Sep 1845
          Lincoln Co., 18 September in 17th y.

WATTS, Elizabeth, youngest daughter of the Rev. Henry, at the home of Richard Poston in St. Francois Co. 26 May, ae 15m.   MORE 28 May 1851

Samuel Boyer, ae 1y 2m 17d, on 2 February.   MORE 10 Feb 1829

WEAR, children of Pleasant and Tryphena of Cooper Co., late of Sevier Co. TN:
Helen M., ae 6y 4m, 31 March.
Margaret, ae 4y, on 4 April.   WEM 11 Apr 1839

WEBER, children of Mahlon and Ellen M., St. Louis:
Claudius Mahlon, ae 4y 9m 7d, 10 January.   MORE 13 Jan 1845
Philadelphia pc
Farmer Emanuel, ae 3y 20d, on 6 April.   "   8 Apr "

WEBSTER, Horace Bourne, son of Benjamin and Rhoda, 5 Oct. ae 11m 26d. Boston pc   MORE 8 Oct 1851

WELCH, Lemuel A., an attorney; tribute by Lincoln Co. Bar. "Untimely death."   LADB 17 May 1847

Lewis G., son of William H. and Elizabeth W., of VA, 1 April in Boonville ae 2y 2m 3d.   WEM 4 Apr 1839

WELLING, children of Charles and Elizabeth, Jackson:
Joseph F. ae 4½ on 22 November.
Ellen G. ae 2 on 24 November.   CGWE 1 Dec 1848

WELLS, children of Claiborne (Clayborn), Marion Co.:
John Thomas, ae 3, on 14 February.   PWH 22 Feb 1840
Claiborne S., ae 2, on Friday last.   "   27 Jul 1848

Hyman G., son of the late Edward of Hartford CT, 17 Nov. in Franklin Co. ae 8.   MORE 21 Nov 1845

John, son of Richard of St. Louis Co., 18 October in CA ae 22.   MORE 3 Jan 1850

Samuel Charles, son of Samuel and Caroline, 27 July ae 7. Philadelphia pc   MORE 28 Jul 1853

Solomon, at his home in Gravois, 15 Sept. ae 58.   NERA 28 Sep 1849

WENDOVER, Joseph Reed, son of J. R. and Harriet, 6-Carr, ae 5m 6d.   MORE 15 Jul 1846

WENDT, Auguste in Cape Girardeau Co. 3 June, ae ca 40.   SLMD 23 Jun 1854

WEST, John P., Broadway near Chambers, in his 33rd year.   MORE 12 Jul 1849
Josephine, daughter of John P. and Harriet, ae 10m. Baltimore pc   SWERE 7 Aug 1848

Temple, estate in Barry Co.: Letters of Adm. to Edwin Pyle, 5 October.   MOAR 1 Nov 1838

Children of Thomas, St. Louis:
Amanda Ann, Sunday last.   MORE 2 Jul 1833
Louise Marion, ae about 6y.   "   15 May 1832

WESTON, sons of David, St. Louis:
Franklin, only child, Sat. ae 21m; 4th-Green.   MORE 15 Nov 1841
Frank, only son, 24 Dec. ae 2y 8m. (mother shown as Phoebe A.).   " 27 Dec 1844

WESTON, Nelson of Parkville, Platte Co., 22 April at   LADB 7 May 1851
          Samuel Shaw's boarding house, in his 39th y.
          St. Louis pc

WETMORE, Charles Leonard, infant of Thaddeus and Caroline,   MORE 3 Jan 1852 ·
          1 January ae 10m.

      Leonidas, aboard the <u>Highland Mary</u>, 18 Nov. ae 33.   "   21 Nov 1849

WETZEL, Philip, at the home of his son John C., of the   SPRIG 26 May 1849
          Greenfield vicinity; tribute by
          Washington Lodge #87 (Masonic).

WHERRY, Mrs. ___ wife of Mackey, last Saturday.   MORE 8 Aug 1825

      George P., son of Joseph A., Elm St. betw 5-6,   MORE 15 Dec 1841
          yesterday ae 3y 5m.

WHIPPLE, Samuel, family of, in Oregon, Holt Co. MO:
          3 children burned when their home caught
          fire, one child survived. Names not   SJA 20 Dec 1850
          given; oldest child was 12.

WHITAKER, Mrs. Jane ae 56. (cholera epidemic?)   MORE 21 Aug 1849

WHITCOMB, Luke, formerly of Townsend VT, 21 June.   MORE 22 Jun 1850

WHITE, children of E. C. and Euphemia, St. Louis:
          Julia Chauvin, ae 5y 7m 22d, yesterday.   SWERE 20 Mar 1848
          Edward, only son, 30 March ae 3y 9m 24d.   "   3 Apr "
          Lived #69 5th St. Catholic Cemetery.

     Clara B., daughter of Robert and Isabella, 9 March   MORE 16 Mar 1853
          ae 3y 10m 2d. Wheeling pc

     Children of Thomas J., St. Louis:
          John Lilbourn, ae 4, on 20 January.   MORE 28 Jan 1836
          Octavia, of scarlet fever, at the Univ.   "   1 Apr 1843
          of VA 5 March.

     Laura, consort of Jerome, 24 February in   SLMD 10 Mar 1855
          St. Charles Co. ae 21.

WHITEHEAD, Anna Eliza, daughter of James R. and Jane G.,   STGAZ 27 Jul 1853
          19 July ae 1y 29d.

      Martha Ann, oldest daughter of James W.,   "   21 Dec 1853
          24 November ae 15y 10m 5d.

WHITEHILL, children of John, St. Louis:
          John D., infant, Monday morning.   MORE 16 May 1838
          Laura M., infant, Sunday last.   "   28 Jun 1831
          Ellen Sophia (mother shown as Laura)   "   26 Jul 1847
          25 July ae 1y6m; lived 156 N. 4th.

WHITELAW, Don Carlos, 2nd son of James H., 146 S. 5th,   SLMD 1 Jun 1854
          31 May of typhoid ae 6y 6m 25d.
          Buried Wesleyan.

WHITESIDE, Adam J., "an old citizen," 27 July near the   MOSN 4 Aug 1838
          mouth of the Missouri River.

WHITING, Ellen Maria Nickerson, ae 9y 11m 20d, Monday last;   WARV 3 Mar 1849
      youngest daughter of Marcus and Eunice N.

WHITMER, Mary, at Richmond, 16 February ae 79.   SLMD 24 Feb 1855

WHITMORE, Bulkley, only son of Noah H. and Mary, ae   illeg. MORE 14 Aug 1844
          Middleton CT & VA Free Press pc

WILCOX, __, daughter of Henry, of cholera in Palmyra.   MORE 28 Jun 1833 .

          Zoe, youngest daughter of J. B. and Henrietta,   SLMD 7 Aug 1857
          6 Aug. of whooping cough ae 6m 30d (sic).

WILES, Benjamin F., son of Benjamin F. and Mary Ann,   MORE 10 Sep 1847
          10th betw Carr-Biddle, 9 Sept. ae 1y 2m.

WILGUS, James, of St. Louis Co., in passage from   MOSN 2 Jun 1838
          Cincinnati to his home, ae 45.

WILKESON, Eugenia, only daughter of J. J. decd, 10 July   NERA 15 Jul 1849
          of cholera in her 15th year.

WILKIE, daughters of Auguste and Dorothe A., Cole Co.:
          Augustina, infant, 2 January.   JEFRE 6 Jan 1844
          Rosetta, ae about 3, 5 January.

WILKERSON, Lucy Ann, only child of Edward, ae 11m 18d.   MORE 21 Jul 1851

          William W., son of Elizabeth, 15 February   MORE 16 Feb 1853
          ae 4y 6m 6d.

WILLI, children of Samuel, St. Louis:
          James T., infant, yesterday morning.   MORE 8 Sep 1829
          Eleanor, ae 18m, at the home of Eli Musick,
                   Gravois settlement.   SCOMB 19 Aug 1835

WILLIAMS, Aquilla, in Warren Co., 30 August.   NERA 23 Sep 1845

          Charles, near Clarksville, 18 July of consumption
                   ae about 75; left a large family.   LADB 26 Jul 1847

          Henrietta Isabella, only daughter of F. A. and   MORE 29 Jun 1847
                   Cornelia, 21 June in New Orleans ae 23m.

          John Thomas, infant of John H. and Emily A.,   BORE 20 Aug 1844
                   ae 16m.

          Sarah W., daughter of Francis E. and Martha   BOLT 22 Oct 1842
                   Ann, 14 October in her 5th year.

          Thomas, youngest son of Dr. Charles and Mary
                   Bell, at the home of his uncle Wm. J.   MORE 19 Aug 1845
                   Ross in Tuscumbia AL 25 July ae 21m 16d.

          Mary Matilda, daughter of Walter, 9 January   MORE 15 Jan 1833
                   in St. Louis Co.

          Amy Ann, daughter of Willis L. and Sarah M.,   SWERE 13 Dec 1847
                   10 December ae 5y 10m.

WILLIAMSON, ___, returning home from Jefferson Barracks
                   night before last, shot through the   MORE 9 Dec 1842
                   mouth; two soldiers and a civilian in
                   the attack. Not dead but "lingering."

          Mrs. Sarah, ae about 80, Tuesday; funeral from   SLMD 6 Sep 1855
                   home of son-in-law John F. Detzold.

WILLIAMSON, Victoria, daughter of William and Mary, at
          Jefferson Barracks 16 Oct. ae 9y 2m 5d.   MORE 13 Oct 1848

WILLIS, Ezekiel Price, only child of Ezekiel P. and
          Eleanor, 22 May ae 15m 9d.   MORE 25 May 1841

WILLOCK, David, son of Gen. David, Saturday night of
          typhoid, ae about 9.   PWH 14 Oct 1847

WILLIBY, WILLEBY, John, estate in Chariton Co.: Final
(WILLOUGHBY?)   Settlement by L. Applegate, P.A.   BRUNS 1 Sep 1855

WILLS, William H., son of Benjamin F. and Mary Ann, 10th- MORE 23 Apr 1850
          Carr, 22 April of congestive fever ae 10.

WILMINGTON, William, son of Henry and Emma, Saturday
          last ae 8.   MORP 4 Mar 1845

WILMOT, Edward Selwyn, youngest child of N. N. and Ursula, MORE 25 Jun 1850
          24 June ae 11m. Boston & Lowell pc

WILSON, ___, son of Dr. A., ae 5, drowned near Sarcoxie,
          Jasper Co., while trying to cross Centre   MORE 1 Apr 1844
          Creek on a log.

        Francis Richard, son of George W. and Mary Louisa, SLMD 12 Jun 1854
          2 June ae 4.   /LaCompt/

        J. Frank, only son of Wesley and Ann, near Paris,   SLMD 12 Dec 1854
          Monroe Co., Thursday last in his 7th y.

        James, youngest son of Mark, 22 October ae 9m 18d. MORE 24 Oct 1838

        Margaret, daughter of Dr. Andrew of St. Charles,   SCMO 8 Jul 1820
          ae 7y 3m 8d.

        Margaret B., daughter of Ephraim, ae about 10.   PWH 15 Mar 1849

        Susan, only surviving daughter of Elder Alfred,   SLMD 20 Aug 1853
          of Paris, 12 August in her 17th year.

        Theodore H., son of John H. and Margaret, killed   MORE 22 Dec 1841
          by the kick of a horse Saturday last
          in his 7th year.

        William Henry, infant of William H. and Sarah   MORE 11 Feb 1842
          Marie, Tuesday ae 16d.

WIMER, children of George A. and Elizabeth, St. Louis:
          Catherine Elizabeth 13 May ae 13y;   MORE 14 May 1853
          funeral St. Francis Xavier.
        Samuel Franklin, ae 14m, 22 July.   "   23 Jul 1851

        Isaac, brother of John, funeral notice; buried   NERA 4 Dec 1849
          Presbyterian Cemetery.

WINCHESTER, Texanna P., daughter of Maj. P. H. and Julia,   MODE 5 Jan 1848
          at Carlinville IL 27 Nov. ae 2y 10m 22d.

WINFREY, William Nicholas, son of Isaac and Kitty, in   SLMD 26 May 1855
          Boone Co. 13 May ae 9.

        Samuel in Boone Co. 14 April.   NERA 25 Apr 1845

WINTER, children of Samuel and Mary Jane, St. Louis:
        Virginia Elizabeth, only daughter,
           ae 9m 10d, yesterday. Lived 5 S. 4th.   MORE 18 Sep 1840
        Laura Josephine, ae 14m, 16 October.   "   18 Oct 1842

WINTERS, ___ son of James drowned in a well in
        Stringtown, Sullivan Co.   STGAZ 13 Jul 1853

WINWRIGHT, Margaret Josephine, daughter of John and Hannah, MORE 16 Nov 1847
        15 November ae 22m 15d.
      Thomas Jefferson, son of John and Hannah, 14 June. " 16 Jun 1849

WISDOM, B., at his home near Huntsville of congestive   SLMD 29 Aug 1853
        fever, ae about 50.

WISHART, Dr. James ae 62; buried Wesleyan Cemetery.   MORE 8 Jul 1849

WITHERS, John Richard, son of Milton and Julia Ann,   MODE 27 Jun 1848
        12 June ae 11y 2m.

     Charles Berrian, only child of W. P. and Mary   "   17 Feb 1847
        Eliza, at Bloomington IL 22 Jan. ae 2y1m6d.

WITT, sons of David H., Howard Co.:
        ____, ae not given, crushed last Thursday when MODE 10/8
         a wagon overturned.   Nov 1847
        Samuel, ae 2, Thursday last of scarlet fever. " 13 Jun 1848

WOERNER, Adolf, son of J. Gabriel and Emilie, 13 July SLMD 14 Jul 1854
        ae 7m 9d.

WOLFE, Ada, only child of Col. William and Margaret J.,
        late of Weston, 12 December of scarlet fever MORE 16 Dec 1845
        ae 23m 14d.

WOOD, Caleb, judge of the Monroe Co. Court, 29 March.   NERA 9 Apr 1845

    Elizabeth, in her 14th year, at the home of her   JEM 26 Sep 1848
        uncle Judge P. H. McBride, 23 September.

    Ellen, wife of W. D., late of Pittsburgh, at the NERA 16 May 1849
        home of Miss Audrain on 4th St.

    Mrs. James, in Andrew Co., 1 November ae about 40. JEM 26 Nov 1848

    James Hampton, son of Capt. Ephraim and Caroline, MORE 23 Jun 1853
        22 June ae 3y 6m.

    Martha Jane, daughter of G. F. and Martha Jane,   MORE 13 Feb 1853
        yesterday ae 3y 7m 26d.

    John B., estate in Daviess Co.: Letters of Adm.   MOAR 20 Aug 1838
        to Andrew McHaney, 5 June.

    Laura H., daughter of Robert L. and Georgiana,   SJA 21 Jun 1850
        18 June ae 8m.

    Samuel Thomas, son of Thomas decd., yesterday
        ae 8m 4d.   SWERE 29 Nov 1847

    Children of William M. and Theresa, St. Louis:
        Ann Sylvania, ae 10m 12d, on 26 July.   MORE 28 Jul 1841
        Alvarez, ae 10m 10d, 14 August.   "   14 Aug 1844
        George, ae 3y 6m.   SLMD 18 May 1854

WOODRUFF, Mary H., wife of James E., 6 July; age illeg.   NERA 6 Jul 1849
        Funeral from Christ Church.

WOODS, Ann Eliza, daughter of John C., 8 January in   SLMD 17 Jan 1855
        Glasgow ae 5y 2m 3d.

    Elizabeth Alice, wife of William Shepard, 13 July.   NERA 14 Jul 1849
    and Esther Alice, their infant, 19 July.   "   24 "

    Children of James and Lucretia, Howard Co.:
        Julia, ae 10y 7m, on 12 January.   SLMD 31 Jan 1855
        William, ae 3y 3m, 21 January.
        James Kavanau, ae 10m, 26 January.

    Jymes M., eldest son of Christopher I. and Rebecca   BRUNS 3 Mar 1849
        in Howard Co. 24 March ae 9y 11m 20d.

    Mary Louise, daughter of Joseph L., Monday last   MORE 23 Aug 1833
        ae 1y 4m 16d.

WOODWARD, David K., at the home of his brother E. K.,   MORE 18 Aug 1849
        ae 24. (cholera epidemic?)

    Jane T., daughter of H. M. and L. T.,   SLMD 14 Oct 1857
        13 October ae 10m 11d.

    Theophile, of St. Louis, at Hannibal 4 August   NERA 10 Aug 1849
        in his 25th year.

WOOLDRIDGE, Mary P., consort of John P. and daughter of
        P. D. Brooks of Saline Co., in   JEM 14 Sep 1847
        Howard Co. 30 August ae 22.

WOOLFOLK, Martha Margaretta Ann, only child of Maj.Richard,   MORE 24 Sep 1844
        in Scott Co. 29 August.

    Charley, only child of Charles and Sue, in   SLMD 28 Dec 1854
        Weston 11 December at the home of
        T. P. Abell, ae 4m 19d.

    Montrose Pallen, youngest son of Z. T. and   NERA 26 Jul 1849
        Anna, 25 July.

WORSHAM, Mary Virginia, only daughter of Henry M. and   SLMD 31 Dec 1856
        Mary, 29 December ae 1m 20d. Lived at
        198 Morgan. Buried Bellefontaine.

WRIGHT, Edward Beebe, son of William F., 4 January; lived   SLMD 5 Jan 1855
        Olive-11th. Ae 10m. Buried Bellefontaine.

    Elizabeth, consort of James, late of KY, in   HAG 19 Aug 1847
        Hannibal Saturday last.

    I., of Taney Co., 2 July 20 miles east of   MORE 7 Oct 1850
        Fort Laramie, ae 18m.

    Children of Leland and Catherine Ann, Boonslick area:
        Eva Frances, ae not given, 24 February. BOLT 1 Mar 1845
        Ada Ann, ae nearly 23m, Wednesday last. MODE 10/12 Aug'46

    Martha Elizabeth, daughter of Edward and Eliza,   MORE 3 Nov 1842
        2 November ae 5m. Troy NY pc

WRIGHT, Lodawick, only son of Hon. Foster P. and Nancy, of Benton Co., ae 15m.   JEFRE 14 Dec 1839

     Nancy, of Taney Co., at the crossing of the South Platte 22 June, ae 8.   MORE 7 Oct 1850

     Rosa, youngest daughter of Richard, formerly of Washington DC, 27 Oct. in her 5th year.   MORE 28 Oct 1840

     Sarah E., consort of John A., at her home in Peno Twp. 30 October.   LADB 29 Nov 1847

     Tiery Joseph, son of James and Louisa, 24 December ae 1y 7m 14d. Funeral/Cathedral.   SLMD 25 Dec 1857

XAUPI, children of Edward and Frances A., St. Louis:
     Joseph Wright, ae 5m, 17 August.   MORE 18 Aug 1843
     Frances A., ae 1y 10m, 18 August.   " 19 "

YANCY, Elizabeth, daughter of C. H., in Greene Co. ae 2.   JEM 26 Oct 1848

     Mary Louisa Lucy Phebe, daughter of J. R. and Mary, at Orleans, Polk Co., 20 January ae 2y 6m.   WEM 7 Feb 1839

YANTIS, Priscilla, relict of Col. John, in Lafayette Co. 1 September.   JEM 28 Sep 1847

YEATMAN, children of James and Angelica, St. Louis:
     Jane Bell, Saturday. Nashville & Baltimore pc   MORE 18 Aug 1845
     (shown as youngest daughter, no age)
     Peyton Thompson, ae 16m, 26 June.   " 30 Jun 1848

YOSTI, Mary Louise, daughter of Louis, 30 Nov. in 13th y.   MORE 1 Dec 1845

YOUNG, David M., of cholera, 28 May in his (34? 35?th) year. Lived Washington betw 2nd-3rd.   MORE 29 May 1850

     J. I. W., of Carroll Co., ae 11, apparently on the western trail. Date not shown.   MORE 7 Oct 1850

     John Page, son of Rev. John F., in Ralls Co. 11 March ae 4y 5m.   PWH 23 Mar 1844

     Sarah Cassandra, daughter of James. C., ae 6m, on 3 October.   PWH 7 Oct 1843

     Dr. Thomas L. in Savannah 20 Dec. in his 36th y. Graduate of St. Louis U. Medical School, had been demonstrator of anatomy there.   SJA 27 Dec 1850

     William, son of John, ae 2y 5m. Lived on Elm bet Main-2nd.   MORE 20 May 1848

ZIMMERER, Ignatz, a little German boy, fell from the Clermont and drowned.   MORE 23 Mar 1849

✝

ADDENDA FOLLOWS.

These records were taken from the St. Louis Missouri Democrat (SLMD), which we did not find until typing had started on the book. As a result, names from A through G for this newspaper, through the period 1854-1857, are found in this addenda. The rest are in the body of the book. Since all are from the same newspaper, only the date is shown.

	SLMD
ADAMS, Mrs. Ann, native of Belfast, 12 October of dropsy ae 31. NY pc	12 Oct 1857
ALEXANDER, Cynthia May, daughter of B. W. and Octavia C., 28 September ae 1y 5m 8d.	29 Sep 1857
ALLEN, Albert, son of T. R., 23 July at Allenton, of typhoid, ae 12y 2m. Buried Wesleyan Cem., St. Louis.	24 Jul 1854
William Henry, son of John and Julia, Gratiot St. betw 9-10, 20 December ae 3m 3w.	21 Dec 1857
AMISS, Marietta, of typhoid, ae 8.	8 Nov 1855
AMOS, Mary, widow of Charles, 18 October in her 66th year. Funeral from home of son-in-law L. Thirwell.	19 Oct 1857
ANDERSON, Capt. John, at the County Farm in Callaway Co., 3 March ae 80.	24 Mar 1855
APPERSON, Miss Mary E. 12 February ae about 14. (Greene Co.?)	3 Mar 1855
ASBURY, Horace, of Johnson Co., froze to death near Rose Hill 4 November - cause "alcohol." (from the Warrensburg Standard)	12 Nov 1856
BALLANCE, James in Weston 6 May, ae about 33; short illness.	25 May 1854
BARNES, Algernon Sydney, son of Dr. A. F. and Mary, 27 August ae 2.	29 Aug 1854
Isaac, in Hannibal, 10 May.	26 May 1855
BARNETT, Thomas in Savannah MO 15 March, ae about 21.	29 Nar 1854
BARNS, Martha, wife of Thomas A. and daughter of the Rev. James Barns (sic) in Randolph Co. 17 December.	17 Jan 1855
BAUER, George, a former engineer on the Polar Star, shot in Jefferson Co. Had spent holidays with friends; a group came, called him out, shot him.	12 Jan 1855
BAUGHER, Ann C., wife of F. A. and daughter of Jacob Baugher (sic) of VA, in Savannah 26 Nov. ae 29y 6m.	12 Dec 1854
BEDFORD, Mary, wife of William, 10 September of consumption in her 44th y. NY City and Galena IL pc	12 Sep 1857
BELT, Fanny Woods, youngest daughter of T. W. and Maria, of Weston, 12 January ae 1y.	31 Jan 1855
Thompson W. in Weston 22 January in his 35th year.	8 Feb "
BENSON, Sallie, eldest daughter of Jesse and Maria, 4 June of cholera ae 6y 4m 15d.	7 Jun 1854
BERGIN, Marcellis, youngest son of C. S. and Mary, 15 March ae 2y 11m. Louisville & NY pc	17 Mar 1857

BISCHOFF, Francis Xavier, ae 17m, 6 July.   8 Jul 1854

BISSELL, Mary Morrison, daughter of Capt. Lewis and Mary J.,   28 Jul 1856
   27 August in her 5th year. Bellefontaine Cem.

BLACH, Albert, a merchant, at his home in Ste. Genevieve   1 Feb 1856
   10 January ae 49.

BLAIR, James, son of Edward and Marion, 30 July ae 6m 21d.   2 Jul 1855

BLAKEY, Ellen W., youngest daughter of John, in Boonville 13 May. 9 Jun 1855

   Lucinda Frances, consort of Y. C., 24 November in   8 Dec 1857
    Cole Camp ae 34y 2m 19d.

BLAKSLEY, Ida, youngest daughter of Henry and Mary Elizabeth,   10 Apr 1855
   47 Walnut, ae 21m. Bellefontaine Cem.

BLATCHFORD, Rev. John at the home of his son-in-law Morris   10 Apr 1855
   Collins, 144 S. 5th. Resident of
   Quincy (MO? IL?); buried there. In 56th y.

BLOW, Webster, 2nd son of William T. and Julia, 5 November.   6 Nov 1857
   Buried Bellefontaine.

BONNER, Cordelia, wife of Samuel, 7th St. betw Walnut-Elm,   20 Feb 1855
   18 February ae 24.

BOUCHARD, Florence, wife of Stephen of St. Louis, at the home   28 Jul 1854
   of S. D. Clairoux in Detroit 22 July ae 39.

BOURGOYNE, John, suddenly, 14 January at Parkville. A Mason.   24 Jan 1855

BOWMAN, Lucy Ann, wife of Alfred and daughter of John R.   21 Jun 1854
   Craghead, 3 June in Callaway Co.
   ae about 26.

BOYD, Sarah Elizabeth, daughter of Dr. E. H. and Mary S., at   24 Mar 1855
  (Eliza?) the home of John S. Waddill in
   Springfield MO 6 March ae 10m 2d.

BRADFORD, Mary Frances, daughter of (H.E. or H. F.) 9 May   11 May 1854
   in her 6th year.

BRAMBLE, children of H. L. and C. E., St. Louis:
   William Henry ae 10y 3m 11d, of brain
    congestion, 18 June.   20 Jun 1854
   Emma Cora, ae 20m, of consumption, 16 Dec.   17 Dec 1857
    Lived at 189 Morgan.

BRANDFORD, Virginia, daughter of L. and E. C., 13 Aug. ae 1y 11m.15 Aug 1854

BRASHEARS, Miss Sarena in Greene Co. 8 February.   3 Mar 1855

BRONAUGH, Cary, asst. engineer on the Iron Mountain RR,   24 Nov 1853
   recently on the Black River in Reynolds Co.

BUCK, George D., son of Charles and Caroline, Ashley-Collins,   4 Jul 1854
   ae 6m 2d.

BURGESS, Henry Taylor, son of John Z. and Sarah Ann of Jackson,   24 Feb 1855
   Cape Girardeau Co., 16 January ae 6y 14d.

BURNS, Henry P., of Warsaw, 9 December.   21 Dec 1854

BUSBY, Mary Jane, daughter of John and Ellen, Broadway betw Morgan-Green, 13 February ae 9m 11d. — 14 Feb 1856

BYRNE, John Francis, son of Daniel and Anne, 23 August of brain inflammation ae 7m 7d. Lived 13-Olive. — 24 Aug 1857

BYRON, Cecelia, daughter of Richard and Eliza LaCompt, 10 June ae 2y 11m. — 12 Jun 1854

CAFFERATA, Victoria, of St. Louis, in Genoa 7 November; had gone with husband and child to visit relatives. — 4 Dec 1857

CALDWELL, Edward Thomas, son of Thomas and Kitty Ann, 30 Dec. at Fulton ae 1y 10m. — 9 Jan 1855

CAMPBELL, Kate, daughter of Thomas and Adaline, 7 March in Cheltenham, of measles, ae 14m 7d. — 10 Mar 1857

CARD, Webster N., only child of Nathan and Ann, drowned 22 May. Ae 10y 8m; lived 104 Collins. Body recovered, buried Bellefontaine. — 9 Jun 1857

CARRINGTON, Mrs. __, wife of John, in Callaway Co. 10 June. — 21 Jun 1854

Kate, wife of Dr. (E or R?) of Bremen, 29 Nov.; late of Philadelphia. Fun/home of A. T. Drysdale. — 30 Nov 1853

CARROLL, Lizzie, daughter of William and Mary, 18 Dec. ae 14; funeral/mother's home, 5th betw Cerre-Poplar. — 20 Dec 1854

CASEY, Margaret, wife of John, 6 July in her 48th year. — 14 Jul 1854

CASTLEMAN, Gordon Simon Jacob, only son of William S. and Amanda, at Independence 8 January, ae 5y 20d, of malignant quinsy. — 22 Jan 1855

CAYOU, Frank, ae 11m, in Bremen. — 6 Jul 1854

CHAPMAN, Emily, wife of William, in Monroe Co. 11 August in her 41st year, leaving 12 children. — 20 Aug 1853

CHURCH, James, a journeyman printer, many years' resident of St. Louis, 20 April of cholera. — 2 May 1855

CLARK, Dr. M. H., at St. Mary, 16 April in his 45th year. — 5 May 1855

CLEMENT, Edward Bacon 17 May in his 8th year. Funeral from Church of the Messiah. — 18 May 1855

CLIFFORD, Elizabeth Catherine, ae 7, on 1 September. Funeral from Mr. Devereaux' home, Market betw 9-10. — 2 Sep 1856

CODY, William, only child of William and Margaret, 4 July ae 1y 10m 27d. CA pc — 6 Jul 1855

COLLINS, James A., son of Dr. G. T. of St. Louis, 9 August in Taunton MA ae 16y 6m. — 23 Aug 1856

Sophronia, wife of Dr. George T., in her 31st year. Lived Washington-Ninth St. — 8 Dec 1854

COMSTOCK, George Henry, son of E. H. and Emma, 4 May ae 21m. Lived se corner of Pine-9th. — 5 May 1855

COONEY, Catherine, infant of Michael and Jane, no date.   18 Jul 1856

COOPER, Thomas Roberts, son of Thomas and Eurania, living on   8 Dec 1854
       11th betw Jefferson-Monroe, ae 2y 5m.

CORNELIUS, Susanna, daughter of Dr. W. W. and L. J., 10 May   15 May 1857 ·
       ae 3y 5m.

COVERT, Cora, youngest daughter of Jacob and Phebe, 6 July   8 Jul 1854
       of cholera ae 6y 5m 13d.

COVEY, Mrs. Hannah, ae 31, 27 Dec.; Marshfield & Cleveland OH pc   29 Dec 1854

COWEN, Charles, son of John and Rosine, 7th betw Biddle-   2 Jun 1857
       O'Fallon, 1 June ae 5y 8m. Holy Trinity Cem.

COX, Eugene Thomas, son of John and Bridget, 178 8th St., of   1 Aug 1854
       cholera infantum, ae 1y 10m 17d. Rock Spring Cem.

CRAFT, Josephine Elizabeth, only child of M. B. and E. A.,   9 Aug 1854
       7 August ae 6.

CRAIG, Mrs. Juliann B. at the home of her father, Samuel Riley,   17 Mar 1855
       in Callaway Co. 16 February in her 20th y.

CRANE, Georgianna, daughter of J. W., 12 April ae 4y 8m.   13 Apr 1857

CROSS, William B., eldest son of Anderson, of Randolph Co.,   17 Mar 1855
       of typhoid, ae 24y 6m 17d.

CULLEN, Catherine, daughter of James and Ellen, granddaughter   17 Mar 1857
       of William and Ellen Lawler, ae 14m.
       Lived 6th-Spruce.

CURTIN, Catherine, wife of Dennis and daughter of William and   27 Aug 1857
       Catherine Clifford, formerly of St. Louis,
       6 August in St. Joseph.

DAVIS, Augustus, son of James and Euphemia, 8 March; his twin   26 Mar 1856
       brother Adolphus died in Glasgow last August.

       John Christopher, son of Martin and Mary, 10 November   11 Nov 1857
       of scarlet fever ae 3y 10m 25d.

DICKENSON, Wayne Walton, youngest son of L. C. and H. G.,   1 Jan 1855
       30 December ae 2y 10m.

DICKEY, William, of Holladay and Dickey, in Weston, 24 January.   8 Feb 1855

DILL, Mary Elizabeth, only child of W. E. and Anna E., 28 June   29 Jun 1857
       ae 1y 25d. Lived on Barlow betw Orchard-
       Gratiot. Covington & Cincinnati pc

DONOVAN, Timothy, inquest: supposedly a fit. Ae 21.   6 Feb 1855

       William, late of St. Louis, formerly of Clonmel, Co.
       Tipperary, in San Francisco 21 October   15 Mar 1856
       of Panama fever.

DRIGGS, Clarence Leslie, son of Edward N. and Jesselia, in   21 Mar 1856
       Jefferson City, 2 March of brain inflammation.

DUNN, Matthew Louis, only son of John and Mary Ann, 102   23 Feb 1856
       Green St., 22 Feb. of brain congestion.
(see p. 124)

DUNN, Mary Jane, infant of John and Mary Ann, yesterday. 27 Feb 1855
        Lived Green St. betw 4-5. (see p. 123)

DUNSTER, Thomas 8 January of pneumonia, in St. Joseph, ae 55. 31 Jan 1855 .

DUSENBURY, Richard, son of Henry and Mary E., 4 May ae 3y 5m. 5 May 1856

ELDER, Hamer, son of Dr. and Mrs. Edwin Elder of Carondelet,
        at Brookville IN 8 January of brain 1 Feb 1856
        congestion, ae about 16m.

    Francis Ignatius, son of Joseph C. and Elizabeth, 11 Mar. 12 Mar 1856

EVILL, Charles, only son of John and Martha, Olive St. betw
        15-16, on 18 August ae 1m 18d. 19 Jul 1856

FLANNIGAN, Catherine, daughter of John and Sallie,
        43 N. Levee, 15 May ae 2y 6m. 16 May 1857

FOGARTY, Edward, son of John and Margaret, 28 September
        ae 2y 7m 19d. 30 Sep 1857

FREEMAN, Carrie, only child of Elisha P. and Cynthia, of
        measles, ae 7m 12d; lived 15 N. 14th St. 8 May 1857

FULTON, Josephine, youngest daughter of John and Elizabeth,
        ae 4y 1m 3d. Lived Rosatti St. 7 Dec 1857
        betw Park-Marion.

GARESCHE, Julius John Regis, son of Alex J. P., 23 July
        ae 21m. Buried Calvary. 23 Jul 1857